ASIA PACIFIC
SECURITY OUTLOOK
1999

edited by
Charles E. Morrison
coedited by
Richard W. Baker

cosponsored by

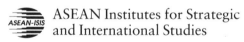 ASEAN Institutes for Strategic
and International Studies

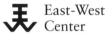 East-West
Center

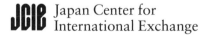 Japan Center for
International Exchange

AN APAP PROJECT

Tokyo • Japan Center for International Exchange • *New York*

The surnames of the authors and other persons mentioned in this book are
positioned according to country practice.

Copyediting by Byron Monasmith and Pamela J. Noda.
Cover and typographic design by Becky Davis, EDS Inc.,
Editorial & Design Services. Typesetting and production by EDS Inc.

Printed in Japan.
ISBN 4-88907-027-3

Distributed worldwide outside Japan by Brookings Institution Press,
1775 Massachusetts Avenue, N.W., Washington, D.C. 20036-2188 U.S.A.

Japan Center for International Exchange
9-17 Minami Azabu 4-chome, Minato-ku, Tokyo 106-0047 Japan

URL: http://www.jcie.or.jp

Japan Center for International Exchange, Inc. (JCIE/USA)
1251 Avenue of the Americas, New York, N.Y. 10020 U.S.A.

Contents

Foreword   7
Regional Overview   9

  1 Australia   21
  2 Canada   32
  3 China   43
  4 European Union   55
  5 India   65
  6 Indonesia   79
  7 Japan   91
  8 Republic of Korea   104
  9 Malaysia   112
 10 New Zealand   121
 11 Papua New Guinea   130
 12 Philippines   138
 13 Russia   149
 14 Singapore   162
 15 Thailand   171
 16 United States   182
 17 Vietnam   194

List of Abbreviations   202
The APSO Project Team   205
Index   207

Foreword

The Japan Center for International Exchange, the East-West Center, and the ASEAN Institutes for Strategic and International Studies are pleased to present the 1999 edition of the *Asia Pacific Security Outlook,* the third in an annual series.

The *Outlook* is distinct from other regional and global security reviews in that it does not seek to come up with a consensus view, but rather places national perspectives side by side. It is hoped through this process not only to increase mutual understanding among the security analysts involved with the project but also to identify those key areas where perceptions differ or where information is lacking.

The security analysts associated with the project are drawn from academic or research institutions in the individual countries analyzed herein, not from government bureaucracies. This means that the views expressed in each country chapter do not necessarily represent the views of that country's government. However, each author has tried to describe the mainstream points of view in the government and society as a whole in his or her country, and most have indicated those issues characterized by significant internal debate.

The *Outlook* does not provide chapters on all ASEAN Regional Forum member countries. However, this 1999 edition of the *Outlook* includes for the first time a chapter on India, which therefore is somewhat longer than the other chapters to permit the inclusion of more background information. We will continue to try to expand the *Outlook*'s country coverage in future editions.

We wish to express our appreciation to several people who made this year's *Outlook* possible. Nishihara Masashi continued to serve as one of the directors of the *Outlook* project, along with Charles E.

Morrison and Jusuf Wanandi. Richard W. Baker of the East-West Center assumed a much larger share of the day-to-day work of editing this year than in previous years, in addition to providing a background paper on the United States. Without his input, the *Outlook* would not have been completed. Wada Shūichi of the Japan Center for International Exchange (JCIE) coordinated the activities associated with the project, and Pamela J. Noda, also of JCIE, again oversaw the entire copyediting and publications process. The Ilmin International Relations Institute of Korea University provided indispensable staff support during the November 1998 Seoul workshop.

The organizing institutions are again grateful to the Nippon Foundation for its financial support of the *Asia Pacific Security Outlook* as a continuing part of the Asia Pacific Agenda Project, a multipronged initiative designed to promote policy-oriented intellectual dialogue among nongovernmental analysts in the Asia Pacific region.

CHARLES E. MORRISON
PRESIDENT
EAST-WEST CENTER

JUSUF WANANDI
FOUNDING MEMBER
ASEAN INSTITUTES FOR
STRATEGIC AND INTERNATIONAL STUDIES

YAMAMOTO TADASHI
PRESIDENT
JAPAN CENTER FOR INTERNATIONAL EXCHANGE

Regional Overview

By most conventional standards, the socioeconomic environment for security in Asia Pacific could hardly be worse. In 1998, for the first time in many decades the gross national product of many countries in the region plunged to large negative figures. Unemployment grew to levels unprecedented in recent years in Hong Kong, Indonesia, Japan, South Korea, and Thailand. However, despite the deepening economic crisis the political systems and international relations of the region have proved remarkably resilient, which bodes well for the future. Nevertheless, the security outlook in the coming years remains uncertain, and multilateral security cooperation, in particular, faces significant challenges.

One broad area of future concern was highlighted by two separate developments during 1998: the successive nuclear tests conducted by India and Pakistan in May, and the launch of a multistage missile by North Korea in late August. These two events served to heighten general consciousness of and to refocus governments' attention on the related long-term issues of the proliferation of weapons of mass destruction and the growing availability of advanced technologies for delivering such weapons.

THE ECONOMIC CRISIS

Asia Pacific Security Outlook 1998 identified the economic crisis as a serious security concern and noted three areas of its politico-security impact: domestic stability, interregional relations, and trans-Pacific relations. The crisis has indeed affected all three of these areas, although to differing degrees. So far, the impact of the crisis has been greater on individual or human security than on traditionally defined national security.

Initially manifest mostly in foreign exchange and currency markets, the crisis and its impact on the real economies of the affected countries deepened in 1998. Interest rate hikes implemented to defend these countries' currencies had the negative effect of dampening business activity. In addition, imports collapsed in many countries, thus affecting the exports of others, and both unemployment and underemployment rose.

So far, however, the domestic political impact of the crisis has been limited, except in Indonesia. In Thailand, the Chavalit government fell as a consequence of the economic difficulties and other factors in late 1997, but the Thai political system proved durable: The successor Chuan Leekpai government has fought off political pressures and pursued its International Monetary Fund (IMF) program. Similarly, in South Korea and the Philippines regular constitutional changes of presidential government took place, and in neither case is the political system threatened by the economic crisis. In Malaysia, the crisis aggravated political tensions between Prime Minister Mahathir bin Mohamad and his former deputy and finance minister, Anwar Ibrahim, each of whom advocated quite different responses to the crisis. Although Mahathir's decision to oust Anwar from office and bring him to trial on corruption and sex-crime charges sent reverberations throughout the Malaysian political system, it has not threatened the system as such. Thus, Indonesia provides the only example of systemic collapse—a special and far-reaching case that will be considered separately below.

In the area of international relations, the economic crisis has intertwined with other influences to place stress on some relationships as well as on regional institutions. In particular, Japan and the United States have both come under criticism from some of the affected countries for not doing enough individually or together to help avert the crisis and bring about recovery. However, despite significant changes in foreign exchange rates, export and import patterns, and unemployment, there had been no significant effect on intraregional or trans-Pacific trade relations by the beginning of 1999. Rather, virtually all the region's economies were vowing to fight protectionism, although the tolerance for rapid liberalization was waning.

Regional institutions, such as the Association of Southeast Asian

Nations (ASEAN) and the Asia-Pacific Economic Cooperation (APEC) forum, have come under particular criticism for their failure to respond effectively to the crisis. Both these institutions before the crisis' onset were pursuing largely trade liberalization oriented agendas, which were buttressed by expectations of continued growth. As a consequence, both had difficulty in adjusting to a new set of concerns about the financial crisis, and in both considerable disagreement existed as to what should be done. In the ASEAN region, stresses re-emerged in relations among the original five ASEAN member countries —Indonesia, Malaysia, the Philippines, Singapore, and Thailand— most noticeably between Malaysia and Singapore, but ASEAN ended the year with a relatively successful leaders' meeting in Hanoi. Conversely, APEC's November ministerial and leaders' meetings were the least productive of all such meetings in the organization's history, for two chief reasons: Member economies could not agree on an Early Voluntary Sectoral Liberalization scheme, and the summit was overshadowed by the controversy over remarks encouraging the Malaysian political opposition made by U.S. Vice President Al Gore at a business forum associated with the meeting.

On the other hand, the crisis clearly underscored the interdependence of the region's economies and the consequent need for regional economic dialogue and cooperation. For these reasons, there seems to be little threat to the existence of either ASEAN or APEC. These economic organizations have traditionally been venues for leaders to deepen their personal acquaintance with each other and for the holding of side meetings that cover political and security topics. It is difficult to discern to what degree regional economic cooperation is a cause of, and to what degree a consequence of, good political and security relations. Since the two seem typically to go together, renewed commitment to and confidence in regional economic cooperation are in the security interests of the region.

By the beginning of 1999, there was growing optimism in Asia that the crisis had hit bottom, a view supported by the relative stability of stock and foreign exchange markets as well as by significantly lower interest rates. After a long delay, Japan seemed to be tackling the bad-loan problems in its banking sector in some earnest, although strong deflationary pressures continued to afflict the Japanese economy and spread outward in the region through decreased Japanese imports. For their part, South Korea and Thailand continued to pursue IMF programs. The collapse of domestic spending produced a

large balance-of-payments surplus for South Korea, thereby allowing it to begin to repay its IMF debt. In fact, some concern existed in
international financial circles that South Korea was recovering so well
that the government as a result might become complacent and fail to
carry through the more politically difficult reforms. In Malaysia, controversial currency controls did not harm the economy in the short
term, although expert opinion about their longer-term impact remains
mixed.

Despite the air of cautious optimism, the economic outlook for the
region remains sober. Much of the region's economic problems reflect
overlending and bad bank debt, and banking crises are notoriously
slow in working their way through the economy. Where growth does
occur, as seems likely in South Korea and the Philippines, it will be
modest. Because much of the job of restructuring still lies ahead, questions about the political ability of governments and leaders to meet
the forthcoming challenges remain unanswerable. Also, there is a
fear of extraregional shocks that could further weaken the global financial system and stretch the limited remaining resources of the IMF.
For all these reasons, the economic stabilization and recovery of East
Asia are still weak or nascent and must continue to be closely moni-
tored.

INDONESIA

The distinctiveness of the Indonesian situation, so different from that
of the rest of the crisis-affected Asia Pacific economies, should be highlighted. The resignation of President Suharto in May 1998 marked not
only a transfer of presidential power but also a collapse of the New
Order system that he had built. This is in stark contrast to the changes
of leadership that have occurred within the systems of other affected
Asian economies, including the Philippines, South Korea, and Thailand. As well, it differs from the testing going on in Malaysia, which
is a challenge to a long-established leader but not to the Malay-domi-
nated political system.

Indonesia thus faces the need to rebuild its political system in addition to its economy. As already demonstrated in Russia, one cannot
succeed without the other. B. J. Habibie, who succeeded Suharto as
president, initially was widely regarded as a transitional figure who
would tend to protect the remnants of the previous system rather than

to rebuild anew. However, the new president has forged a partnership with the military leadership and at the same time accommodated rather than resisted pressures to move forward in establishing a more democratic framework for national parliamentary elections in June.

Opinion is mixed concerning the degree of economic desperation in Indonesia. While the end of the El Niño drought has ameliorated some of the effects of the economic crisis in rural areas, the politically important middle and professional classes have been and remain significantly affected by the crisis. Signs of deteriorating order have been visible in the periodic flare-ups of ethnic and religious violence as well as the general increase in banditry and lawlessness. Moreover, Indonesia is likely to face mounting security challenges before and after the June election.

Further instability in Indonesia has serious implications for broader Asia Pacific security and regional relations. Indonesia not only is Southeast Asia's most populous country but also occupies a strategic location astride the main passages between the Indian and Pacific oceans. In addition, it has played a leading role in regional cooperation as a principal architect of ASEAN, while in the APEC context Suharto's influence was key to winning support in 1994 for the goal adopted at the Bogor meeting of developing "free trade and investment in the region" by 2020. Consequently, his departure as president removes from the APEC scene the leader most committed to the realization of this vision. Further turmoil in Indonesia, or weak future leadership, would be a significant detriment to the region as a whole.

WATCH LIST ISSUES

Aside from the economic crisis/recovery and Indonesian issues, the *Asia Pacific Security Outlook* analyst team continues to watch four issues dating from the inaugural 1997 edition of the *Asia Pacific Security Outlook*: the Korean peninsula, large power relations, territorial disputes, and weapons procurement.

THE KOREAN PENINSULA   Of these issues, all were seen as improving except the Korean peninsula situation, where a slight majority of the *Asia Pacific Security Outlook* analysts believed that the security situation had deteriorated during 1998. New South Korean President

Kim Dae Jung's "Sunshine Policy" toward North Korea was a stabilizing element in South-North relations, but the lack of a strong and positive North Korean response weakened political support for the new South Korean approach. On the contrary, infiltration incidents, North Korea's missile launch over Japanese territory, and the discovery by American intelligence of an underground facility apparently usable in nuclear weapons production tested Kim's resolve and raised doubts about the ability of the United States and Japan to continue to support the 1994 Framework Agreement.

In 1998, the U.S. Congress became increasingly impatient with appropriating funds for the fuel supplies promised to North Korea under the aforementioned agreement and passed legislation demanding that the U.S. president provide assurances in March and June 1999 of the North's continued adherence to the agreement. On its side, Pyongyang argued that the United States had failed to lift trade and investment sanctions. Given the brinkmanship that has characterized past U.S.–North Korean negotiations, it seemed highly likely that tensions between the two countries would mount. However, it also seemed unlikely that such tensions would lead to military conflict. To head off the threat to the Framework Agreement, the Clinton administration appointed the highly respected former secretary of defense, William Perry, to reassess and make recommendations for U.S. policy. Compromise and cooperation by North Korea also remain essential to surmounting the current difficulties.

LARGE POWER RELATIONS   Fortunately, the containment of tensions on the Korean peninsula has been facilitated by improving relations among the large powers. The era of good large power relations, especially evident at the end of 1997, continued in 1998 with another round of summit meetings. The leaders of China, Japan, Russia, and the United States all met the leaders of the other three countries on at least one bilateral visit during the year. Of these visits, the most significant was U.S. President Bill Clinton's June trip to China, the first visit by a U.S. president since the 1989 Tiananmen Square events. Featuring a public debate between the two leaders on human rights issues, the trip was widely regarded as successful in both countries and the region. Clinton's assurances that the United States would not support Taiwanese independence also helped defuse the Taiwan issue in Sino-American relations. Another factor helping to dampen Taiwan as a Sino-American issue was the resumption of the high-level but unofficial mainland-Taiwan dialogue in October 1998 after a five-year hiatus.

The six-day visit to Japan by Chinese President Jiang Zemin, the first ever by a Chinese head of state to Japan, marked the 20th anniversary of the 1978 treaty of peace and friendship between the two countries. In this instance, the lead-up to the visit was accompanied by hard bargaining over the language of the Japanese statement on Taiwan policy and of Tokyo's expression of apology for past aggression in China, which reflected deeper mutual frustrations over what each side considers to be the other's inflated view of its position. Nevertheless, substantial Japanese assistance to China is in place, and the infrastructure of economic, cultural, and political ties between East Asia's two leading countries continues to deepen.

Despite the impressive series of high-level leadership exchanges, the root sources of tensions among the large powers in the region remain. Aside from the demarcation of the Sino-Russian border, no serious issues among the large powers have truly been resolved. The most complicated and unpredictable bilateral relationship remains that between China and the United States. The strategic analysts associated with the *Asia Pacific Security Outlook* noted that prevailing American and Chinese views remain fundamentally opposed on such basic issues as the value of the American forward presence in the region, the future of the U.S.-Japan Security Treaty, and the need for theater missile defense systems for South Korea and Japan. Moreover, basic differences in economic and political systems continue to generate tensions. For example, underlying rivalries between Japan and China were evident during Jiang's Japan visit. Finally, while Russia's power has drastically diminished, Russian diplomatic alignment remains an uncertain element in the relations among the large powers of the Asia Pacific region.

TERRITORIAL DISPUTES   Conflicting territorial claims, especially in the sea, remain time bombs that threaten to derail improving international relations in the region. With the exception of Mischief Reef, a part of the Spratly Islands west of the Philippines, little attention was given to territorial issues during 1998. The Mischief Reef issue resurfaced when it was discovered by the Philippines that China had substantially built up its structures on the reef. The Chinese maintain that these structures are for the use of fishermen, while the Philippines argues that they violate a code of conduct under which the two countries had promised to inform each other before undertaking uni-lateral actions in the area. The Philippines has had little alternative but to protest and to consider whether and how to strengthen its own meager defense forces. There has also been some discussion of joint use of the facilities.

Over the past two years, the *Asia Pacific Security Outlook* strategic analysts have tended to give a reduced significance to territorial disputes as a potentially disturbing factor in the security outlook for the region. In general, the status of such disputes is regarded as symptomatic of the overall state of relations, rather than a causal factor. However, since many of these disputes involve China, China's posture toward such claims is frequently regarded as a litmus test of China's overall foreign policy toward its neighbors. This gives particular significance to the Spratly Islands, where China has broad claims that overlap with those of four Southeast Asian countries, and to the Senkaku/Diaoyu Islands, where China's claim conflicts with Japanese possession. Moreover, where other stresses are at play in a given relationship, a latent territorial conflict may suddenly escalate. Such disputes are perennial targets of opportunity for nationalist movements or for opposition groups that wish to embarrass current governments. Thus, the failure of governments to finally resolve these disputes means they continue to bedevil Asia Pacific international relations.

WEAPONS PROCUREMENT   As pointed out in previous issues of the *Asia Pacific Security Outlook*, the strategic analysts associated with the project have generally not regarded the acquisition of weapons by Asia's modernizing militaries as a significant source of regional tension. This is because most such acquisitions appeared to reflect plausible defense missions, such as those associated with patrolling large maritime Exclusive Economic Zones, and did not involve competitive purchases fueled by perceptions of specific external threats.

As the individual country chapters indicate, since the onset of the Asian economic crisis a number of governments, particularly in Southeast Asia, have had to scale back their defense modernization programs. Exercises and training have also suffered. These cuts may come at the expense of the effectiveness of Asia's military forces in carrying out missions associated with the maintenance of law and order and the control of illegal fishing or smuggling. This practical concern is probably of greater contemporary significance than is the concern about possible arms races in the region.

In addition to these, there are other concerns associated with the impact of the economic crisis on weapons procurement programs. For example, the region's poorer countries will not be able to finance the technology necessary to keep abreast of the Revolution in Military Affairs, and thus there may be increased perceptions of a growing balance-of-power disequilibrium. Further, widening disparities in technology can also create problems in developing and sustaining interoperability or engaging in practical cooperation at a time when many militaries are seeking to intensify engagement with their counterparts.

The competitive nuclear testing programs in South Asia, combined with renewed doubts as to whether North Korea's nuclear weapons program has truly ended, have raised the level of concern in the region over the related longer-term issues of the proliferation of weapons of mass destruction and technological advances in delivery systems for them. Given that several Asian states are capable of producing nuclear weapons but have acceded to the strictures of the nonproliferation regime, a weakening or collapse of this regime could have serious consequences, especially in Northeast Asia. The key task for the region is to restore confidence that North Korea is abiding by its pledges. The South Asian nuclear issue poses a global challenge—to bring the now explicitly acknowledged nuclear states in South Asia into the nonproliferation, comprehensive test ban, and missile control regimes.

ASIA PACIFIC SECURITY OUTLOOK 1999

1 Australia

THE SECURITY ENVIRONMENT

The events of 1998 shook some of the more fundamental—and comfortable—assumptions that have underlain Australia's security policy in recent years. The nuclear tests in South Asia, the expanding economic crisis in Southeast and East Asia, and, most pointedly, the dramatic deterioration of economic and political conditions in Indonesia have all raised the specter of broad and long-term uncertainties in the region's security environment.

By virtue of geography alone, Australia is one of the more secure countries in the world. The Australian government has therefore been able to focus considerable attention on regional and global security issues, while also maintaining a small but technologically advanced armed force as well as alliance arrangements that would provide direct deterrence and defense should strategic conditions deteriorate.

At the same time, the Australian government and defense policy community recognize that Australia's security cannot be divorced from that of the broader Asia Pacific region, that the region is rapidly changing and subject to considerable uncertainties beyond Australia's direct control, and that Australia's own resources available for defense purposes are quite limited. Thus, Australia's interests are best served by building long-term stability in the region, but its efforts toward this end remain highly vulnerable to unwelcome surprises.

There were a number of such surprises in 1998. One of these, the nuclear tests by India and Pakistan, was not entirely unexpected. Both countries had been for years classed as "threshold" nuclear weapons states. Although neither India's nor Pakistan's nuclear capability is seen as posing a direct threat to Australia, the Australian government reacted more strongly to the tests than it had to North Korean nuclear developments in the mid-1990s, primarily in the hope that a strong international reaction would deter other states from crossing the nuclear threshold in the future. Australia supported actions by the United States and others in defense of international norms on nonproliferation.

More importantly, the fallibility of intelligence and monitoring systems demonstrated by developments on the subcontinent, together with the continuing confrontation between the United Nations and Iraq over the issue of that country's weapons of mass destruction, leave unresolved questions about how the proliferation of such weapons is to be effectively restrained in the future. Australia's foreign minister, Alexander Downer, indicated Australia's concern when he stated at a conference in May 1998 that "Nuclear proliferation and the attainment of nuclear weapons by rogue states or political movements may in time constitute the greatest threat to Australian and global security."

A second, broader setback to the prospects for long-term regional stability was the deepening of the Asian financial crisis, which has moved well beyond being primarily a problem of foreign exchange markets, or merely a regional problem. In the most fundamental sense, the crisis has eroded the belief that economic interests would bind regional states together in relationships of interdependence that would eventually grow into broader economic, social, and political convergence.

Of all the aspects of the crisis, the most significant for Australia has been the combination of economic collapse and political upheaval in Indonesia, Australia's closest Asian neighbor. Instability in Indonesia could affect Australia's security even without there being any hostile intent on the part of the Indonesian government. The rapidity and depth of the deterioration in Indonesia have exceeded almost everyone's expectations. Food shortages affecting possibly half the population, widespread politically and economically motivated violence, the uneasy transition from the now thoroughly discredited Suharto regime, and the increased political access and assertiveness of the largest Muslim population in the world—all these factors contribute to the uncertainty. The evolving situation in Indonesia will be a continuing major focus of Australia's security outlook.

Australia has its optimists and pessimists regarding the ultimate impact of the broader economic crisis on regional security and strategic stability. The optimists anticipate a resumption of growth in most Asian countries (except Indonesia) over the next two or three years, thereby allowing a return to development-oriented policies bolstered by more effective prudential monitoring and regulation and with only minor political adjustments. On the other hand, the pessimists see the economic damage as so substantial, and the recovery period so long, that fundamental political and social stability are at risk.

Many Australian observers have noted somewhat troubling changes in the relative weights of the major powers in the region. Japan has not been able to play an active international leadership role and, notwithstanding the strengths of its manufacturing industry, will not be able to do so until its financial sector is restored to health. By contrast, China has so far been able to resist the adverse trends in trade and investment flows and to maintain the value of its currency. More important, China has acknowledged a solidarity of interests with its more vulnerable neighbors in Asia, thus overtly playing a stabilizing role in the region. However, it remains uncertain as to how long China will be able to hold to this course in the face of the pressing need to reform its own inefficient state-owned enterprises and reduce the accumulation of bad debts in its financial system.

Less unsettling has been the evidence of the preeminence of the United States, now not only the world's only remaining military superpower but also the natural leader in financial matters. As Downer put it, "U.S. involvement in the region remains the single most important factor in regional strategic planning and, of course, is crucial to the region's stability." It is ironic, therefore, that unrelated domestic developments in Washington are causing doubts about this leadership potential being fully realized for some time, possibly not until a new administration takes office in 2001.

The Association of Southeast Asian Nations (ASEAN) has long been seen as a major positive factor in Australia's security, chiefly because it has served to stabilize relations among Australia's neighbors to the north, thus enabling them to concentrate on economic development without undue concern about external threats. It has also given birth to the ASEAN Regional Forum (ARF), which has stimulated multilateral dialogue on regional security issues and has substantially raised the region's profile in global forums, as well.

However, ASEAN and, by extension, ARF have been weakened by strains stemming from the economic crisis. In particular, the magnitude of the damage done to the economies of Indonesia, Malaysia, and Thailand has shaken confidence. The cohesion that so marked ASEAN in the past has been challenged as members of the newly expanded group have had to focus on issues of economic and political survival rather than regional affairs. In this environment, ASEAN is less able to play a stabilizing role in relations among its members, even such core members as Indonesia, Malaysia, and Singapore. A number of events in 1998—including Malaysia's refusal to allow Singapore to use its airspace and its withdrawal from a scheduled multilateral military exercise, together with rising concerns over violence in Indonesia and the arrest and trial of the former deputy prime minister of Malaysia—threatened the existing patterns of ASEAN cooperation.

DEFENSE POLICIES AND ISSUES

DEFENSE POLICY   Despite the changing security environment, the conservative coalition government's major review of defense policy, entitled *Australia's Strategic Policy,* contained little change. Rather, the government adhered to the basic analysis contained in its 1997 *White Paper on Foreign and Trade Policy* in its efforts to identify the trends to 2020 and beyond against which decisions on military capabilities could be made. The government's review postulated continued strong economic growth in the region, rather than major setbacks. Also, it reiterated Australia's interest in the security of the region in familiar terms while placing a "re-emphasis on the importance of Northeast Asia" for Australia's security, noting China's emergence as "a powerful economic force in our region." Finally, it described U.S.-China relations as "fundamental to stability in the future."

Australia's Strategic Policy gives highest priority to the "knowledge edge" in the development of defense capability, that is, exploiting information technology for intelligence, command systems, and surveillance. Approved projects to achieve this objective include airborne early warning and control aircraft, enhanced satellite communications, an advanced secure military messaging system, an army battlefield command support system, and an automated command support system for joint operations.

The defense minister has spoken of directing the Australian Defense Force (ADF) to "the forefront of the revolution in military affairs," and progress on the above priority items is deemed essential to the maintenance of interoperability with U.S. forces. This approach seeks to exploit Australia's developed economy and high skill levels, thereby compensating for limited military personnel, and takes the opportunity of a relatively benign security environment to invest for the future. It runs the risk, however, of diverting efforts from more pressing near-term defense requirements, and it could also reduce the ability of Australian forces to interact with regional partners.

A second priority goes to developing capabilities to dispel threats to Australia's maritime approaches. This goal stresses air superiority and the enhancement of surface and subsurface maritime capabilities.

The government's third priority is the ability to operate "proactively against enemy forces." Projects to this end include keeping the F-111 fleet in service until 2015–2020 and acquiring standoff weapons to use with it.

A fourth priority is the development of land capabilities to counter threats on Australian territory. The approach here is to develop highly mobile joint task forces, a limited amphibious capability, improved land surveillance equipment, aerial fire support and reconnaissance helicopters, additional light armored vehicles, and, for special forces, improved counterterrorist and other capabilities.

In presenting the government's review to Parliament in December 1997, the defense minister stated that "current spending levels will allow us—with savings from the Reform Program—to substantially modernize our existing defense platforms like the surface fleet, to acquire airborne early-warning aircraft, and to give the army greater mobility." He made it clear, however, that acquisitions of new fighter aircraft or a new surface combatant for the navy would not be possible within current funding levels.

It is unclear how long it will take to implement the projects listed by the defense minister. Some of the items have appeared on similar lists for years. In addition, the actual savings achievable through the Reform Program, which transfers resources from noncombat areas to combat-related activities, are difficult to assess. In any case, transition costs are expected to consume the bulk of anticipated savings in the early years.

Further, the proportion of gross national product allocated to defense is projected to decline, from an already low 1.9 percent in 1998–1999 (and in the preceding two fiscal years) to 1.8 percent in 1999–2000 and 1.7 percent in 2000–2001. The Parliamentary Joint Standing Committee on Foreign Affairs, Defense and Trade expressed concern on this point, noting that measuring defense as a proportion of GDP does not take into account the security environment or the defense tasks required. Accordingly, the committee argued for a real increase in the defense budget of 1.5 to 2.5 percent annually for the next five years.

Given the absence of debate on this matter during the 1998 election campaign, however, it can be assumed that the current level of defense spending enjoys broad public and bipartisan support and therefore is unlikely to change in the absence of some major external shock. Moreover, the substantial reductions in military spending in many Asian countries due to the economic crisis, and the consequent deferral of modernization programs in these countries, have probably further weakened support for increased defense spending in Australia.

THE DEFENSE BUDGET   Funding for defense in fiscal year 1998–1999 is essentially unchanged from the previous year in real terms, with total outlays of A$10.95 billion (US$6.68 billion at A$1 = US$0.61). This represents a nominal increase of A$589.2 million (US$359 million) over 1997–1998. At 1.9 percent, defense spending as a share of Australia's GDP is now the lowest since the 1930s.

Operating costs have generally been held constant. Funding for equipment and stores, accounting for 43 percent of total outlays, has increased 15 percent. Personnel costs account for 35.8 percent of defense spending: Permanent (regular) forces are scheduled to be reduced 3.1 percent, to 54,035; reserves will increase 2.3 percent, to 30,143; and civilian personnel will decrease 2.5 percent, to 17,131.

Capital investment expenditure, which includes most capital equipment as well as all capital facilities, in 1998–1999 remains healthy, at 31.7 percent of total defense spending, or A$3.47 billion (US$2.12 billion). Some A$2.68 billion (US$1.64 billion) will be directed to projects already approved, including navy frigates, mine hunters, a submarine, fighter and airlift aircraft, helicopters for the frigates, updated P-3 surveillance aircraft, modernized communications, and an active missile decoy.

In addition, new projects totaling A$1.77 billion (US$1.08 billion) have been approved, with A$45.7 million (US$28 million) to be spent in 1998–1999. These include:
- upgrades of F/A-18 fighters and M113 armored personnel carriers
- antiship missiles for ship-borne helicopters
- electronic chart display and information systems for the navy

- upgrades of Collins-class submarines
- additional spares for the F-111 fleet
- development of a deployable intelligence database.

Approved major capital facilities projects total A$377.6 million (US$230 million), with A$26.5 million (US$16 million) to be spent in 1998–1999. A further A$716.6 million (US$437 million) is to be spent in 1998–1999 on other capital projects.

ALLIANCE RELATIONSHIPS   The ANZUS alliance with the United States and New Zealand continued to receive high priority. The annual Australia–United States Ministerial Consultations (AUSMIN), held in Australia in June 1998 with both the U.S. secretary of state and secretary of defense in attendance, was highly profiled by the Australian government. This enhanced profile, intended to reflect the "reinvigoration" of ANZUS under the coalition government, can be viewed in partisan terms as an effort to show "product differentiation" vis-à-vis the Labor Party. Be that as it may, in the 1998 election campaign there was remarkably little questioning by the Australian public of alliance cooperation with the United States, although some commentators have urged that a similar level of priority and vigor be directed to regional matters.

The most important development in the alliance relationship during the year was the agreement to extend by ten years the Pine Gap Treaty covering the intelligence-gathering facility in central Australia. Further, the AUSMIN communiqué stated that cooperation previously undertaken at the Nurrungar Joint Defense Facility would continue "in new ways, including Australian involvement in the management of the relay ground station for early-warning data to be located at Pine Gap, in the data processing operation in the United States, and in associated research development."

Other agreements mentioned in the communiqué concerned cooperation in maintaining the "knowledge edge." A "particularly close and productive partnership" in the intelligence area was noted, with long-term cooperation agreed upon in wide-area surveillance. Other measures mentioned would broaden the exposure of Australian personnel to U.S. theater commands other than that of the Pacific, further explore the implications of the Revolution in Military Affairs, and "facilitate access to particular U.S. technologies important to the ADF and its capacity to contribute to coalition operations, notably in the submarine, airborne early-warning and control, and combat aircraft fields." Also, the communiqué called for the establishment of a committee to coordinate and promote cooperation in equipment acquisition, technology, and support.

Finally, the ministers agreed on an extensive series of policy positions that closely align the two countries on regional and global security issues, ranging from nonproliferation, the U.S. alliance with Japan, U.S.-China relations, and the U.S.–South Korea security relationship to the roles of the International Monetary Fund and the Asia-Pacific Economic Cooperation forum in dealing with the economic crisis in Asia.

The communiqué took particular note of developments in Indonesia, expressing support for the Indonesian government's "commitment to political reform and the staging of early elections" and pledging continuing help, "including increased humanitarian assistance." The ministers also "urged all parties to exercise utmost restraint in pursuit of a lasting solution to the future of East Timor."

Australia's security relationship with New Zealand is predominantly bilateral and proceeds under the Closer Defense Relations program to seek more effective ways of enhancing cooperation and interoperability between each country's forces. In 1998, the two sides agreed to a series of positions for exchange officers and to the joint development of military equipment and support strategies. The gap between Australia's and New Zealand's individual defense efforts has provided both an incentive to seek greater defense integration and a constraint on its practical benefits.

CONTRIBUTIONS TO REGIONAL AND GLOBAL SECURITY

RELATIONS WITH SOUTHEAST AND EAST ASIA   The high media profile gained in 1996 and 1997 by the populist One Nation Party, headed by Pauline Hanson, an outspoken member of Parliament, raised anew longstanding questions about the Australian public's attitudes toward Asia, particularly opposition to Asian immigration. These questions were largely answered in 1998, as other parties distanced themselves from the One Nation Party during the federal election campaign: Hanson was defeated and the One Nation Party won no seats in the federal House of Representatives, although the party will have one federal senator from mid-1999.

At the official level, Australia in recent years has been steadily developing bilateral security dialogues and cooperation with other Asian countries. For example, intensified dialogue with Indonesia on regional security and arms control issues has been conducted since the conclusion of the bilateral security agreement in 1995. In addition, political and military dialogues with Japan and South Korea date from 1996, while those with the Philippines and China began in 1997. Similar exchanges with Vietnam and Thailand started in 1998.

Following the downfall of Indonesian President Suharto in mid-1998, Australian military exercises with Indonesia's special forces, which had been involved in abuses against Suharto's opponents, were suspended. However, Defense Minister John Moore reaffirmed during a visit to Indonesia in late 1998 that Australia intends to maintain a close working relationship with Indonesia's armed forces.

Although Australia's relations with China experienced a brief period of uneasiness after the 1996 change of government in Australia, they continued to improve during 1998. The first-ever visit to Australia by a Chinese defense minister took place in February and produced agreement on regular ministerial-level meetings, enhanced dialogue on strategic developments and defense policies, and further junior- and mid-level officer exchanges.

Australia continues to participate actively in regional multilateral security forums, although economic matters have taken priority among regional issues since the start of the crisis. Australia participates in the Korean Peninsula Energy Development Organization arrangements, as well as in the Five Power Defense Arrangements with Malaysia, New Zealand, Singapore, and the United Kingdom. In addition, Australia is active in ARF, with Downer recently pointing to the desirability of ARF "taking forward the agenda for developing preventive diplomacy in the region."

ARMS CONTROL AND DISARMAMENT Australia also continues to be an active supporter of multilateral arms control measures, paying particular attention to the control of weapons of mass destruction. Australia ratified the Comprehensive Test Ban Treaty (CTBT) in July 1998. Also, it deployed a ground force unit (SAS) and two B-707 refueling aircraft to Kuwait for several months in 1998 in support of the international coalition's response to Iraq's refusal to cooperate with the United Nations Special Commission investigating stockpiles of weapons of mass destruction.

Downer made nuclear proliferation the priority issue when he addressed the Conference on Disarmament in Geneva early in 1998. He argued strongly for a Fissile Material Cut-off Treaty, which would include an agreement not to produce weapons-grade fissile material or to assist others to produce such material; and an agreement by all parties, including nuclear weapons states, to accept international safeguards on all facilities capable of producing weapons-grade fissile material.

A treaty along these lines would put a quantitative restraint on the development of nuclear weapons, parallel to the qualitative restraints called for by the CTBT. Also, a cut-off treaty would pressure the nuclear weapons states to curtail nuclear weapons development in accordance with the Nonproliferation Treaty and create an environment of greater transparency conducive to reducing nuclear weapons stocks. By bringing nuclear facilities in the nuclear weapons states under international verification, such a treaty would address the discrimination implicit in the existing nonproliferation regime. In this regard, effective verification will be crucial to any new treaty regime, and the elimination of existing stocks remains a distant goal.

The 1998 nuclear tests on the Indian subcontinent not only defied such forward-looking efforts but also undermined progress already made. Downer went so far as to assert that the tests "challenge the foundations of the nuclear nonproliferation structure. . . They could touch off a nuclear arms race in South Asia with serious implications for regional security. And . . . a weakening of the nuclear nonproliferation regime could threaten other global mechanisms for the control of weapons of mass destruction. . . ."

Australia reacted to the Pakistani and Indian tests with a combination of multilateral and bilateral measures, supporting those taken by the United States and others. Australia's heads of diplomatic missions to both Pakistan and India were recalled for consultations, and defense cooperation and all visits by ministers and senior officials, as well as nonhumanitarian aid, were suspended.

PEACEKEEPING, DISASTER RELIEF, AND HUMANITARIAN ASSISTANCE Australia was particularly active in peacekeeping in 1998 on both the Indonesian and Papua New Guinean sides of the island of New Guinea and on the island of Bougainville. Australia contributed the commander and some 250 personnel to the Bougainville Peace Monitoring Group. In disaster relief, after a tsunami struck the

northern coast of Papua New Guinea, Australia deployed a total of
130 defense personnel to the area for a period of two weeks. In addition, drought in Irian Jaya prompted the deployment of some 150 defense personnel to deliver aid by helicopter, in conjunction with the
Indonesian Armed Forces.

2 Canada

THE SECURITY ENVIRONMENT

GLOBAL SECURITY   Canadians entered 1999 with a fuller realization of the broad range of events that can impinge upon their security. The forces of globalization and economic transformation that brought prosperity and relatively benign domestic conditions to much of the world throughout the 1990s are now responsible for stark reversals to both economic and social orders abroad, which have in turn reverberated throughout the North American economy. Entrenched communal conflicts in other countries have reignited, demonstrating both their intractability and the inability of the international community of nations to mobilize itself to protect populations at risk. Moreover, progress toward the nonproliferation of both conventional and nonconventional weaponry was countered in 1998, most pointedly by the open nuclearization of two additional countries. Finally, confronted by the social damage caused by the international drug trade and the influx of persons trafficked illegally across its borders, the Canadian public has become increasingly aware of the reality of transnational crime and its impact on social well-being.

Thus, although the risk of military threat to Canada remains remote, most Canadians would agree with their defense minister's characterization of the world as "complex and dangerous."

At the same time, this has not caused Canadians to become more insular or isolationist. On the one hand, such a turn inward is impossible. With a heavily export-driven economy, Canadians are affected by economic trends abroad and thus cannot be immune to the social and political circumstances that fuel them. With policies that invite immigration (necessary to sustain the Canadian labor force) and accept refugees, Canada is directly influenced by upheavals abroad inasmuch as they both bring in more people and touch the lives of growing communities in Canada with direct ties to foreign conflicts. On the other hand, Canadians in general, and their current foreign minister in particular, sense and espouse a responsibility to act to stop destruction and promote conflict resolution at both intra- and interstate levels.

On the domestic political front, separatist pressures in Quebec and related federal-provincial tensions have abated from levels of several years ago. Although the Parti Quebecois was returned to power in Quebec in 1998, the election results did not indicate strong public interest in another referendum or in other dramatic actions toward separation.

REGIONAL SECURITY   Through its historical, cultural, and economic ties, Canada has interests in Africa, Europe, the Americas, and Asia. Regarding Asia, two developments occupied Canadian attention in 1998. First was the financial crisis, which quickly became a full-blown regional economic crisis threatening not only the economic security of Asian peoples but also their social and political security. Canadians were particularly concerned over the collapse of the Indonesian economy and the subsequent civil disorder chiefly targeting ethnic minorities. As well, developments in Malaysia raised doubts about the health of civil society in that country.

Ottawa is concerned that the Association of Southeast Asian Nations (ASEAN) may be losing its regional leadership capacity. With Indonesia currently unable to exercise its traditional role, and with most member states preoccupied with domestic economic problems and intra-ASEAN affairs, Canadian observers worry that the ASEAN Regional Forum (ARF) and other regional institutions may lose momentum.

The Asian economic crisis has been felt directly in Canada through a sharp decline in exports (especially of natural resource products from western provinces) and a dramatic rise in imports. Because the bulk of Canadian economic transactions are with the United States, the overall Canadian economy remains quite healthy, but if U.S.-Asian trade flows were to be significantly affected there might be ripple effects in the Canadian economy. In a December 1998 report, the Canadian Senate Committee on Foreign Affairs highlighted these points, as well as the importance of "non-traditional security threats" including environmental degradation. The committee stressed "the domestic repercussions of instability and conflict within Asia Pacific," stating that drugs, AIDS, illegal immigrants, gangs, and terrorism had become serious concerns.

The second critical development in Asia that focused Canadian attention was the overt nuclearization of South Asia. For the Canadian government, this development constitutes "a clear and fundamental threat to the international security regime." India's and Pakistan's nuclear tests invoke security concerns on four dimensions. First, South Asia is a less stable place with the new threat that an outbreak of conflict over perennial hot spots such as Jammu and Kashmir could escalate into nuclear annihilation. Second, global nonproliferation regimes have been set back substantially. Third, these actions fly in the face of one of the primary lessons of the cold war and an emerging post–cold war norm—that nuclear weapons have neither political utility nor useful military purpose. Fourth, the new reality in South Asia has implications for Northeast Asia: The Chinese have had to reassess their strategic situation, and North Korea may draw unfortunate conclusions.

On the fourth point, Canadian analysts see the primary security threat in Northeast Asia as the breakdown of relations on the Korean peninsula. While South Korean President Kim Dae Jung's "Sunshine Policy" toward North Korea is regarded as a bold and positive gesture, genuine progress is uncertain, especially in light of continued provocations by the North testing the patience of the South Korean public and the other parties involved in peninsular diplomatic efforts. With the reciprocal state visits of President Bill Clinton and President Jiang Zemin in 1997–1998, U.S.-China relations appear to have regained a more even keel, although the threat of disruption due to developments on Taiwan lurks in the background.

Relations among the major powers have progressed substantially over the past several years. Analysts speak of "concerted bilateralism," or suggest that an ad hoc ensemble of powers operate to defuse threats to regional or global stability (such as the threat posed by North Korea's nuclear program). However, security multilateralism has had difficulty taking root in Northeast Asia/North Pacific. This may be about to change, though, with Moscow, Seoul, and Tokyo all calling for the creation of a six-party (between China, Japan, North and South Korea, Russia, and the United States), or six-plus-one (i.e., with Mongolia), security dialogue at the track one level. Canada currently cochairs the only functioning "full house" dialogue in the subregion, the track two Council for Security Cooperation in Asia Pacific (CSCAP) North Pacific Working Group, and Ottawa would view its exclusion from a track one grouping with some concern.

HUMAN SECURITY   Foreign Minister Lloyd Axworthy has gained both national and international prominence in recent years for his articulation of an agenda for human security. This agenda is built on a few key premises, chiefly, that security goals should be focused around the security of people rather than states or regimes; that traditional military force is of declining utility in promoting security; and that there is a particular urgency to attend to the victims of conflict, especially civilian populations. Advancing human security, in turn, calls for new initiatives, methods, and actors—proceeding, if necessary, outside the more established channels of diplomacy and international organizations. Finally, human security stresses values. The following is an excerpt from the Department of Foreign Affairs and International Trade (DFAIT) circular announcing Canada's accession to a nonpermanent UN Security Council seat in 1999–2000:

> The notion of human security is made up of a broad range of concepts, including democratic development, human rights and fundamental freedom, the rule of law and good governance. Canada believes that the Council must move to encompass this wider view of the root causes of conflicts in order to address more effectively our new security environment, where threats to international peace and security arise more and more from conflicts within states than between them, and where these threats increasingly affect civilian populations.

The human security agenda views traditional modes of conflict management and peacekeeping as inadequate to contemporary intra- and interstate security challenges. Rather, the focus should be on peace building, that is, creating or restoring conditions that allow civilians to lead secure and productive lives. Axworthy argues that the application of "soft power" through skillful diplomacy, the delivery of humanitarian and development assistance, confidence-building mechanisms, and the promotion of good governance is more effective for Canada than a reliance on traditional "hard power" tactics. While Axworthy's assertions have involved him in a lively critical debate with certain academics and defense experts, the foreign minister shows no signs of abandoning his proactive agenda. Furthermore, enthused by successes to date such as the land mines treaty and the establishment of the International Criminal Court, the attentive Canadian public continues to support such international activism.

Defense Policies and Issues

POLICY AND MISSIONS   Canada's formal defense arrangements remain within the framework of the North Atlantic Treaty Organization (NATO) and its North American partnership with the United States. In the latter context, the government has renewed its North American Air Defense (NORAD) agreements regarding continental air defense surveillance and warning. Canada has supported the enlargement of NATO, as well as specific NATO-led undertakings in the former Yugoslavia. However, regarding the development of NATO's new Strategic Concept, Canada has generated controversy by calling for consideration of a "no first use" nuclear policy. A November 1998 report by the House of Commons Standing Committee on Foreign Affairs, which advocates a rethinking of nuclear policies, ensures that this issue will remain on the agenda in 1999.

In line with general government priorities in the 1990s, the Canadian forces have continued to increase attention to and deployments in Asia Pacific. Roughly half of the navy (including five frigates, two destroyers, and five Maritime Coastal Defense Vessels, or MCDVs) will be stationed on the west coast, and staff resources for briefings and policy advice for the Maritime Command Pacific have been strengthened. The navy has regularized its program of ship visits to Asia, an initiative started in 1995 that has raised Canada's profile in the region. WESTPLOY '98 took in ports in Japan, South Korea, the Russian Far East, and China—the first such visit to the People's Republic in over a decade. In addition, Canada participates in joint naval activities in the Pacific, specifically the U.S.-sponsored biannual RIMPAC (Rim of the Pacific) exercises and other multinational exercises such as MARCOT '97, which involved Australian, Canadian, Chilean, and U.S. forces.

FUNDING, PROCUREMENT, AND TECHNOLOGY   The 1994 defense white paper continues to provide the framework for Canadian security and defense policy. The government is committed to the principle of maintaining "multi-purpose, combat capable" air, land, and maritime forces, trained and able to respond to a wide spectrum of mission requirements at home and abroad. While acknowledging the need for upgrading capital equipment and training, the white paper set out a stringent five-year defense budget plan. Reflecting the government's priority effort to reduce national indebtedness, the Department of National Defense (DND) was slated to have its budget cut by 23 percent (30 percent in real terms) from 1994 to 2000. To date, the cuts have been implemented as planned, with additional, one-time cuts in some years. The defense budget for 1998 was Can$9.4 billion (US$6.1 billion at Can$1 = US$0.65), just under 1.1 percent of gross national product. Since the government has now exceeded its overall deficit reduction targets, however, the DND is optimistic that the decline in real defense spending will be halted.

Budget cutbacks have hit hardest in two areas: personnel and equipment expenditure. The Canadian military has now nearly reached its downsizing targets, having reduced uniformed personnel about 20 percent from the 1993–1994 level of 75,000 to around 61,000 in 1998. (Current breakdowns by force are 10,500 maritime, 23,200 land, and 20,100 air, with the remainder not identified by service). Over the same time period, the civilian defense work force has been cut about 40 percent, from 35,000 to 20,000.

After several years of delaying essential acquisition decisions, the government in 1998 moved forward with some major announcements. In April, it confirmed that Canada would acquire four Upholder diesel-electric submarines from Great Britain to replace its aging Oberon-class vessels, thereby reaffirming a commitment to sustaining submarine capabilities for the navy. The government also announced the purchase of 15 Cormorant helicopters for search-and-rescue duties but has not moved on the necessary decision to provide much-needed maritime helicopters. The army received light armored reconnaissance vehicles and also achieved its full complement of 100 tactical helicopters. The navy's major capital expenditure programs of the 1980s and 1990s are winding down: All 12 frigates have now been commissioned, and 12 new MCDVs (designed for minesweeping, interdiction, and coastal patrol) will be completed within a year. Late in 1998, a billion-plus dollar plan was floated for updating the air force's aging F-18s.

The Canadian military, like many others in the region, faces serious challenges in meeting broad mandates with reduced resources.

Concerns regarding this issue have been voiced more loudly after several incidents involving a lack of equipment were publicized in the media. Even the government auditor, generally a supporter of cost-cutting, has concluded that the Canadian forces are underequipped to fulfill their mandate.

The defense establishment has begun to carefully consider the implications of the high-tech Revolution in Military Affairs, although questions remain regarding expense, roles, interoperability within multilateral contexts, and the overall capacity of the Canadian military to sustain the state-of-the-art command and information capabilities appropriate to its missions.

CONDUCT AND MORALE Revelations and subsequent investigations of a number of incidents involving serious misconduct by Canadian military personnel, particularly in the Somalia mission of the early 1990s, badly tarnished the image of the military and shook public confidence. The military appears to have turned a corner in this regard in 1998, however. An official inquiry into the Somalia incidents was ended, the government implemented numerous changes in command and training practices, and over a 12-month period many senior military leaders (including the chief of defense staff) were replaced. More positively, the military's image and morale received a boost from the superior performance of armed forces personnel in assisting civil authorities during catastrophic storms in Quebec and floods in Manitoba. In addition, the federal budget presented in 1999 is to include salary increases for the rank-and-file members of the forces, whose standard of living has eroded over the past decade.

CONTRIBUTIONS TO GLOBAL AND REGIONAL SECURITY

GLOBAL CONTRIBUTIONS Continuing their long-standing involvement in peacekeeping operations, Canadian forces in 1998 participated in 20 missions abroad. By far the largest number of personnel (about 1,500) were involved in NATO operations in the former Yugoslavia, while just under 200 were assigned to the UN Disengagement Observer Force (UNDOF) in the Golan Heights.

Reflecting both the Canadian public's support for an enhanced Canadian international role and the priorities and commitment of the current foreign minister, the government has been pursuing a higher-profile strategy on global security matters. This strategy has two dimensions: a self-conscious determination to assume leadership roles, and a refocusing of the security agenda toward human security and peace building.

The keystone of the former dimension in 1998 was the government's successful campaign to secure a nonpermanent seat on the UN Security Council for 1999–2000. Axworthy announced that Canada's main objective during its term will be to focus Council attention on matters of human security: conflict prevention, peace building, and respect for human rights and fundamental freedoms. An additional priority, in line with Ottawa's impatience with UN operations in recent years, is "to make the Council more effective, transparent and responsive to the legitimate concerns of the entire UN membership."

Cognizant of the limitations of established international institutions, Canada is also promoting new avenues of international activism. Specifically, it is seeking to build partnerships with nonstate actors, particularly nongovernmental organizations (NGOs), and exploiting the opportunities for direct communication created by the revolution in information technology. These approaches, dubbed the "Ottawa process," were used in the international campaign leading to the convention on the banning of antipersonnel land mines.

Witnessing the growing reluctance of many countries to engage in peacekeeping activities, and the concomitant reduction in the number and scope of UN initiatives, Canada has adopted an alternative strategy of focusing on building "coalitions of the willing," that is, identifying and working with countries that are willing and able to commit to action on particular issues. Canada's natural (dubbed middle-power) partners in this regard include the Scandinavian countries and Australia. The successful campaign for a land mine convention led to the Lysoen Declaration in May 1998, in which Canada and Norway agreed to a framework for coordinating action on a variety of issues. These include land mines, the establishment of an International Criminal Court, human rights, international humanitarian law, women and children in the midst of armed conflict, small-arms proliferation, child soldiers and child labor, and Northern and Arctic cooperation.

Nonproliferation of weapons of mass destruction has long been a priority issue for Canada. Ottawa moved quickly to ratify the Comprehensive Test Ban Treaty and supports all efforts to enhance global nonproliferation regimes and to tighten and enforce supplier agreements. However, disappointing developments in 1998, particularly in Asia, have forced even the most optimistic Canadian observers to realize that the strategies of denial and sanctions invoked by these nonproliferation regimes do not address the underlying, and overriding, concerns of national states impelling them to develop and deploy biological, chemical, and atomic weapons.

REGIONAL CONTRIBUTIONS   Canada's engagement in Asia Pacific security-related matters in the 1990s has evolved along three general lines: promoting a broadened definition of security, developing the norms and processes of security multilateralism, and working with Asian states to promote the institutionalization of track one and track two security dialogues and mechanisms.

Canada continues active participation in ARF and its track two counterpart, CSCAP. Canadians have been particularly engaged in inter-sessional and working group meetings on such issues as confidence-building measures, demining, peacekeeping, disaster relief, and search and rescue. Canada welcomed the creation of the CSCAP Working Group on Transnational Crime and continues to cochair the North Pacific Working Group, which held two meetings in 1998: in January in Tokyo, and in November in Beijing.

Also in track two, Canada continued to sponsor the Asia Pacific Roundtable and, with Indonesia, a program of technical workshops on the South China Sea. Canada has funded these programs, as well as its long-standing support of the ASEAN Institutes for Strategic and International Studies, through the Canadian International Development Agency. In the past several years, it has undertaken innovative projects concerning human security in Southeast Asia and has announced funding for a new initiative in 1999—a Northeast Asia Cooperation Program that will focus on nontraditional security concerns.

Canada has sought to ensure inclusivity in regional and subregional multilateral forums. Thus, Canada has supported the participation of Vietnam, Mongolia, and Laos in regional security dialogues.

In addition, Ottawa has attempted to respond to the human security dimension and the threats to social order of the economic crisis in Southeast Asia, providing humanitarian and food assistance, particularly to Indonesia. Further, it has arranged programs through international financial institutions such as the Asian Development

Bank focused on building institutional infrastructure and regulatory capacities in the financial, judicial, and legislative areas. Finally, Canada has supported and promoted the preservation of institutions of civil society and the rule of law in Indonesia and Malaysia.

Over the past several years, Ottawa has altered the ways in which it approaches Asian countries on the issue of human rights protection. Current emphasis is on bilateral engagement, in particular with Indonesia and China. Regarding China, Canada has established a joint committee on human rights and bilateral projects on legal reform. On the other hand, the Canadian government has remained adamant regarding Myanmar. Unless democratic processes are respected by the Myanmar regime, Ottawa will continue to refuse to engage in relations with it and will actively support those dedicated to creating an open, civil society in that country.

Although Canada does not have a direct voice in the arduous reunification process on the Korean peninsula, it shares the interests of regional states in preserving stability and ensuring a smooth transition on the peninsula. To that end, it has looked for opportunities to engage the North Koreans in regional affairs. In particular, Ottawa regards the Korean Peninsula Energy Development Organization as an important instrument within the context of the Framework Agreement to end North Korea's nuclear programs and as a functional mechanism for the integration of North Korea on the peninsula and in the subregion.

On the bilateral level, DND and DFAIT have worked together to organize workshops on arms control and on peacekeeping with South Korea, Japan, and ASEAN states. Of particular note in 1998 was progress by Ottawa and Tokyo toward the development of an agenda for security consultation and collaboration recommended by a jointly commissioned 1997 experts report. Activities during the year included a visit by Canada's chief of defense staff to Japan, military staff talks, a peacekeeping seminar in Japan, and a high-profile workshop in Vancouver exploring possibilities for bilateral action on peacekeeping, peace building, and nonproliferation. Officials in DFAIT believe that this bilateral initiative may become the model for Canadian engagement with other key actors in Asia Pacific. For example, productive seminars on security multilateralism were held in 1997 and 1998 with representatives of Chinese ministries and institutes.

In response to overtures from Latin American countries on the Pacific Rim and in keeping with Ottawa's interests in developing fuller relations with the Americas, an increasing number of military-to-military contacts and ad hoc track two meetings have taken place with hemispheric partners. For example, the joint MARCOT '97 exercise off the Canadian west coast, which includes Chile, simulates peace-keeping responses to regional emergencies.

In Europe in 1998, Canada joined with its U.S. and European allies in attempts to resolve the crisis in Kosovo. Canada provides ground troops for the NATO Stabilization Force (SFOR) and devotes a substantial portion of its peace-building and foreign assistance programs to rebuilding Bosnia and generally supporting democratization in Eastern Europe. Through its membership in the Group of Eight and its involvement in the World Bank and International Monetary Fund, Canada has helped shore up Russian President Boris Yeltsin's fragile regime and supported programs of economic reform in Russia.

Canadian experiences with the complex humanitarian emergencies in Africa during the past decade have been frustrating. As Ottawa learned in 1997 during its efforts to engineer an international response to the crisis in Zaire, sufficient "coalitions of the willing" no longer exist among non-African states to intervene in such situations. Canadian attention, therefore, has focused on selective human security oriented initiatives such as support for the International War Crimes Tribunal on the Rwanda genocide, land mine removal and mine victim assistance in Angola and Mozambique, and civil society building in South Africa.

3 China

The year 1998 was difficult for China, as for other nations in Asia Pacific, with the Asian economic crisis affecting China's internal and external economic environment. However, the Chinese government undertook actions to further push its economic reform programs and to improve its diplomatic relations with Japan, the United States, and other countries in the region. Relations across the Taiwan Strait also progressed during the year. These internal and external efforts served as the background for developments in China's security policy.

THE INTERNAL ENVIRONMENT   China has been less severely affected than most Asian countries by the Asian economic crisis. Although not as healthy as before, the Chinese economy in 1998 was still sound and rapidly developing.

The Chinese government's economic goal has been to maintain an 8 percent annual growth rate. A 20 percent increase in infrastructure investment was the major mechanism used to achieve this objective during the year under review. By the middle of 1998, the central government had spent 100 billion yuan (US$12.1 billion at renminbi 1 = US$0.12) on infrastructure. The strategy seems to be working, as the growth rate in 1998 was 7.8 percent. Agriculture achieved a record harvest, despite the difficulties caused by serious flooding in northeast China. Foreign trade grew at an annualized 2.4 percent in the first three quarters, down from 20 percent growth the previous year. Foreign currency reserves stood at more than US$140 billion, second only to Japan, and the Chinese currency remained stable throughout the year.

43

Political stability was maintained. The 9th National People's Congress, held in March 1997, completed the post-Deng leadership transition, with personnel and institutional changes in the central government. Li Peng completed the two terms as prime minister allowed by the Constitution and became chairman of the People's Congress. Zhu Rongji took over as prime minister and launched various reforms to the economy and government. Major programs include state enterprise reform, bureaucratic restructuring, housing reform, and changes in grain policy. The full implications of these reforms remain to be seen, but they appear likely to have deep and lasting impacts.

Social stability remains a major internal security concern to the Chinese government. The reforms and restructuring of the Chinese economy and bureaucracy and the associated layoffs are creating socioeconomic problems for millions of Chinese citizens. However, the government is also trying to establish a social safety net to assist those who are adversely affected by the reform and restructuring process.

After five years of ups and downs, high-level cross-Strait talks resumed in a meeting in Shanghai in October between Wang Daohan, president of the Beijing-based Association for Relations Across the Taiwan Strait (ARATS), and Koo Chen-fu, chairman of the Taipei-based Strait Exchange Foundation (SEF). The second Wang-Koo Talk, although not formally labeled as such, was in important ways more significant than the previous meeting, held in Singapore in 1993. First, this meeting took place on Chinese soil. Second, Koo talked not only with Wang but also with Chinese President Jiang Zemin, Foreign Minister Qian Qichen, and other high-level mainland officials, making these the first talks at such a high level since 1949.

Wang and Koo reached a four-point agreement: (1) Wang accepted Koo's invitation to visit Taiwan sometime in the near future, possibly in 1999; (2) ARATS and SEF will hold a dialogue covering both political and economic topics; (3) ARATS and SEF will strengthen exchanges and contacts; and (4) the two organizations will improve cooperation and arrangements for mutual aid in the event of accidents on either side of the Taiwan Strait. To what extent and how quickly the cross-Strait relationship will improve remain uncertain, but the resumption of high-level dialogue is in any case a positive development.

THE EXTERNAL ENVIRONMENT   China sees its current external environment as basically positive. Although the economic crisis in Asia creates instability in the economic environment, the political and security environments remain fundamentally healthy. China's relations with all the major regional and world powers—Japan, Russia, and the United States, as well as France and the United Kingdom—are normal. China also enjoys good relations with most of its neighbors in Asia, India being the major exception.

Sino-American Relations. U.S. President Bill Clinton's visit to China in late June–early July completed the first exchange of visits by the leaders of the two countries in the post–cold war era (Jiang had visited the United States in October–November 1997). It also completed the work of renormalizing the relationship and putting an end to the "Tiananmen period" in Sino-American relations. The gap between the two countries on human rights and arms proliferation has been narrowed thanks to increased dialogue and cooperation on these issues, although major differences remain. A Sino-American agreement to not target strategic weapons against the other country was a symbolic but significant confidence-building measure.

On the issue of Taiwan, the fundamental differences between China and the United States have not narrowed, but both sides seem more willing to recognize the danger to their relationship posed by this issue and are therefore trying to control and manage it. Clinton's enunciation in Shanghai on June 30 of the "three no's" policy ("We don't support independence for Taiwan, or two Chinas—or one Taiwan, one China—and we don't believe that Taiwan should be a member in any organization for which statehood is a requirement") was very helpful in stabilizing the Taiwan factor in Sino-American relations. The compatibility of Chinese and American positions on the Asian economic crisis, India's and Pakistan's nuclear tests of May 1998, and other issues indicates that strategic cooperation is becoming the major theme in the Sino-American relationship, at least from the viewpoint of the two administrations. Problems that potentially could harm the relationship are domestic political factors in the United States, adverse economic developments in either country, and the mounting U.S. trade deficit with China. Taiwan, as well, remains a troublesome and unpredictable factor.

Sino-Russian Relations. China's relations with Russia are almost problem-free because the two countries have no major differences on any international or bilateral issue. Both countries oppose hegemonism and power politics in international affairs, as well as the use of force in the Persian Gulf and Kosovo. In bilateral relations, border issues have been almost completely resolved, and along with other

Central Asian states the two countries are engaging in arms reduction and confidence-building measures in the border areas. The only disappointing aspect of Sino-Russian relations is the fact that bilateral trade is not growing as quickly as the two governments would like. The goal of US$20 billion in total Sino-Russian trade by 2000 seems difficult to reach, especially considering that in 1998 trade (including border trade) appears unlikely to have exceeded US$7 billion.

Sino-Japanese Relations. The relationship between China and Japan is one of the major factors shaping the security environment of the entire Asia Pacific region. And, importantly, China's relations with Japan today are more complicated than its relations with any other major power. On the one hand, fewer issues actually separate China and Japan than most people perceive. On the other hand, feelings, attitudes, and public opinion in China and Japan vis-à-vis the other have become less friendly. History, Taiwan, Japan-U.S. security cooperation, and the Diaoyu Islands (called the Senkaku Islands by the Japanese) are the major problems.

Japanese and Chinese defense leaders exchanged visits during the year, and Jiang's state visit to Japan in November improved the atmosphere of Sino-Japanese relations. However, the two sides did not move far on the key political problems of Taiwan and history, or on economic matters.

Relations with Southeast Asia. China enjoys basically sound political and security relations with the countries of Southeast Asia, even though trade relations have been weakened by the regional economic crisis. Numerous political and military contacts, visits, and dialogues between China and Southeast Asian countries took place in 1998.

Differences still exist on sovereignty issues in the South China Sea, but all the parties have exercised restraint. China and Vietnam held their sixth round of border talks in September, with the result that the two countries committed to sign a border agreement on land boundaries and the Gulf of Tonkin (Beibu Wan). Chinese Vice President Hu Jintao reconfirmed this commitment in talks with Vietnamese leaders during his visit to Hanoi in connection with the Association of Southeast Asian Nations (ASEAN) summit dialogues in mid-December. With the Philippines, a problem arose in November–December 1998 over construction by China on Mischief Reef. To resolve the issue, the two governments engaged in talks through diplomatic channels, with China eventually offering cooperative use of the disputed island, including the structures it had built.

Beijing condemned the mistreatment of ethnic Chinese Indonesians during the civil unrest in Indonesia in a statement that was issued largely in response to expressions of concern by overseas Chinese communities in a number of regional and Western countries. The Chinese government itself, however, considers this issue to be basically an internal matter and the responsibility of the Indonesian government. At root, China does not want to see the issue have a negative impact on its relations with Indonesia and other Southeast Asian countries.

Relations with India. China's relations with India in 1998 encountered difficulties, chiefly owing to statements by Indian officials about a "China threat" and to India's nuclear tests and weaponization program. However, the overall picture of Sino-Indian relations did not change fundamentally, particularly as both China and India understand that good relations are in their respective national interests. For its part, Beijing believes that current difficulties in the relationship can be overcome in a relatively short time.

DEFENSE POLICIES AND ISSUES

DEFENSE POLICY   A major step by the Chinese government in the security area in 1998 was the publication of a defense white paper entitled *China's National Defense*, released in July by the Information Office of the State Council. Although the second such document released in recent years, the first having been *China's Arms Control and Disarmament Policy* published in 1995, it is the first standard-form defense white paper issued by China. As such, it marked a major step toward enhancing the transparency of China's defense doctrine and budget, military structure, and other aspects of security policy.

The white paper states the following five major points as fundamental to China's defense policy:

1. The basic objectives of China's defense policy are to consolidate national defense, resist aggression, curb armed subversion, and defend the state's sovereignty, unity, and territorial integrity. China's defense modernization program is entirely for self-defense, and China is committed to resolve international disputes and questions left over by history through peaceful means. China follows a policy of independence and self-reliance in national defense.

2. National defense work is subordinated to and serves the nation's overall economic development. The armed forces are to actively

participate in and support economic development, and improvements in national defense are coordinated with economic development.

3. China pursues a military strategy of active defense, emphasizing self-defense and gaining mastery by striking only after the enemy has struck. China will adapt its defensive capabilities in the light of advances in military technology, especially high technology.

4. China will both reduce the quantity and improve the quality of its army in the Chinese way, with the objective of forming a revolutionized, modernized, and regularized people's army with Chinese characteristics. The Chinese army will make the transition from a numerical superiority approach to a technology-intensive approach.

5. China seeks and supports efforts by the international community to promote world and regional peace, security, and stability, to fairly and rationally solve international disputes, and to achieve arms control and disarmament. China does not seek hegemony, military blocs, or military expansion. China does not station troops or set up military bases in any foreign country. China believes that effective arms control and disarmament must be carried out in accordance with the principles of fairness, rationality, comprehensiveness, and balance.

IMPLEMENTATION OF 500,000-TROOP REDUCTION PLAN AND THE ORGANIZATIONAL CHANGE   The Chinese military, the People's Liberation Army (PLA), engaged in moderate organizational and structural changes in 1998. The plan announced by President Jiang at the 15th Party Congress in 1997 for a reduction of 500,000 troops is under way. The PLA is reported to have cut more than 100,000 soldiers in 1998, with additional cuts in the officer corps, military schools, troops, and headquarters being planned. The objective is to reduce the PLA from 3 million to 2.5 million personnel between 1998 and 2000. (According to the defense white paper, this figure includes all border and coastal defense forces, military service mobilization organs, military-run agricultural and other economic operations, civil cadres, and active service personnel in the reserves.) Reductions in land, naval, and air forces are to be 19 percent, 12 percent, and 11 percent, respectively. Steps are also being taken to optimize the structure and adjust the composition and interrelationships of the Chinese armed forces.

The Central Military Committee decided in March to establish a new PLA general headquarters unit, the General Armament Department of the PLA, at the same level as the General Staff Department, the General Political Department, and the General Logistics Department. The new unit is to be responsible for weaponry and equipment development as well as military purchasing.

Another significant development was a decision by the Party Central Committee in mid-1998 to disengage the Chinese military, armed police, and law enforcement organizations from business activities. This major policy decision will have significant impacts on political, economic, and military developments in China. In effect, it will enhance the rule of law, help the government fight corruption, help establish a real market system, and make the PLA become a more "modern, regular," and professional armed force. The central leadership stated that the government would ensure that all the necessary funding is provided, which means that funds will be added to the defense budget to make up for the loss of income to the military and related organizations arising from the termination of their business activities. At the time of the decision, the disengagement process was projected to be completed by the end of 1998. According to a *People's Daily* report, the handing over of military enterprises from PLA to civilian control was actually completed by December 16.

SEARCH FOR A "NEW SECURITY CONCEPT"   The Chinese government and scholarly community continue to search for a "new security concept" for post–cold war regional security in Asia Pacific. In his remarks to the ASEAN Regional Forum (ARF) meeting in Manila in July, Chinese Foreign Minister Tang Jiaxuan stated that China is seeking a new security approach and ways of safeguarding peace. He praised ARF as the main government-level channel for maintaining security dialogue and enhancing mutual confidence in the Asia Pacific region under the new post–cold war world order. Also, he stated that China will continue to participate in multitiered and multichanneled dialogues and security cooperation in the region.

U.S.-JAPAN SECURITY COOPERATION   On the general subject of alliances, the Chinese defense white paper states, "Under the new international situation, enlarging military blocs and strengthening military alliances are not helpful in maintaining peace and safeguarding security." The white paper specifically criticizes U.S.-Japan security cooperation; the Chinese government has continued to object to the new Guidelines for U.S.-Japan Defense Cooperation announced in late 1997.

When General Chi Haotian, China's defense minister, met with his American and Japanese counterparts in January, February, and May, he raised this issue and stated the Chinese position. Chi made clear to his Japanese counterpart in February that the major reason for China's concern over U.S.-Japan security cooperation is its relationship to the Taiwan issue. More specifically, he stated that clarification by the Japanese side on the relationship between the U.S.-Japan Security Treaty and Taiwan would help to reduce Chinese suspicions of U.S.-Japanese security cooperation and thus help develop Sino-Japanese relations. Other Chinese military and civilian officials repeated these points in talks with their Japanese counterparts during the year.

The Chinese government argues that Japan should abandon its "cold war mentality" and confine Japan-U.S. security cooperation to bilateral relations, thereby not allowing it to have anything to do with Taiwan or infringe on China's sovereignty and security interests. China also opposes the development of theater missile defense (TMD) in Asia by the United States and Japan. Regarding TMD development, Chinese strategists worry that it will trigger an arms race both in Asia and around the world inasmuch as it will force others to increase their offensive capacity to outpace the capacities of the new defense system. The Chinese are also concerned about TMD's implications for Taiwan. Continuing support for Taiwan in the U.S. Congress, coupled with the fact that the U.S. and Japanese governments do not exclude Taiwan in their TMD development and deployment plan, would appear to indicate that the two countries want to use TMD to protect Taiwan. China fears this sends a political signal to the Taiwanese independence movement that the United States will protect them from a mainland attack.

DEFENSE BUDGET ISSUES   The officially announced Chinese defense budget for 1998 is 90.99 billion yuan (US$10.99 billion), up 12.8 percent over the figure for 1997. Defense expenditure in 1998 accounted for 17.13 percent of the total state budget of 530.92 billion yuan (US$64.13 billion); this equals 1.2 percent of China's total gross domestic product of 7.48 trillion yuan (US$903.58 billion) in 1997. As noted above, the government has indicated that it may allocate additional funding to the defense budget to compensate for the military's disengagement from business activities.

According to the defense white paper, the composition of China's defense expenditure in 1997 was 36 percent for personnel expenses, 33 percent for operations, and 31 percent for equipment. No official figure has been given for the categories of defense expenditure in 1998.

CONTRIBUTIONS TO REGIONAL AND GLOBAL SECURITY

THE KOREAN PENINSULA Beijing maintains balanced relations with both North and South Korea because it believes such an approach to be in the interest of maintaining peace and stability on the Korean peninsula. China continues to give economic aid to North Korea in recognition of the latter's difficult economic situation. In 1998, the Chinese government provided emergency aid of 150,000 tons of grain, 20,000 tons of fertilizer, and 80,000 tons of oil, in addition to normal trade and assistance between the two countries. The two countries exchanged visits through a number of party, government, and military delegations during the year. China's assistance to North Korea goes through bilateral channels, not multilateral mechanisms such as the Korean Peninsula Energy Development Organization (KEDO), to which China does not belong because it is not a party to the 1994 Framework Agreement between the United States and North Korea on the nuclear issue that led to the establishment of KEDO.

China has actively participated in the Four-Party Talks (with North and South Korea and the United States) for building lasting peace on the Korean peninsula. The second round of talks was held in March in Geneva, chaired by the Chinese delegation, and the third round of talks took place in late November and produced an agreement to establish two working groups. The parties agreed to hold a fourth meeting in January 1999.

CAMBODIA The Chinese government sent personnel to observe Cambodia's national elections in July. Agreeing with the judgment of ASEAN and the international community that the election was fundamentally fair and free, Beijing urged all political parties in Cambodia to accept and respect the result and to cooperate in forming a new government. China believes that the question of how to deal with the leaders of the Khmer Rouge is an internal affair of Cambodia and accordingly takes no position on this matter.

SOUTH ASIA The May 1998 nuclear tests by India and Pakistan were a negative development, in China's view. Beijing strongly condemned the tests, based on the view that they are inconsistent with the global trend of banning nuclear tests and the nonproliferation efforts of the international community. Also, the Chinese government believes that nuclear tests and weaponization will lead to an arms race and jeopardize peace and stability in South Asia. China consults and cooperates with Russia, the United States, and other members of the UN Security Council on the South Asian situation; in fact, Jiang and Clinton made the first use of their new hot-line link to discuss the South Asian nuclear crisis. China chaired the meeting of the permanent members of the Security Council that issued a joint communiqué on Indian-Pakistani nuclear testing, and helped pass the UN resolution on the subject. During Clinton's June–July visit to China, he and Jiang issued a joint statement condemning the nuclear tests in South Asia and urging India and Pakistan to stop nuclear development and accede to the Comprehensive Test Ban Treaty.

Nevertheless, China is not fundamentally antagonistic toward either India or Pakistan; rather, it favors improving relations with both. Beijing believes that it is in the national interests of all three countries to maintain good trilateral relations and to maintain peace and stability in South Asia. In China's view, then, the nuclear testing issue is only a short-term difficulty and can be overcome.

THE MIDDLE EAST AND THE BALKANS As a permanent member of the UN Security Council, China claims some responsibility for maintaining peace and security in such areas as the Middle East and the Balkans. Beijing supports a peace settlement in the Middle East, as well as the UN inspection program in Iraq concerning weapons of mass destruction. However, it does not support the use of military force to reach the goals set by the UN resolutions and favors the lifting of sanctions against Iraq when clear progress is made toward compliance with the resolutions. China's position and efforts helped to avoid a military showdown in early 1998, and it strongly condemned the U.S.-British attack on Iraq in mid-December, reflecting its belief that such military action is not helpful in resolving the problems of inspection and nonproliferation.

The Chinese government regards Kosovo as an internal affair of the former Yugoslavia, and therefore does not support the use of force against Yugoslav army operations there.

ARMS CONTROL, DISARMAMENT, AND NONPROLIFERATION The Chinese government maintains an arms control and export control regime in order to fulfill its nonproliferation responsibilities. On June 10, the government issued a regulation controlling the export of dual-use nuclear materials and related technologies. Shortly thereafter, it issued for the third time a list of oil and chemical materials whose export is to be supervised by the central government.

Jiang and Clinton signed a Joint Statement on Biological Weapons during Clinton's state visit, thereby reaffirming their countries' strong support for the global elimination of biological weapons. They also signed a joint statement on antipersonnel land mines, reiterating their commitment to ending the human suffering caused by the indiscriminate use of such devices. China and other nuclear powers—France, Russia, the United Kingdom, and the United States—issued a joint statement in May committing themselves to gradually reduce and eventually eliminate nuclear weapons. Also during Clinton's visit, China pledged to further study the issue of joining the missile technology control regime.

On September 23, Zhu Bangzao, spokesperson for the Chinese Foreign Ministry, warned against a possible arms race in Asia in a comment on the decision by Japan and the United States to develop a joint missile defense system to protect Japan in light of North Korea's satellite launch in August. "We are opposed to any country precipitating an arms race under the pretext of countering the move [by the Democratic People's Republic of Korea]," Zhu stated.

MILITARY-TO-MILITARY EXCHANGES The Chinese military engaged in extensive exchanges with foreign militaries in 1998, as Chinese military leaders paid visits to Asian, North American, European, and even Latin American countries and many military leaders of other countries visited China. Chinese naval ships made port calls in Australia, New Zealand, the Philippines, the United States, and other countries. In addition, Chinese foreign ministry and defense officials have held regular security dialogues with their American, Japanese, Russian, and Australian counterparts. As an example, PLA General Staff officers and their Russian counterparts held a second round of strategic and security consultations in July. Finally, the Chinese military also had contacts with counterparts in India, the Philippines, South Korea, Vietnam, and other neighboring countries.

These exchanges have produced some specific results, important examples of which are the signing of a Sino-American agreement on maritime security consultation, invitations to foreign military officers to observe military exercises between the Chinese and American militaries, and plans for joint work on environmental security, disaster relief and humanitarian assistance, and maritime search and rescue. All these steps should serve to enhance trust and cooperation between the Chinese and American militaries.

MULTILATERAL SECURITY DIALOGUE AND COOPERATION In 1998, China continued to support and participate in various multilateral security dialogues in the Asia Pacific region, such as ARF, the Council for Security Cooperation in Asia Pacific, and the Northeast Asia Cooperation Dialogue. However, the Chinese government has reservations about proposals for an official triangular security dialogue among China, Japan, and the United States, chiefly because it believes such a dialogue might not be truly triangular but rather a bilateral dialogue between China on one side and the U.S.-Japan alliance on the other. Instead, the Chinese government has suggested that the three parties hold a track two security dialogue first.

4 European Union

The Security Environment

ECONOMIC CRISIS TESTS EUROPEAN COMMITMENT TO ASIA   The
year 1998 was a watershed year not only for Asia Pacific but also for
Europe's relationship with and its commitment to the region. As the
economic crisis, which began with the devaluation of the Thai baht in
July 1997, reverberated ever more menacingly throughout East Asia
and beyond, past achievements by individual European governments
and the European Union (EU) itself in building a stronger and more
diversified relationship with East Asia were put to the test.

The crisis produced ripple effects close to home, such as the financial implosion of Russia and an accumulating impact on European
exporters. These tended only to reinforce the pressures on Europe to
concentrate on its own affairs and its immediate environment. But
continuing high (if somewhat reduced) levels of trade with East Asia,
substantial direct investments, and the painful exposure of European
banks to the turmoil in the region reminded Europeans that their
involvement with East Asia was important enough to maintain and
strengthen previous political commitments. Overall, the year demonstrated to Europe that a closer relationship with East Asia entailed not
only profits but also risks, costs, and responsibilities.

CHANGE WITHIN EUROPE   If the European commitment to building
closer relations with East Asia was tested by entirely new conditions
in that region and in other parts of the world economy in 1998, the
task was further complicated by political change within Europe. The
projects of "deepening" and "widening" the EU continued to absorb

much energy. Although the Treaty of Amsterdam, which provided for institutional reforms to deepen European integration, was signed in 1996, the ratification process is not yet completed. In the meantime, EU enlargement negotiations have formally begun with four Central and Eastern European countries. Moreover, the Economic and Monetary Union project steadily gained momentum, leading to the initiation of a common currency (the euro) on January 1, 1999. On top of all this, in Southeastern Europe the situation in Kosovo deteriorated throughout the year and by the fall had produced another major political confrontation between the North Atlantic Treaty Organization (NATO) and Belgrade.

In addition, domestic political changes in key European countries contributed to foreign policy uncertainty. In France, a new period of "cohabitation" between Gaullist President Jacques Chirac and a Socialist-led government settled into a pattern in which the foreign policy role of the president was considerably reduced. In the United Kingdom, the new Labour government of Prime Minister Tony Blair had to reconcile its strong human rights commitments with Britain's economic and other interests in Asia. In Italy, the center-left coalition government of Romano Prodi fell in October 1998, creating fears about a return of Italy toward political uncertainty and an indistinct policy profile. Perhaps most important, in Germany also in October a new coalition government of Social Democrats and Greens replaced the liberal-conservative government of Helmut Kohl, which had run the country since 1982. Kohl had been one of the most forceful advocates of closer relations between Germany (as well as the EU) and Asia.

In principle, a largely bipartisan approach to foreign affairs and the strength of the foreign policy bureaucracies in all three major European states (France, Germany, and the United Kingdom) should have assured continuity in relations with Asia. However, the real question was over the priority and level of commitment the new governments would attach to Asia, rather than the basic substance of their policies.

EUROPEAN STAKES IN EAST ASIA   European stakes in East Asia continued to be primarily economic, although the broader interests in regional stability and security were driven home painfully by the ramifications of what was initially (and somewhat euphemistically) called a "financial crisis." In fact, the crisis is multidimensional and is affecting all aspects of societies, from grass-roots activities to international security relations.

Perhaps the most pronounced and visible European stakes in East Asia in 1998 were in the form of bank credits. As of the end of 1997, European banks accounted for more than half (US$141 billion) of total outstanding claims held by Western and Japanese banks in the five Asian states most affected by the economic crisis—Thailand, Indonesia, Malaysia, South Korea, and the Philippines. This large exposure chiefly reflected a rush by European banks for a stronger presence in the region in the period immediately preceding the crisis, in addition to the rapidly growing scope of activities in the region by European companies.

Trading relations have expanded considerably in recent years; European trade with East Asia now approximates total U.S. trade with the region. EU exports to East Asia (excluding Japan) in 1997 totaled about €109 billion (US$128 billion at €1 = US$1.17), up 12.8 percent over the previous year, while imports from the region increased by over 20 percent, to €120 billion (US$140 billion), from €99.6 billion (US$117 billion) in 1996. However, large European transnational corporations are still less exposed to East Asian markets than their Japanese or American counterparts are. Very few European transnational corporations make more than 10 percent of their total sales in Asia.

European stakes in East Asia also include regional stability and prosperity, as well as East Asia's full integration in and commitment to regional and global institutions. Europe would be profoundly affected, for example, if the momentum toward trade liberalization and open regionalism were lost in East Asia, or if that region disengaged from active support of a strong World Trade Organization (WTO). As a trading power without large military power projection capabilities, Europe ultimately depends on a stable and well-ordered international environment with strong international institutions.

Finally, Europe also has indirect but tangible security interests in East Asia. For example, exports from Asia of weapons of mass destruction, long-range missiles, or related technology could easily affect European security. Indeed, this has already begun to happen through the export of such capabilities to the Middle East and North Africa.

PASSING THE TEST   By and large, Europe so far has passed the tests of 1998 fairly well. Initial European reactions to the economic crisis in East Asia were colored chiefly by concern about the impact of the crisis on the euro project. Specifically, it was feared that a decline in economic activity resulting from the crisis might complicate the achievement of the stringent performance criteria set up at Maastricht for the euro member countries. These initial fears receded as it became clear that the euro project would not be affected—at least not in the short term. But the more optimistic assessments that the crisis would have only a very minor impact on Europe also turned out to be misguided. Instead, Europe discovered that by rapidly building up its financial and economic presence in East Asia in the years immediately preceding the crisis it had become significantly exposed to the risks of the new situation.

On the positive side, Europe's contributions to financial crisis management in East Asia were considerably more substantive and sustained than is generally acknowledged. From the time the crisis hit Indonesia and South Korea, Europe swung its support behind U.S.-inspired and IMF-led efforts to stabilize the financial and economic situation in those countries. Several elements were involved.

- EU member countries contribute about 30 percent to the resources of the International Monetary Fund (IMF)—with a parallel share in voting rights—as compared with 6 percent for Japan and 18 percent for the United States.
- EU member countries contributed about 30 percent of the total US$35 billion pledged to the IMF-led multilateral front line of defense for South Korea, and another 30 percent (US$7 billion) to the second line of defense. Both amounts exceeded U.S. contributions.
- The EU also holds 40 percent of the World Bank's subscribed capital and voting rights, as well as 14 percent of the subscribed capital of the Asian Development Bank (ADB), in which Japan and the United States each holds 16 percent. These institutions also contributed to the financial rescue packages.
- Finally, several EU member countries, as well as the European Commission, invested considerable political energy and diplomatic resources to underpin the IMF-led effort at crisis management. Thus, in February 1998 telephone calls by heads of state were made and government and high-ranking personal envoys were deployed to dissuade Indonesia's then President Suharto from pursuing the project of a currency board for Indonesia.

Europe also pressed ahead with the Asia-Europe Meeting (ASEM) process. The ASEM London summit in April 1998 was strongly colored by the Asian crisis. The meeting broadly succeeded in demonstrating Europe's continued commitment to East Asia—not so much through its fairly modest specific agreements and undertakings (such as the establishment of an ASEM support fund for human resource development in the financial sector) as by maintaining the momentum of ASEM and its multifaceted dialogue and cooperation processes. The London meeting also included discussions of security issues, such as developments on the Korean peninsula, and took some modest security-related initiatives (for example, a cooperative initiative on organized crime, the international drug trade, and money laundering).

European governments also seemed determined to retain their various commitments to closer relations with East Asia through individual initiatives. The new U.K. Labour government, which had come to office with strong pledges of an "ethical" foreign policy and a commitment to human rights activism, toned down its initial emphasis on human rights issues and began to stress economic and commercial cooperation. Blair's visit to China in October 1998, during which conciliatory and cooperative gestures clearly overshadowed differences over human rights issues, sealed this shift. In addition, several other European countries also intensified their individual efforts in Asia. The level of commitment of the new Italian and German governments to closer relations with Asia remained either less clear-cut or as yet uncertain at the time of this writing.

At the private-sector level, European multinationals have used opportunities offered by the crisis to strengthen their positions in East Asia through acquisitions or joint ventures. There are few signs of companies withdrawing; most now recognize the long-term importance of a substantial presence in East Asia and are determined to stay the course.

DEFENSE POLICIES AND ISSUES

European defense policies and expenditures continue to be driven by Europe's primary security concerns in its immediate geographical vicinity. First, since the end of the East-West military confrontation armed forces have been gradually restructuring to reflect a new security environment characterized by uncertainties and diffuse threats. This suggests the creation of rapid-deployment forces with greater versatility, firepower, and mobility. Second, while military integration continues to be a key operating principle, European NATO forces are being reorganized in ways that will make national forces deployable in different combinations (combined joint-task forces). Third, the military legacy of the cold war requires that arms control and disarmament efforts be continued. And fourth, instability and uncertainties in the former Yugoslavia and in the Southern and Eastern Mediterranean littoral regions (especially Algeria, Libya, and Israel, as well as the neighboring Arab states) are forcing Europe and NATO to focus on ways to export stability to and contain risks in Europe's neighborhood. The continued deployment of substantial forces in Bosnia involving around 33,000 military and civilian personnel from 14 NATO and 17 non-NATO countries, as well as the projected introduction of some 2,000 observers into Kosovo from the Organization for Security and Cooperation in Europe, underline this new reality, which has led NATO to move away from its past concentration on more geographically delimited responsibilities and toward "out-of-area" operations.

Defense expenditures in Western Europe had generally declined in recent years (see table 1). However, they may have bottomed out in 1998, at least in nominal terms. In the United Kingdom, Germany, Italy, and the Netherlands, the 1998 defense budgets showed either a stabilization or even a small increase, although in France there were significant cuts. However, real increases in defense spending are unlikely in the next several years.

Although the importance of the Asia Pacific region to European economic and broader political interests is clear, the goals of security and stability in the region do not figure prominently in European defense policies. European security involvements basically reflect (1) the colonial past in the region, of which a few small military vestiges

Table 1. Defense Expenditures (US$ million, at constant 1997 prices)

Country	Defense Expenditure, 1996	% of GDP	Defense Expenditure, 1997	% of GDP
France	47,401	3.3	41,545	3.0
United Kingdom	35,266	3.0	35,736	2.8
Germany	39,828	1.8	33,416	1.6
Italy	23,947	2.1	21,837	1.9
Spain	8,802	1.7	7,671	1.4
Netherlands	8,022	2.2	6,888	1.9

SOURCE: *Military Balance, 1998/99*. London: The International Institute for Strategic Studies, 1998.

remain; (2) Europe's alliance with the United States, which brought France and Britain into the Korean War and the armistice regime on the peninsula; and (3) an interest in commercial arms sales to the region. France maintains a military presence in the South Pacific through bases in its overseas territories of New Caledonia and French Polynesia. This presence includes three frigates and five Guardian maritime reconnaissance aircraft, as well as some support vessels and aircraft. The United Kingdom still has Gurkha infantry and some helicopters stationed in Brunei and continues to cooperate in the Five Power Defense Arrangements (FPDA) with Australia, Malaysia, New Zealand, and Singapore (although the FPDA has been affected recently by tensions and disagreements between Malaysia and Singapore). France and the United Kingdom in recent years have intensified their participation in joint naval exercises, not least to assist efforts at arms sales. Germany recently has also shown its flag in East Asia through a major naval visit to the region.

In addition, the major European countries are engaged in regular bilateral security consultations with a number of East Asian countries. The most extensive bilateral security dialogues take place between Japan and the major European powers, involving both foreign affairs and defense ministries. The three major European countries have also started bilateral military dialogues with the Chinese armed forces. Motives for such bilateral activities include broader political objectives, as well as these European countries' interests in arms sales.

CONTRIBUTIONS TO REGIONAL AND GLOBAL SECURITY

ARMS SALES European defense industries have become important arms and arms-technology suppliers to countries in East Asia; their market share rose during the 1990s from about 10 percent to more than 20 percent. Depending on circumstances and one's point of view, arms supplies and technology licenses might be seen as contributing just as effectively to regional insecurity as to regional security. Be that as it may, military establishments in a number of countries in the region consider European arms and defense technology, which often is somewhat less advanced and complex than American technology, to be useful additions to their national arsenals. Historical ties, the desire to diversify supply sources, and a European monopoly in certain types of arms (such as diesel-powered submarines) all play a role in this.

With the rise to power of the new left-leaning governments in the United Kingdom and Germany came reviews of the two countries' arms export policies. In the United Kingdom, initial inclinations to pursue a more restrictive or "ethical," to use Foreign Secretary Robin Cook's term, approach to arms sales were quickly countered by powerful industrial arguments for continued arms exports. Consequently, a fundamental change of the United Kingdom's rather permissive policy toward arms exports is unlikely. Germany's arms export policies have traditionally been more restrained, although the sale in the mid-1990s of much of the remnants of the East German navy to Indonesia briefly gave Germany an important position as an arms supplier.

DEVELOPMENT ASSISTANCE   Given a broad definition of security that includes as essential elements resilience, economic prosperity, and political stability, European Official Development Assistance (ODA) to East Asia clearly represents an important contribution to regional security. From 1990 to 1996, total ODA from the EU to East Asia was approximately US$12 billion, equivalent to about 55 percent of Japanese ODA to East Asia during the same period and ten times that of the United States. As mentioned previously, Europe has also contributed generously to official efforts to contain and overcome the financial crisis. Most of this support was channeled through international institutions, including the IMF, the World Bank, and the ADB, although some support was arranged bilaterally or through ASEM.

KOREA   The EU joined the Korean Peninsula Energy Development Organization (KEDO) as an Executive Board member in September 1997. There had been some early reluctance on the part of other members, particularly South Korea, to allow the EU to join in this capacity, primarily because of the statutory veto that the EU would have enjoyed as an Executive Board member. However, the statutory veto principle was subsequently abandoned, thereby removing this source of objection. The EU's contribution to KEDO has been substantial: After initial payments of €5 million (US$5.9 million) in 1995 and €10 million (US$11.7 million) in 1996, the EU's contribution was fixed at €15 million (US$17.6 million) for 1997 and subsequent years. European participation in KEDO formally takes place through both the European Atomic Energy Commission (EURATOM)—which forms part of the European Communities and thus represents an element of the EU's integrated political machinery—and the Council of Ministers, the principal decision-making body of the EU representing national member governments.

In addition, the EU was one of the largest donors of humanitarian aid to North Korea in 1997 and 1998. Its approach toward North Korea is closely coordinated with those of the United States and—through bilateral consultation arrangements—Japan and South Korea.

MULTILATERAL SECURITY DIALOGUE   EU participation at the July 1998 meeting of the ASEAN Regional Forum (ARF) in the Philippines was broadened to include the presidency of the Western European Union (WEU), in addition to the presidency of the EU and a representative of the European Commission. This change reflects the growing role of the WEU as a European defense and security organization, as well as underlines the willingness of Europe to contribute to the security—broadly defined—of Asia Pacific. During the ARF meeting, EU interventions primarily addressed efforts to prevent the proliferation of weapons of mass destruction—the nuclear tests by India and Pakistan were strongly criticized—and to promote international arms control and disarmament in the conventional field, including land mines and arms registers. Human rights and democracy issues in Myanmar were also raised. However, concern about the East Timor issue, which traditionally has loomed large in bilateral relations between the EU and the Association of Southeast Asian Nations (ASEAN), faded into the background as changes in the Indonesian position on this issue suggested movement toward a political settlement.

Europe also organized a track one seminar on peacekeeping operations (to "train the trainers," in Dublin in October 1998) and a track two symposium on land mines. Through the European Council for Security Cooperation in Asia Pacific (ECSCAP), European officials and experts continued to participate actively in the Council for Security Cooperation in Asia Pacific process, of which ECSCAP became a full member in December 1998.

Clearly, then, Europe's relationship with East Asia both through ASEM and through EU-ASEAN cooperation has relevance to broadly defined security in Asia Pacific. ASEM formally includes security issues on its agenda, and EU-ASEAN cooperation has developed a political dimension in which security issues are discussed. However, the

EU-ASEAN relationship continues to be complicated by the contested issue of Myanmar's participation in ASEAN. The ASEM London summit was able to sidestep this issue by referring the question to an ASEM "vision group" of wise men and the Seoul meeting in the year 2000. On a practical level, though, the discussions in London and the agreements resulting from them touched on security issues only at the margins, such as the initiative on organized crime, the drug trade, and money laundering. The core of the debate revolved around economic relations and the Asian economic crisis.

5 India

CHANGING GOVERNMENTS, CHANGING PERCEPTIONS   The end of Congress Party dominance of Indian politics in 1996 also marked the end of the stable parameters of India's foreign and security policies laid down by its first prime minister, Jawaharlal Nehru, at independence in 1947. There were two brief interludes of coalition government in this period, but both had neither the time nor the opportunity to make major policy changes even had they wished to do so. For the next few years, once again, coalition politics and transient governments may well be the reality in the central Parliament. This situation promises new attempts at redefining national security, although such attempts are likely to remain broadly within the bounds defined in the past.

Two versions of a center-left United Front government ruling at the center from mid-1996 to March 1998 gave priority to regional affairs through the consolidation of the South Asian Association for Regional Cooperation (SAARC) and continued the previous government's policy of improving relations with China. The United Front government supported global nonproliferation, but not those arrangements that were against Indian security interests. Its regional policy, named the Gujral Doctrine after Inder Kumar Gujral, who served successively as foreign minister and prime minister, was based on the belief that benign bilateral relations accelerate regional cooperation. The policy emphasized accommodation with and unilateral concessions to smaller South Asian neighbors, dialogue to settle all outstanding disputes, and promises not to allow one's territory to be used to launch hostile acts against another.

The present coalition government was formed in March 1998 by 19 parties led by the Bharatiya Janata Party (BJP, or Indian People's Party). The BJP holds about 34 percent of the seats in the lower house; with its coalition partners it enjoys a slender majority in the Parliament. The BJP is a center-right party representing middle-class values and propagating an ideology of *Hindutva*, or Indian-ness, which its critics consider to have a pro-Hindu bias. While seeking a greater international position for India, the BJP in economics emphasizes self-reliance (*swadeshi*) without giving up globalization. It favors a strong country with a strong defense, and it is this policy that led to the nuclear explosions on May 11 and 13, 1998, breaking a 24-year self-imposed moratorium on such tests. Pakistan followed with six nuclear tests of its own on May 28 and 30. Although there was overwhelming domestic support for the nuclear tests in both countries at first, opinion subsequently became more mixed. India has yet to clearly articulate its nuclear policy or develop its stated doctrine of "minimum deterrence." In any case, the reality of nuclear weapons on the subcontinent is likely to shape India's security environment for the future.

THREAT PERCEPTIONS   India considers its security horizon to be defined by the region including Central Asia, the Persian Gulf, the Indian Ocean community, the member countries of the Association of Southeast Asian Nations (ASEAN), and China. Within this area, major security concerns involve China and Pakistan.

India and China fought a border war in the high Himalayas in 1962. The boundary in the north with China remains unresolved and is defined today by a Line of Actual Control (LAC). Both sides claim large tracts of each other's territory: India considers China to be in occupation of 38,000 sq km of its territory in the northwest, while in the northeast the entire Indian province of Arunachal Pradesh, comprising some 90,000 sq km, continues to be claimed by China. Border talks began in 1981 and have continued ever since. This process received additional momentum with then Prime Minister Rajiv Gandhi's visit to Beijing in 1988. A Joint Working Group (JWG) has been set up to expedite the settlement of the border question.

Two major agreements have been concluded between the two countries in recent years. The first, signed in 1993, was to "maintain peace and tranquillity along the LAC," which expressed both sides' determination to maintain peace along the line separating their two forces while leaving the actual border alignment to be determined in the future. The agreement also set up an Expert Group under the JWG to hasten the ending of the LAC stalemate. Finally, the agreement was strengthened by a number of confidence-building measures (CBMs) that are being implemented by both sides. The second agreement was signed during Chinese President Jiang Zemin's visit to India in November 1996. This Agreement on Confidence Building Measures in the Military Field along the LAC expressed the commitment of both sides not to use their military capability against each other. Also envisaged were major force pullbacks and substantial additional CBMs to strengthen this agreement, the details of which were to be finalized subsequently.

Statements by the current defense minister since April 1998 have changed earlier perceptions of India-China relations. Most pointedly, the minister was quoted as naming China "potential threat No. 1." Although this was a spontaneous reply to provocative questions by an aggressive media and not necessarily correctly quoted, it did give the impression of a changing Indian view of Beijing and its future role. As the defense minister is not from the BJP and is known for taking anti-China positions, Beijing may have discounted his statement. However, a subsequent indirect reference to China as the reason for India's nuclear tests by the prime minister in a letter to U.S. President Bill Clinton suggests a real change in policy. Nevertheless, later statements by the prime minister, the defense minister, and others have been much more moderate.

India is fully conscious of China's military might and, in particular, its nuclear weapons capability. India also sees these capabilities being modernized rapidly, transforming the technological quality and force projection ability of China's armed forces. New Delhi is particularly concerned with China's continuing assistance to Pakistan in the nuclear field, as well as its sale of missiles and missile technology. Beijing's special relationship with Myanmar, including the development of strategic lines of communication and the supply of military hardware, is also seen as detrimental to Indian security.

Although Pakistan is much smaller than India, it remains a security threat primarily because of its contestation of Indian control of Jammu and Kashmir. The accession of Jammu and Kashmir to India on independence has never been accepted by Islamabad. The province remains divided in two parts controlled respectively by India and Pakistan. The two countries have fought three wars over this area in the last 50 years. A spontaneous uprising against the central government in the Indian part of Jammu and Kashmir in December 1989 was subsequently converted into a proxy war through Pakistani support. After three rounds of elections in the past two years and the accession of a popular government in the province, the earlier state of insurgency is over and conditions are returning to normal, although they still remain disturbed.

The 1998 nuclear tests have apparently given rise to a feeling in Pakistan that this is an ideal opportunity to draw global attention to Jammu and Kashmir through calibrated threats of a likely nuclear confrontation. Intense artillery duels occurred during July and August 1998 across the Line of Control (LC). Indians are also concerned that once the Taliban completely secure control of Afghanistan, they may next turn their attention to Jammu and Kashmir with the help of Pakistan's Inter-Services Intelligence. Most terrorists in Jammu and Kashmir now come from countries immediately to the west of India. Indian intelligence claims that a majority of the 28 terrorists killed in the U.S. missile attack in August on Osama bin Laden's training center at Khost in Afghanistan were earmarked for Jammu and Kashmir. Nevertheless, New Delhi remains confident that it can deal with the situation in Jammu and Kashmir without escalating the level or nature of its response to the proxy war.

In its election manifesto and later its "Agenda for Governance" put out in early 1998, the present BJP-led government stated that it would take a holistic view of national security, to be elaborated through a Strategic Defense Review (SDR). The SDR is to assess the threats and challenges to Indian security and recommend suitable policy options, and will be drawn up by a national security council (NSC). In mid-1998, an expert committee recommended a structure and tasks for an NSC, and in November the government approved the formation of an NSC. The SDR, which should be completed in the first part of 1999, will provide for the first time a comprehensive government statement on defense policy along the lines of a white paper.

EXTERNAL RELATIONS   India traditionally has played an active role in world affairs, interacting closely with other leading countries.

The Major Powers. India's relations with the United States gained considerable positive momentum after the end of the cold war, and the period leading up to India's 50th anniversary of its independence in 1997 witnessed a further consolidation of this relationship. Business and economic relations have continued to develop, with the United

States now the largest foreign investor in India, accounting for a quarter of all direct investment. A useful framework of defense cooperation has evolved between the two nations over the years, including annual meetings of a Defense Policy Group, a Joint Technical Group, and steering groups at service-to-service levels.

This emerging relationship was set back after India's May 1998 nuclear explosions, however. As required by its domestic legislation, the U.S. government imposed economic sanctions on India after the tests, including restrictions on technology transfers. An effort was launched in June to resolve the associated issues through high-level dialogue, the seventh round of which took place in Rome in November 1998. While progress has been made in some areas, leading to the partial lifting of economic sanctions by the United States in November, significant differences and important sanctions remain.

India traditionally has had a major defense supply relationship with the former Soviet Union, now Russia. Russia continues to be an important source of aircraft, air defense, naval ships, and armored warfare equipment for the Indian Armed Forces. Russian Prime Minister Yevgeny Primakov visited India in late December 1998 and signed an agreement extending military and technical cooperation to the year 2010. Both sides expect to move toward a strategic partnership, which may be formalized with Russian President Boris Yeltsin in 1999. India also has had cooperative arrangements in defense industry and research and development with several European countries, and in recent years Israel has emerged as another source of military equipment and technology.

The most recent major tension along the India-China border occurred in 1986–1987, in the eastern sector. The Tenth Meeting of the JWG on the boundary question was held in New Delhi on August 4–5, 1997. No breakthroughs were made, and no JWG meeting was held in 1998, for the first time in ten years. The Expert Group met in June 1998 in Beijing but made no progress. High-level military visits continue, however, including visits to China by the Indian army vice chief (presently chief) in 1997 and the navy chief in 1998. The director of the General Staff Department of the People's Liberation Army visited India in 1998 just before the nuclear tests.

India's Neighbors. The implementation of the Gujral Doctrine saw an improvement during the year in India's relations with its neighbors in South Asia. Prime Minister Gujral met with Pakistan's prime minister on five occasions from May 1997 to January 1998. Foreign secretary level meetings with Pakistan, which had been suspended since January 1994, resumed in late March 1997. During the second round of these meetings held June 19–23, 1997, it was agreed that structured dialogues would take place to address eight outstanding issues, namely, peace and security including CBMs, Jammu and Kashmir, the Siachen Glacier, the Tulbul Navigation project, Sir Creek, terrorism and drug trafficking, economic and commercial cooperation, and the promotion of exchanges in various fields. After interruptions due to some difficulties in 1997 and the nuclear tests in 1998, talks resumed under the agreement. The first two issues were discussed at Islamabad in October 1998; the remaining six were discussed consecutively at New Delhi in November. India has been willing to engage in constructive dialogue on all these issues but sees Pakistan as determined to block progress on all items until success is achieved on Jammu and Kashmir, which it terms the "core" issue. However, the facts that talks have taken place at all and that an agreement is in place to continue this dialogue provide hope for the future.

In December 1996, a historic treaty was signed with Bangladesh on sharing the water of the Ganges River, thereby removing a longstanding irritant in bilateral relations. The treaty is being implemented successfully despite an exceptional drought in the summer of 1998 followed by a severe flood. Progress also has been made on a number of other outstanding issues. For example, a motor vehicle agreement now being finalized will enable direct bus service between Dhaka and India. In addition, a Protocol on Inland Water Transit and Trade has been renewed for a period of two years. Also, Chakma refugees long resident in India have been repatriated to Bangladesh. On the military level, the Indian army chief of staff paid a goodwill visit to Bangladesh in August 1997, and the navy chief visited in November 1998. The Bangladeshi army chief visited India in December 1998.

Frequent high-level contacts continue with Sri Lanka, Maldives, and Nepal. The Tenth SAARC Summit was held in Colombo on Sri Lanka's 50th anniversary of its independence in 1998, and trade and economic relations between Sri Lanka and India have grown steadily. The Mahakali River Treaty, signed with Nepal in 1996 and ratified in June 1997, cleared away a long-standing bone of contention that had held up prospects of exploiting the large hydropower potential of the many Himalayan rivers originating in Nepal. With its signing, many other possibilities for cooperation are now open. Over 40,000 Nepali citizens serve alongside Indian soldiers in the regular Indian army, and many more are employed in the numerous police and paramilitary forces in India. Consequently, several hundred thousand former soldiers draw pensions from the Indian government, which is a major source of income to Nepal. India's relations with Bhutan have long been cordial and friendly, an example of harmonious coexistence between two very dissimilar nations. For example, India provides a military training team and equipment to the Royal Bhutan Army.

A substantial strengthening of regional ties in South Asia has occurred in the past few years. The target date for realizing the South Asian Free Trade Area (SAFTA) was advanced recently by four years to 2001, even though it is highly unlikely to be achieved by that date. A report by a SAARC Group of Eminent Persons provides a long-range vision and plan of action, and ministerial meetings take place frequently. As a result, the prospects for a strong regional cooperative organization are brighter than ever.

Southeast and East Asia. India also attaches high priority to its relations with Southeast Asian countries. New Delhi has participated in the ASEAN Regional Forum (ARF) and the ASEAN Post-Ministerial Conferences since 1997. It continues to participate in track one and track two dialogues in the region and is currently setting up a national Council for Security Cooperation in Asia Pacific (CSCAP) committee to help in this process. When this is completed, India will be eligible for consideration for full membership in this organization. In addition, India seeks to develop mutually beneficial defense linkages with the ASEAN countries. One notable recent development was the formation of a Bangladesh-India-Myanmar-Sri Lanka-Thailand Economic Cooperation (BIMST-EC) grouping in June 1997 to enhance economic interaction among these countries. In East Asia, high-level visits between India and Japan continued through 1997, with the Indian navy chief visiting Japan in June 1997.

Central Asia. Following the breakup of the Soviet Union, India resumed its traditional links with various Central Asian countries, including numerous high-level visits. A trilateral transit agreement to facilitate trade was signed in 1997 between India, Turkmenistan, and Iran. India's energy needs are best served by stability in the region and multiple exit routes for energy supplies. Oil and gas pipelines from Central Asia through Afghanistan and Pakistan to India should contribute to general prosperity in South Asia. However, Afghanistan remains an area of concern, with continuing ethnic conflict and the Taliban's religious extremism and support of terrorism abroad.

West Asia. The Persian Gulf region is part of India's extended neighborhood and will remain a vital source of energy for India for many years in the future. Adverse developments in the region therefore directly impinge on Indian security. Annual trade with the region exceeds US$10 billion, and foreign remittances from Indian workers contribute US$4 billion. Peace and stability in the region are thus of paramount concern to India.

Indian Ocean Region. India has a coastline of 7,683 km and an Exclusive Economic Zone (EEZ) of 2.01 million sq km. Ninety-five percent of India's external trade and 84 percent of its oil are transported on its waters. Accordingly, the security of maritime routes is of chief concern to India, making a sufficient naval capability an imperative. While the Indian government strongly supports the Indian Ocean Rim Association for Regional Cooperation (IOR-ARC) as a means to strengthen economic relations with countries in the region, it opposes any security arrangements among them. New Delhi has voiced strong opposition to any foreign naval presence in its surrounding oceans, in particular the U.S. naval base at Diego Garcia.

INTERNAL ENVIRONMENT   India's unique experiment of establishing a nation in a multiethnic, multireligious, and multilingual environment, within an entirely democratic state structure, has not been without its problems. The strains of state building continue to be felt in some parts of the country, particularly on the periphery. Insurgencies smolder in four out of the seven provinces in northeast India, some with a pro-independence goal but most seeking greater autonomy within the existing political system. Remnants of an armed communist movement persist in central India, while the Sinhala-Tamil conflict in Sri Lanka overflows and affects south India. Meanwhile, other related problems of externally sponsored terrorism are exacerbated by porous borders. Although the Indian democratic system has been resilient enough to deal with these problems, at times they heavily strain the nation.

Government-Military Relations. The Indian armed forces have a strong tradition of being apolitical and respecting civilian control, but the end of 1998 brought unaccustomed tension in relations between the military and the government. On December 30, the government suddenly fired the navy chief of staff, who only two days previously had also become chairman of the Joint Chiefs of Staff. Simultaneously, the defense secretary (the senior civil servant in the ministry) was transferred. Although there had been some naval discontent over a senior navy appointment made by the cabinet despite the resistance of the navy chief, this alone seems an inadequate explanation for such unprecedentedly fractious government-military relations in India. The full consequences of these developments are unclear and potentially troublesome.

NONMILITARY DIMENSIONS OF SECURITY   India is located between two of the world's leading narcotics-producing and narcotics-exporting regions: to the northwest lie Pakistan and Afghanistan, and to the east Myanmar. Along with small-arms trafficking and money laundering, narcotics production and export pose major challenges not only to bordering provinces but also to the rest of the country.

Other Indian security concerns relate to uncontrolled population movements, unemployment, inadequate economic growth, ecological degradation, and climate change. Large population movements from Bangladesh and Nepal to India add to regional burdens and damage social cohesion in the new areas of settlement. India achieved a steady annual gross domestic product growth rate of around 7 percent from 1995 to 1997 and has not been greatly affected by the Asian crisis, with growth of about 5 percent likely in 1998. However, 5 percent annual growth is inadequate to absorb new entrants to the labor market or to ameliorate massive poverty. A growth rate of at least 7 percent is probably required to address these fundamental causes of internal insecurity.

Ecological degradation leading to the loss of forest cover in the Himalayas has decreased the ability of the land to hold rainwater. This causes sudden overflows in the monsoon months and flooding in the lower reaches of rivers, destroying crops and reducing food production. Moreover, global warming and climate change leading to rising sea levels have the potential to result in massive human displacements in the coastal areas of the peninsula and in Bangladesh. All these factors are engendering a better appreciation of the interdependence of the region in matters of nonmilitary security.

DEFENSE POLICIES AND ISSUES

DEFENSE POLICY   India considers its security to be best served in a multipolar world, believing that this provides the best environment for nations to interact with each other in a spirit of mutual respect, mutual benefit, and equality. India's overall security aim is for its population to live securely within the country's legally defined borders. Its specific objectives are defined as the ability to (1) defend the country's borders; (2) protect the lives and property of citizens; (3) promote cooperation and understanding with neighbors; (4) work with the Non-Aligned Movement and through ARF; (5) pursue security and strategic dialogues with major powers and key partners; (6) follow a principled policy on disarmament and international security issues based on universality, nondiscrimination, and equal security for all; and (7) maintain a secure and effective deterrent against the use or threat of use of weapons of mass destruction.

Defense Forces. The Indian Armed Forces of the Union Government consist of the army, the air force, and the navy, with total personnel of about 1.2 million. The Coast Guard, also under the Ministry of Defense, is responsible for the defense of coastal waters. Major paramilitary organizations, under the Ministry of Home Affairs, are the Rashtriya Rifles, the Assam Rifles, the Border Security Force, and the Central Reserve Police. Their total strength is about 400,000.

The Army. The primary role of the Indian army is to safeguard the territorial integrity of the nation. An additional responsibility of the army is to assist the civil administration to maintain internal security and law and order, a task which in recent years has frequently been entrusted to it. Monetary resources have not been entirely adequate to address the need for modernization. Most army equipment is produced by the domestic defense industry; however, long-range artillery and air defense systems are imported. New equipment acquisitions include the domestically manufactured Arjun main battle tank and a new family of infantry small arms. The short-range (150 km) Prithvi missile was introduced in 1997.

The Navy. The peninsular nature of the Indian landmass, the importance of territorial waters, and India's large EEZ necessitate a substantial naval capability. However, the Indian navy is the smallest of India's three services and has often been given lower priority owing to more pressing security problems on land. Many shipbuilding projects, including an indigenous submarine and the aircraft carrier program, have been delayed because of a lack of financial support. The Indian navy has always believed in aircraft carriers as the best means of maintaining control over surrounding waters. Currently, however, only one carrier is in service, and it will soon go into an extended refitting program.

The Air Force. India's modern combat air force is the fourth largest in the world both in terms of number of aircraft (762) and personnel (140,000), with a mix of aircraft originating from various sources. The Indian aircraft industry has a good maintenance capability but cannot yet develop new systems entirely by itself. A current major project is the midlife upgrading of some 100 MiG-21 BIS aircraft by Russia in India. In addition, 40 Russian Su-30 K multipurpose combat aircraft have been purchased recently. A major shortcoming of the Indian air force is its lack of an advanced jet trainer. Two ambitious major projects, an advanced light helicopter and a multipurpose light combat aircraft, both fairly advanced, may be affected by the recent U.S. denial of technology transfers.

DEFENSE SPENDING   Defense expenditure details are presented every year to the Parliament in the annual budget. The defense budget is scrutinized by the Expert Committee of the Parliament and by the Parliament itself. The breakdown of the defense budget for the past four years is shown in table 1.

Table 1. Defense Budget for India (billions of current rupees)

	1995–1996	1996–1997	1997–1998	1998–1999
Army	142.52	158.73	189.73	222.59
Air Force	69.31	74.92	91.53	94.02
Navy	37.98	39.76	47.73	59.77
R&D	13.82	13.46	19.9	24.7
Defense production	5.0	7.3	12.2	10.9
Total	268.56	295.51	361.90	412.0*

SOURCE: Indian government budgets.

*Just under US$10 billion at the end-1998 approximate exchange rate of Rs42.47 = US$1.00.

Given India's land area, security responsibilities, population, and GDP, its defense expenditure is comparatively modest, at about 2.3 percent of GDP. The defense budget includes all items of defense spending except pensions, which in 1997–1998 amounted to about Rs49 billion (US$1.15 billion at Rs42.47 = US$1.00). Defense expenditure for 1998–1999 increased about 14 percent from the previous year, mainly because of a substantial, long-overdue pay hike for all ranks. The budget also reflects an annual inflation rate of around

5 percent, rising to 8 percent in 1998–1999, along with a steady devaluation of the rupee, which makes imports more expensive. India recently has been a very modest arms exporter: Sales were Rs5.4 billion (US$127 million) in 1994–1995, Rs0.96 billion (US$23 million) in 1995–1996, and Rs1.6 billion (US$38 million) in 1996–1997.

NUCLEAR POLICY   On May 11 and 13, 1998, India successfully completed a series of five nuclear tests: One was of a thermonuclear device, another of a fission device, and three were of subkiloton devices. Although doubts were raised in the West regarding the yields of some of the explosions, Indian scientists have stuck to their estimates and claim now to have sufficient data to develop a variety of weapons without additional tests.

The BJP has all along favored nuclearization and stated this clearly in its election manifesto. However, this policy might have remained on hold had it not been for continued Chinese assistance to Pakistan's nuclear and missile programs and Pakistan's testing of the medium-range Ghauri missile on April 6, 1998. The Indian order to test reportedly was given on April 8.

India is now a nuclear state, even though it may not be recognized as such under the UN Nonproliferation Treaty (NPT). Subsequent to the tests, India declared a policy of "no first use" and its willingness to extend this formally through bilateral and multilateral assurances. India has also agreed to sign the Comprehensive Test Ban Treaty (CTBT) under certain conditions and does not oppose the treaty's coming into force by September 1999. Having already announced a voluntary moratorium on further testing, India is ready to engage actively in the Conference on Disarmament in Geneva to develop a Fissile Material Cut-off Treaty that will prohibit the future manufacture of fissile material for nuclear weapons use.

India has vaguely articulated a policy of "minimum deterrence," although it has not spelled this out. In any case, it does not believe in entering into a nuclear arms race with its neighbors. At present, its delivery capability is restricted to the Prithvi short-range missile and a variety of aircraft. The third and final test of the medium-range (1,500 km) nuclear-capable Agni missile, which was initially only a technology demonstrator, was conducted in 1994, after which the program was shelved. The project was revived in early May 1998, however, but no further trials had been conducted as of the end of 1998. The range of Agni II is likely to be about 2,500 km.

CONTRIBUTIONS TO REGIONAL AND GLOBAL SECURITY

REGIONAL SECURITY   India's support for regional security cooperation (through SAARC, ASEAN, ARF, and track two efforts) was discussed in the first section of this chapter. In addition to these activities, India engages in confidence-building measures in the region, including goodwill visits by the Indian Armed Forces and joint naval exercises. A unique example of these is an annual gathering of regional navies in the Andaman Islands. Eleven naval ships from Bangladesh, India, Indonesia, Malaysia, Singapore, Sri Lanka, and Thailand met for social, cultural, and sports activities in 1997. Such activities help foster friendship and promote confidence among the larger naval fraternity in the region.

DISARMAMENT AND INTERNATIONAL SECURITY   India has consistently followed a principled policy on disarmament and international security based on universality, nondiscrimination, and equal security. In the 1950s, India advocated a comprehensive nuclear test ban, which if implemented then would have sharply limited the current nuclear weapons stockpile and controlled both vertical and horizontal proliferation. New Delhi has opposed the NPT as unequal and discriminatory, and rejected the CTBT as inadequate both to effect global nuclear disarmament and to ensure the security of all nations.

India has signed the Chemical Weapons Convention (CWC) and was the 62nd country to ratify it, on April 29, 1997. Moreover, India was unanimously elected the first chair of the Executive Council of the Organization for the Prohibition of Chemical Weapons to oversee the implementation of the CWC. As a state party to the Biological and Toxic Weapons Convention, India is actively engaged in developing a verification protocol to strengthen the convention.

Although it recognizes the humanitarian problems posed by the indiscriminate use of antipersonnel land mines, India believes that the legitimate use of land mines as accepted under an amendment to Protocol II of the Certain Conventional Weapons Convention should be permitted until alternative defense means are found. The Indian army has always been a responsible user of land mines, employing them only for legitimate defense purposes. After conflicts, land mines have been lifted and the ground made safe for productive use. No mines are laid during peacetime, even for preventing large-scale hostile infiltration across borders; however, limited numbers of mines from earlier conflicts are still in place in some remote mountain areas. India has never exported land mines and has pledged never to do so; it considers the major problem in this area to be the indiscriminate sale and transfer of such weapons, and would support all measures to prevent this. In the meantime, India believes the focus of international action should be on demining activities.

Small-arms proliferation has emerged as a major cause of instability and violence in the world. The increasing lethality and indiscriminate use of such weapons today pose a major threat to the security of many nations, including India. India therefore favors concerted international efforts on this problem to supplement the ongoing work of many nongovernmental organizations.

GLOBAL SECURITY   India has provided probably the largest number of soldiers to UN peacekeeping operations of any nation—over 50,000 troops to date. It has participated in 21 UN missions, beginning with the UN Forces in Korea in the 1950s, and has provided nine force commanders. It currently provides a battalion to the UN Interim Force in Lebanon (UNIFIL) and military personnel to the UN Iraq-Kuwait Observer Mission (UNIKOM). Fifteen Indian officers and 76 soldiers have died in UN operations. As a matter of policy, India would prefer not to be engaged in peace enforcement operations (under Chapter VII of the UN Charter), or in operations where the UN contingents are under single-nation command. However, Indian forces are available for peace maintenance and observation, as well as for humanitarian missions. In addition, an Indian brigade has been committed to the UN standby arrangement.

6 Indonesia

THE SECURITY ENVIRONMENT

Indonesia, the fourth most populous country in the Asia Pacific region as well as in the world, entered 1999 in a state of extreme uncertainty. The financial crisis and economic collapse that had begun in July 1997, combined with the erosion of confidence in President Suharto over recent years, precipitated a political upheaval in the country in 1998. A wave of violent incidents and student demonstrations led to Suharto's sudden resignation on May 21. The simultaneous economic and political crises constitute the most profound challenge to Indonesia's fundamental stability and security since the chaos and blood bath that accompanied the transition from founding President Sukarno to Suharto in 1965–1966. The succession to the presidency of B. J. Habibie, Suharto's longtime colleague and newly elected (in March 1998) vice president, was widely seen as a transitional phenomenon owing to Habibie's links to the former regime and his lack of independent legitimacy. The near-term outlook is highly uncertain; even the survival of the nation in its current form may be at risk.

Indonesia's perceptions of the security environment, and its own contributions to regional and global security, are inevitably affected by its almost total preoccupation with the ongoing domestic crises. The Indonesian government's ability to exercise the tacit leadership role it had played in the Association of Southeast Asian Nations (ASEAN) and in wider regional and international forums in recent years has been seriously eroded. It is an open question when—or if—Indonesia will be able to recover its internal cohesion sufficiently to resume its former international role. Should the nation disintegrate, it could become a source of instability in the wider region.

DOMESTIC SECURITY   *Economic Collapse.* As 1999 began, the Indonesian economy was in a shambles. Economic growth in 1998 was estimated at negative 15 percent. Although the rupiah had recovered from its crisis lows, at Rp7,000–8,000 to the U.S. dollar it was still worth only one-third of its mid-1997 value. Inflation for 1998 was estimated at over 75 percent, with prices of basic commodities such as food in many cases more than doubling, especially in the hardest-hit cities and regions. Estimates of unemployment ranged from just under 10 percent to over 20 percent of the total labor force, or 10–20 million people. The numbers of unemployed were particularly high in the volatile major cities—the Jakarta manpower office estimated over 800,000 unemployed in the capital, with urban-bound inflows of unemployed from the countryside running as high as 300,000 in December 1998 alone. The number of people living at or below the poverty line, which had been estimated at 22 million, or 11 percent of the population, in 1997 before the crisis, also increased dramatically: Estimates as of the end of 1998 ranged from nearly 40 million to over 100 million, or half the population. Even the lower ranges of these estimates indicated an environment of abject poverty, desperation, and social volatility in the capital and elsewhere.

Meanwhile, the new Habibie government was working closely during the year with the International Monetary Fund (IMF) and the World Bank on a program of economic reconstruction and reform, and making reasonable progress toward agreed-upon goals. However, much of the banking system was under government supervision or at best on very shaky financial footing, most Indonesian private enterprises remained technically bankrupt (the cost of imported raw materials generally exceeding the local market price of the finished products), and the government was attempting to privatize or sell off (at heavily discounted prices) most government-owned enterprises— with highly mixed success to date. Despite emergency loans from the IMF, other international institutions, and bilateral donors, as well as special commercial credits and guarantees from Indonesia's major trading partners, economic activity showed few signs of recovery. Clearly, the economic collapse alone would have been sufficient to pose a grave danger to national stability.

Primordialism and Conflict. The series of incidents beginning in mid-1996 and continuing up to the present—with high points being the May 1998 rioting that precipitated Suharto's resignation and the confrontations between government security forces and student demonstrators during the November 1998 special meeting of the People's Consultative Assembly (MPR, Majelis Permusyawaratan Rakyat) to call new elections—revealed the persistent depth of ethnic, religious, and other primordial divisions within Indonesian society. The small ethnic Chinese minority, a perennial scapegoat in internal Indonesian conflicts, was the most visible though not the only target. Conflicts also occurred between Moslems and Christians, between different Moslem factions, and between other ethnic groups throughout the archipelago, to varying degrees echoing or stimulated by splits within the national leadership. In addition, small but determined secessionist movements in Aceh Province in the far north of Sumatra, as well as in Irian Jaya and East Timor at the eastern end of the archipelago, gained renewed confidence and increased their activities. Finally, opportunistic actions by criminal elements taking advantage of the loss of control by the security authorities, score-settling in local disputes, and violent outbursts by the disaffected poor who have suffered most acutely from the economic meltdown complete the picture of growing anarchy. Thousands of people may have died in the violence of 1998.

Political Maneuvering. As 1998 ended, new laws on political parties, the composition of the central and provincial representative bodies, and the electoral system were being debated in the national parliament (DPR, Dewan Perwakilan Rakyat) and among the political elite. In the meantime, over a hundred new political parties had been established since the outbreak of the crisis, many representing parochial interests or extremely small groups. Given this situation, if a genuinely fair and competitive election is held as scheduled on June 7, 1999, five or six major parties are likely to have a significant representation in the new DPR, but with none holding a majority. (Should the government political vehicle Golkar overcome current internal frictions and its formal disengagement from the military and manage to mobilize its former bureaucratic machine to win a dominant position in the new DPR, this outcome would be widely seen as illegitimate, likely triggering further protests and instability.)

President Habibie plausibly could form a coalition between Golkar and one or more of the larger parties and thereby win reelection as president by the MPR in December 1999. However, in his first six months he did not appear able to exercise firm control over his diverse cabinet, and lacking a strong political constituency of his own he would be in an even weaker position heading a coalition government. Habibie's effective power still depends primarily on a tacit alliance with the armed forces chief, General Wiranto.

Role of the Military. In the meanwhile, the Indonesian Armed Forces (ABRI, Angkatan Bersenjata Republik Indonesia), the power base of the former Suharto regime and still the ultimate guarantor of national stability, have been undergoing their own grave crises of identity and confidence. Charged with maintaining order, ABRI has repeatedly failed to prevent or effectively respond to the recent eruptions. Worse, military personnel also have been accused of inciting violence for their own political purposes. A government-appointed fact-finding team investigating the May 1998 riots implicated Suharto's son-in-law, General Prabowo, in instigating violence, including the rape of dozens of (mostly ethnic Chinese) women. Prabowo's troops are also accused of kidnapping 24 student protest leaders, and possibly killed 15 of them. A wave of mysterious killings of religious figures in East Java, and revelations of atrocities committed by the army over the span of a decade in Aceh, further reduced public respect for, and morale in, ABRI. Finally, the army was forced to reduce its deployments in Aceh and East Timor, triggering renewed incidents in both provinces.

Wiranto, at the top of the ABRI command, played a key role in orchestrating both Suharto's resignation in May and the smooth takeover by Habibie, but his own position within the military is not completely secure. The dismissal of Prabowo from the command of the Strategic Reserve immediately after Suharto's resignation, and his forced retirement from the military later in the year (following the fact-finding committee report), removed Wiranto's major rival. Also, a subsequent series of personnel shifts in ABRI further strengthened Wiranto's position. However, Prabowo is believed to retain supporters among his former elite troops and elsewhere, and other military officers close to Habibie can also challenge Wiranto.

Indonesia is now a weak state with a weak government; its survival as a nation is not guaranteed. Uncertainty about both Indonesia's economic viability and political stability is a serious concern for Southeast Asia and the broader Asia Pacific region, as well.

THE EXTERNAL ENVIRONMENT   A Department of Foreign Affairs seminar in late 1998 concluded that the relative complacency of recent years in Indonesia about the security environment has been replaced by a new wariness and tension. There is a greater recognition that economics is inseparable from politics and security, and that economic growth and dynamism are important to maintaining peace and stability in the region. The economic crisis has also demonstrated the importance of regional and global institutions such as the IMF and the World Bank.

The Major Powers. One common view is that the economic crisis and the new uncertainties in the region are changing the relative balance of power among China, Japan, and the United States. The United States, with its overwhelming political, economic, and military power, has become more powerful in the region as a result of the economic crisis. An increased U.S. role is inevitable, because no other nation has the same reach and leadership position in the region. Some Indonesians favor more active support of the United States in its expanded role. For example, the vice chairman of the parliamentary security commission suggested that Indonesia provide military facilities to the United States. On the other hand, many other Indonesians remain ambivalent about the U.S. role, indicating danger of a backlash if the United States becomes too assertive. A balanced American policy toward the region, combining economic, political, and security roles, would be most likely to win sustained acceptance.

Japan, as the second largest economy in the world, has been widely expected to take the lead in the region's economic recovery—first of all, by reflating its domestic economy. In general, Indonesians would like to see Japan play a leadership role in the region; the problem has been weak leadership in Japan. That much said, though, Indonesians clearly prefer that the Japanese role be limited to economics, as many are still reluctant to accept a Japanese military role. (However, support exists for the U.S.-Japan security alliance because it provides a reliable basis for Japanese participation in regional security.)

China's response to the economic crisis has shown understanding. Beijing's participation in providing financial assistance to Thailand as part of the IMF deal, and its pledges not to devalue the renminbi (which would deal another blow to the Asian economies affected by the crisis), were well received. However, this is also a somewhat mixed picture. If China manages its economy well, then its political and strategic (and presumably military) weight will increase vis-à-vis the rest of East Asia. How Beijing uses this greater weight will affect the future regional power balance.

Indonesians attach less regionwide significance to Russia and India. A lack of financial resources plus a preoccupation with more pressing domestic issues and with Europe will likely limit Russian engagement in Asia to the North Pacific area. Indonesia has long historical links with India, but the country has never entered into Indonesia's security calculus except for minor concerns about India's naval power.

Because the U.S.-Japan security alliance limits concerns about Japan, the primary security concern for Indonesia in the region undoubtedly is China. The general Indonesian perception is that China views Southeast Asia as its traditional sphere of influence. Accordingly, although the ideological threat of Chinese communism has faded (as affirmed when Indonesia restored normal diplomatic relations with China in 1990), the traditional strategic fear of China remains. China's nuclear status is a general concern, and its claim to the Spratly Islands reflects its geographic proximity and interest in the region. Moreover, the influential ethnic Chinese minorities in the countries of the region are seen by Indonesians as conduits for Chinese influence.

Southeast Asia/ASEAN. The 1998 leadership change in Indonesia and other stresses associated with the regional economic crisis and its political fallout produced brief verbal flare-ups during the year at the leadership level between Indonesia and both Singapore and Malaysia. When Habibie became vice president, former Singaporean Prime Minister Lee Kuan Yew questioned his fitness to serve as president. Habibie, after succeeding Suharto, reciprocated by describing Singapore as an insignificant dot on the map. With Malaysia, the dismissal and subsequent arrest of former Deputy Prime Minister Anwar Ibrahim led to a public expression of sympathy from Habibie, who has a long-standing personal friendship with Anwar. This was followed by suggestions that Habibie might not attend the November Asia-Pacific Economic Cooperation (APEC) meeting in Kuala Lumpur, much to the chagrin of Prime Minister Mahathir bin Mohamad. In the end, Habibie attended and his reservations about the treatment of Anwar were put aside for the sake of the larger national interests involved. Regarding ASEAN, some disappointment exists among Indonesians that the grouping has done little to help Indonesia in its present crisis. Nevertheless, the government continues to attach major importance to ASEAN.

DEFENSE POLICIES AND ISSUES

Domestic and external changes in the security environment have directly affected Indonesia's defense policies and agenda.

THE DUAL FUNCTION   A major debate is now under way about the military's dual function (*dwifungsi*) concept. This concept, which dates from the struggle against communism in the 1950s and 1960s, holds that the military has civil and political as well as security responsibilities. It is the theoretical basis for the military's long domination of the Indonesian government and policy making. Many outside ABRI, including retired senior military figures, today argue that the military must become more professional and should deemphasize *dwifungsi* in order to concentrate on its security role. Such arguments have increased following Suharto's downfall.

The issues involved are fundamental and complex. The dual function concept is deeply entrenched. The Indonesian military, to its benefit, has been less sectarian and more pro-nation in its operations than other sociopolitical groups. There is an inevitable tendency, however, for the military to interpret all opposition activities as threats to national interests. Consequently, over time the military's *dwifungsi* role has come to be equated with resistance to change for the sake of preserving the military's privileged position.

In practice, the dual function fell primarily to the army. It is therefore not surprising that the navy and air force have been in the forefront supporting the case for increased professionalism. Basically, they argue that the army's role should be limited to guarding the country against external threats and that the police should be separated from ABRI (a change now in process).

A related issue is the role of ABRI in the DPR. The number of DPR seats allocated to ABRI was reduced from 100 to 75 in 1997; draft legislation proposed by the government for the 1999 election provides for a further reduction to 55 seats. Nongovernment parties have demanded even further reductions, and the November 1998 MPR session endorsed a gradual phasing out of ABRI seats in the future. In addition, there is growing criticism of ABRI's long-standing involvement in commercial activities as yet another distraction from its professional mission as well as a bottleneck to a competitive economy and democratization.

TECHNOLOGY AND DOCTRINE   The Indonesian military also faces pressures to modernize its technology and weapons systems. This will entail a smaller number of more highly trained personnel. According to the publication *Military Balance 1998/99*, from the International Institute for Strategic Studies, the Indonesian Armed Forces now comprise approximately 300,000 personnel: 235,000 army, 45,000 navy, and 20,000 air force. In addition, there are approximately 175,000 police. A change in the size and structure of the force would also necessitate revisions to current military doctrine, which is still essentially based on the experience of the independence revolution, when poorly equipped Indonesian forces supported by the local populace mounted a stubborn and ultimately successful opposition to the militarily superior Dutch.

Generally speaking, direct attacks on a country's core territory seem increasingly unlikely in today's world. Furthermore, the concept of "total people's defense" derived from the experience of the Indonesian revolution is difficult to apply to strategies for protecting Indonesia's Exclusive Economic Zone or its small outlying islands such as the hydrocarbon-rich Natunas near the South China Sea. Rather, expanded roles for the navy and the air force seem more appropriate for these situations. However, the army has resisted efforts to prepare for these contingencies and instead is reemphasizing the people's defense concept. The proposal advanced in late 1998 by Wiranto to recruit and train a new paramilitary force of 40,000 men to reinforce security during the 1999 election seems to reflect this more traditional approach to security.

The adoption of a modernization agenda would inevitably lead to decreases in the size of the army. But at a time when the security forces—primarily the police and the army—are having difficulty controlling the social upheaval in the country, army leadership is understandably reluctant to reduce its force levels. Complicating this debate, then, are differences over priorities among missions as well as institutional interests.

SPENDING AND PROCUREMENT   The economic crisis had already constrained military procurement in 1997—the 1997 defense white paper ruled out new acquisitions other than those already approved. Habibie, for some time the leading advocate of developing a domestic high-technology and defense-related industry, was obliged during the year to reduce the governmental priority given to high technology. As a result, government spending on the national defense industry has plummeted.

The overall military budget was cut in July 1998 to the equivalent of US$1.7 billion (down from US$2.3 billion in 1997), a level sufficient only to maintain routine expenditures. The ratio between routine and development expenditure is unusually high, at 3 to 1. About 43.3 percent of routine expenditure is for personnel costs, and the remaining 56.7 percent covers operations and maintenance.

A purchase of Russian Sukhoi fighter aircraft, approved in 1996, was canceled in 1997; no alternative purchase has yet been decided. Indonesia now has a smaller air force than Singapore, Thailand, and Vietnam. On the other hand, it has the strongest navy in ASEAN.

DEFENSE COOPERATION Although officially pursuing an "independent" foreign policy, Indonesia carries out long-standing defense cooperation activities, including joint exercises, with a number of other countries. In 1998, however, owing to economic problems and domestic unrest no joint exercises were held. Indonesia's defense cooperation partners include its immediate ASEAN neighbors, Australia, and the United States. Nevertheless, Indonesia continues to reject multilateral security cooperation under ASEAN.

CONTRIBUTIONS TO REGIONAL AND GLOBAL SECURITY

Given the difficult and unstable domestic situation in Indonesia in 1999 and the unknowable outcome of the parliamentary and presidential elections now scheduled for June and November, respectively, it is impossible to predict with certainty Indonesia's future policies on regional and global issues. If conditions continue to deteriorate, it is possible that there will be a rise of nationalistic sentiment and a tendency—likely to be encouraged by some politicians—to blame foreign countries or other external actors for Indonesia's problems.

Nevertheless, a reversion to adventurism abroad along the lines of the confrontation against Malaysia under Sukarno in the early 1960s seems highly improbable. Neither Sukarno's daughter, Indonesian Democratic Party leader Megawati Sukarnoputri—the natural heir to her father's nationalist credentials—nor Amien Rais or other modernist Moslems who have criticized former President Suharto for not aligning more closely with the Islamic world, nor any other visible contenders for national leadership now advocate such radical nationalism. Except within some fringe groups with no significant leadership or influence on policy making, the desirability of wide-ranging engagement with the outside world is not seriously questioned. Most segments of Indonesian society recognize the importance of ASEAN and other multilateral arrangements. Similarly, most business leaders accept the need for Indonesia to continue engaging in trade liberalization through the ASEAN Free Trade Area, APEC, and the World Trade Organization; to work with international financial institutions; and to remain open to foreign investment.

Overall, 1998 saw a reprioritization rather than a redirection of Indonesia's foreign and security policy. Despite the Habibie government's primary focus on domestic concerns, the Foreign Ministry led by longtime minister Ali Alatas continues to pursue the basic policies of regional and global cooperation established during the Suharto period. As an example, regarding the most contentious foreign policy issue that potentially could be used as a lightning rod for nationalistic emotions, East Timor, the Habibie government has continued discussions of a negotiated resolution with Portugal, the former colonial power, through the United Nations. Absent a total collapse and the emergence of an entirely new leadership configuration, it is likely that Indonesia will remain strongly committed to the maintenance of stability and the building of regionalism in Southeast and East Asia.

REGIONAL SECURITY   Indonesia's primary contribution to regional security remains its participation in ASEAN. Increasing awareness of the power of interdependence has led to significant changes in outlook among Indonesian policymakers even within the usually conservative security establishment. For example, ABRI used to support only an evolutionary approach to developing the ASEAN Regional Forum (ARF) but has now begun to argue that it is necessary to develop as wide and full a range of partnerships as possible at all levels of society in order to strengthen a network of direct links.

ARF is the most important Asia Pacific institution for confidence-building endeavors. Indonesia strongly supports the ARF agenda including confidence-building measures and preventive diplomacy. Other desirable areas include exercise procedures and coordination on procurement and operations, for instance, in maritime surveillance capabilities. Invitations to observe exercises and other activities are another important mechanism. In the future, ARF countries may agree to allow their navies direct communication to coordinate exercises, search and rescue, patrols, and antipiracy measures. All this is aimed at creating a real community of security interests, to promote regional resilience based on a comprehensive security concept.

The track two processes that have proliferated throughout the 1990s provide another channel for the exploration and dissemination of ideas that is consistent with the less formalized strategic culture of the Asia Pacific region. Thus, Indonesia also actively participates in the nonofficial regional track two dialogues such as the Council for Security Cooperation in Asia Pacific (CSCAP). In this context, CSCAP's Maritime and Comprehensive Security Working Groups are seen as particularly important. In addition, Jakarta continues to support informal dialogues to help resolve conflicting claims in the South China Sea.

The Indonesian government believes that a country's most fundamental contribution to regional and global security is to keep its own house in order. However, when the Thai and Philippine foreign ministers in 1998 broached the possibility of modifying ASEAN's long-standing policy of noninterference in members' internal affairs, Indonesia joined other conservative ASEAN member countries favoring continuation of the noninterference policy. Domestic considerations seem to have figured prominently in this decision. Nevertheless, at the diplomatic level ASEAN has in fact engaged in a form of domestic intervention vis-à-vis new and prospective members. For example, an ASEAN troika, including Indonesia, was formed to handle discussions of controversial domestic political matters with the Cambodian and Myanmar governments.

GLOBAL SECURITY   At the global level, Indonesia continues to support the international role of the United Nations, but sent no military personnel to UN peacekeeping missions in 1998. In 1997, it contributed noncombat personnel to operations in Bosnia, Croatia, and Georgia, where these civilian police and/or observers remain, although there are no plans to send others. Preoccupation with internal affairs and a lack of resources have significantly reduced Indonesia's role and initiatives in these areas.

Indonesia also supports efforts toward nuclear nonproliferation and the elimination of weapons of mass destruction. In April 1998, the government ratified the Chemical Weapons Convention. Also, Indonesia criticized the nuclear tests in May 1998 by India and

Pakistan on the basis that the tests not only create a regional arms race and increased tension in South Asia but also pose a serious threat to the global nonproliferation regime, including the Nonproliferation Treaty and the Comprehensive Test Ban Treaty, as well as the Southeast Asian Nuclear-Weapons-Free Zone.

7 Japan

THE SECURITY ENVIRONMENT

Japan's security environment outlook in 1999 mirrors both positive and negative developments in the previous year. On the positive side, Japan's relations with the United States, China, Russia, and South Korea improved as a result of leaders' visits and increasing security dialogues primarily at the bilateral level, reflecting Tokyo's resolve to play a key role in constructing a new regional order based on dialogue and cooperation. On the negative side, Japan still found itself mired in chronic economic recession and political muddle. Moreover, Japan's regional security outlook was substantially worsened by North Korea's test launch of a Taepodong-1 ballistic missile (claimed to be a satellite launch by Pyongyang) on August 31, part of which landed in the Pacific Ocean after flying over the main Japanese island of Honshu. Other negative developments included the prolonged economic crisis in Asia as well as Indian and Pakistani nuclear tests in May, which raised serious concerns about nuclear proliferation in the region.

DOMESTIC DEVELOPMENTS   Despite extensive media reportage on the seriousness of Japan's financial crisis and its international ramifications, Japanese politicians and bureaucrats were slow in formulating effective policy measures to restore the banking sector to health and revive the domestic economy. A series of scandals revealing widespread unethical dealings between bureaucrats and financial institutions indicated deep-rooted structural defects in Japan's financial system. In April 1998, amid growing criticism both at home and abroad of Japan's economic recovery efforts, then Prime Minister Hashimoto Ryūtarō announced a public works stimulus package amounting to ¥16 trillion (US$138 billion at US$1 = ¥115.70), which, however, proved to be insufficient to resuscitate the economy.

The Hashimoto administration's haphazard management of economic and financial problems led to a major defeat for the ruling Liberal Democratic Party (LDP) in the July 12 House of Councillors (Upper House) election, forcing Hashimoto to resign. Discontented voters gave the Democratic Party of Japan and the Japan Communist Party new strength in the Upper House. The LDP, which still controls the House of Representatives, chose Obuchi Keizō, a leader of the LDP's largest faction, as the party's new president, and the Diet designated him prime minister.

Initial major tasks for the Obuchi administration were to address Japan's financial problems, including a huge amount of bad loans held by major banks, and to stimulate the domestic economy. In the face of mounting domestic and international pressure, the Diet passed a bank recapitalization law and a set of financial revitalization laws in October 1998. The bank recapitalization law, which empowers the government to nationalize failing banks, has already been applied to the Long-Term Credit Bank of Japan and the Nippon Credit Bank. The financial revitalization laws are designed to help capital-poor but still-viable banks with an injection of public funds, for which purpose ¥25 trillion (US$216.08 billion) has been earmarked. Coupled with ¥18 trillion (US$155.57 billion) set aside for nationalization and a ¥17 trillion (US$146.93 billion) fund created early in 1998 to protect depositors at failed banks, the whole plan costs ¥60 trillion (US$518.58 billion). Obuchi noted that these laws were "two parts of the legal framework needed to stabilize the banking sector and restore confidence at home and abroad in the Japanese economy." In addition, in mid-November the Obuchi cabinet announced a ¥24 trillion (US$207.43 billion) emergency economic stimulus package, including income and corporate tax cuts, government loans, job-creation schemes, merchandise coupons, public spending for social infrastructure projects, and assistance to Asian economies facing economic difficulties. With this stimulus package, the government aims to put the Japanese economy on the track to recovery by fiscal year 2000.

REGIONAL SECURITY AND FOREIGN POLICY DEVELOPMENTS
Several incidents in 1998 heightened security concerns in Japan. Chief

among these was North Korea's test launch in August of a ballistic missile through Japanese airspace with no prior notice, which increased Tokyo's apprehension about Pyongyang's intentions and potential military capabilities, including the development of weapons of mass destruction and long-range missiles to deliver them. Tokyo reacted with unusual vigor, lodging a strong protest with North Korea, suspending food aid and charter flights, freezing diplomatic normalization talks, and suspending cooperation with the Korean Peninsula Energy Development Organization (KEDO). In view of the importance of KEDO's Framework Agreement as the most realistic and effective effort to prevent North Korea from developing nuclear weapons, however, Tokyo subsequently agreed to resume cooperation with KEDO on cost sharing for the construction of two light nuclear reactors for North Korea. Japan is expected to offer about US$1 billion to the KEDO program.

Strong antinuclear sentiment in Japan was aroused by Indian and Pakistani nuclear tests in May 1998. Tokyo was particularly concerned about the tests' potential impact on Northeast Asian stability in light of the North Korean situation. Characterizing the tests as "extremely regrettable," the Japanese government responded by imposing economic sanctions, including the freezing of grant aid to the two countries with the exception of emergency and humanitarian aid and support for grass-roots projects. Tokyo also froze yen loans for new projects to the two countries, and decided to review its position on lending to India and Pakistan by international financial institutions.

The Asian financial crisis remained a serious problem, with profound ramifications for the region and the whole world. In response, in 1997–1998 the Hashimoto administration dispensed a total of US$44 billion in crisis aid to several East Asian countries, the largest contribution of any single country. Furthermore, in October 1998 Finance Minister Miyazawa Kiichi announced an additional aid package worth US$30 billion.

Japan's relationship with the United States remains vitally important not only for Japan's security but also for peace and stability in the Asia Pacific region. Summit meetings between Obuchi and U.S. President Bill Clinton in September and November 1998 reaffirmed the two countries' shared view of the Japan-U.S. security relationship as "the cornerstone of stability and prosperity in the Asia-Pacific region." The alliance, which also provides Japan with diplomatic leverage in developing cooperative relations with China and Russia, was strengthened by the adoption in 1997 of the revised Guidelines for U.S.-Japan Defense Cooperation. In April 1998, the Japanese government submitted to the Diet bills to implement these guidelines, as discussed below.

Japan's persistent—and once again growing—trade surplus with the United States, as well as Tokyo's delay in effecting deregulation, structural reform, and market-opening measures, continued to be the outstanding issues between the United States and Japan. The continual criticism flowing from Washington and the U.S. mass media in regard to these issues has aroused nationalistic and anti-American sentiment among many Japanese, including politicians, bureaucrats, and journalists. This is part of an increasing resentment in Japan toward "American triumphalism."

Japanese observers have mixed feelings about recent developments in U.S.-China relations. Some Japanese saw the fact that Clinton did not stop in Japan when he visited China in June–July 1998 as an indication that Washington was prioritizing the China relationship. Be that as it may, the mainstream view remains that better U.S.-China relations are good for Japan, as are better Japan-China relations for the United States. Also, it is widely understood that the Japan-U.S. alliance relationship is qualitatively different from the U.S.-China relationship.

Japan's relations with South Korea improved significantly in 1998. In a joint declaration signed and issued by Obuchi and South Korean President Kim Dae Jung on October 8, 1998, Obuchi acknowledged the historical fact that Japan's colonial rule caused tremendous damage and suffering to the Korean people and expressed his "deep remorse and heartfelt apology for this fact." Then Prime Minister Murayama Tomiichi's remarks made in August 1995 on this subject also included "remorse," but the joint declaration formally documented Japan's apology for the first time. Strains still exist between the two countries over issues of history and conflicting claims to Takeshima Island (Tokdo Island to the South Koreans). Nevertheless, the results of Kim's visit, including the joint declaration, suggested that the two countries recognize the importance of forging a broader, new partnership encompassing political, security, economic, and cultural cooperation.

Japan's relationship with China was also enhanced by President Jiang Zemin's trip to Japan in November 1998, the first visit to Japan

by a Chinese head of state in the more than 2,000 years of relations between the two countries. In a joint declaration announced on
November 26, the Japanese government acknowledged "the responsibility for the serious distress and damage that Japan caused to the
Chinese people through its aggression against China during a certain
period in the past" and expressed "deep remorse." However, although
Obuchi offered a verbal apology to Jiang during the summit meeting,
the joint declaration omitted the word "apology," thereby perpetu-
ating controversy and discord over this issue. The omission presumably reflected Obuchi's concern about possible negative repercussions
from factions of the LDP, where resentment of China's persistent
harping on Japan's war guilt persists.

The apology issue notwithstanding, the two leaders agreed on
building a "partnership of friendship and cooperation for peace and
development" by strengthening high-level dialogue between Japan
and China through annual leader visits and the establishment of a
Tokyo-Beijing government hot line. The two countries also agreed on
a variety of other measures, including youth exchanges, environmental cooperation, and security dialogue and exchanges.

In addition, further positive development in Japan's relations with
Russia has followed on the November 1997 summit meeting in Krasnoyarsk, when then Prime Minister Hashimoto and Russian President
Boris Yeltsin agreed to make efforts to conclude a peace treaty by the
year 2000 based on the 1993 Tokyo Declaration. However, no substantive progress has been made in resolving the thorny issue of the
disputed Northern Territories. At an April 1998 summit meeting between Hashimoto and Yeltsin in Kawana, Hashimoto proposed that
the two countries agree to draw a new boundary north of the islands,
with Russia granted temporary administrative rights. When Obuchi
visited Moscow in November, Yeltsin presented a counterproposal
suggesting that the territorial issue be resolved separately from the
peace treaty, which accordingly would include only a pledge to settle
the territorial issue. This, in effect, would postpone the settlement of
the territorial issue indefinitely.

With the territorial issue still pending, Japan and Russia signed a
Moscow Declaration, aimed to "build a creative partnership which
is consistent with [their] strategic and geopolitical interests." In the
declaration, the two countries reaffirmed their intention to conclude
a peace treaty by the year 2000, and agreed to create two subcom-
mittees within the existing Joint Japan-Russia Federation Committee

on the Conclusion of the Peace Treaty. One subcommittee will deal with border demarcation, the other with joint economic activities on the disputed islands. The two leaders also agreed in principle to allow visits by former residents of the disputed islands. Other significant bilateral activities in 1998 included an exchange of visits by top-level military officers as well as joint training between the Japanese Self-Defense Forces (SDF) and the Russian Armed Forces in search-and-rescue operations.

Japan has also been actively forging new partnerships with the countries of the Association of Southeast Asian Nations (ASEAN) by promoting dialogue and cooperation on politics and security, trade and investment and other economic matters, cultural exchanges, and global issues. In particular, Tokyo considers multilateral forums such as the ASEAN Regional Forum (ARF) and the ASEAN Post-Ministerial Conferences to be important mechanisms for security policy consultations among countries in the Asia Pacific region. As mentioned previously, Japan has made considerable financial contributions to the troubled Asian economies. In a December 1998 speech in Hanoi during the ASEAN meetings, Obuchi enunciated the "Obuchi doctrine," wherein he stated that Japan's Asia policy would focus on three areas: (1) Asian economic recovery; (2) "human security," that is, responding to "all threats to human survival, life and dignity" and helping "the socially vulnerable" most affected by the crisis; and (3) the promotion of intellectual dialogue.

DEFENSE POLICIES AND ISSUES

DEFENSE POLICIES   Japan's defense policies are circumscribed by Article 9 of the Constitution renouncing the use or threat of force, and the Japan-U.S. alliance providing the ultimate security guarantee. The main features of Japan's basic defense policies, set out in its annual white paper on defense, are (1) an "exclusively defense-oriented policy"; (2) a pledge not to become a military power; (3) adherence to the three nonnuclear principles of not possessing, producing, or permitting the introduction into Japan of nuclear weapons; and (4) civilian control of the military. Within these basic policies, the Japanese government has been building up its defense capability on the one hand and strengthening the Japan-U.S. security arrangements on the other.

The new National Defense Program Outline (NDPO) adopted in 1995 substantially expanded the roles and missions of the SDF to include response to large-scale disasters, terrorist attacks, and "various other situations that could seriously affect Japan's peace and security" (potentially including regional military contingencies), as well as participation in UN peacekeeping operations. Based on the new NDPO, a Mid-term Defense Program (MTDP) for fiscal years 1996 through 2000 provides for a substantial increase in defense capabilities.

The revised Guidelines for U.S.-Japan Defense Cooperation, issued in September 1997, provide a comprehensive framework for defense cooperation between Tokyo and Washington both in peacetime and in times of crisis. The new guidelines considerably enhance Japan's roles, which now include noncombatant rear-support operations for U.S. military forces in regional contingencies. As previously noted, the Japanese government formulated and submitted to the Diet in April 1998 bills to establish a legal basis for implementing the guidelines. The bills included a revised Japan-U.S. Acquisition and Cross-Servicing Agreement signed by Tokyo and Washington in April, which will enable the SDF to provide rear support to U.S. forces in regional emergencies. The formation of a coalition government between the LDP and the Liberal Party in January 1999 improved the circumstances for actualizing the guidelines legislation. Tokyo and Washington have begun to establish two institutions envisaged in the guidelines: a "comprehensive mechanism" for joint defense planning and the establishment of common standards and procedures, and a "bilateral coordination mechanism" for specific activities in times of crisis.

One serious practical difficulty resulting from the guidelines has been China's continued strong objections to the expanded scope of Japan-U.S. cooperation in regional contingencies, potentially including a crisis in the Taiwan Strait. Tokyo has sought to develop a triangular security dialogue among Japan, the United States, and China to allay Chinese misunderstandings or tension over this and other issues. To date, China has not agreed to participate in such an official dialogue, although it did agree to a track two triangular dialogue that began in 1998.

DEFENSE SPENDING AND PERSONNEL   Japan's difficult recent financial situation led the Japanese government to review the fiscal

1996–2000 MTDP in December 1997, resulting in a reduction of the planned increases in defense spending for fiscal 1998–2000. Total planned expenditure of ¥25.15 trillion (US$217.37 billion) over the five years was cut ¥920 billion (US$7.95 billion). The defense budget for fiscal 1998 was ¥4,939.7 billion (US$42.69 billion), a 0.2 percent decrease from the previous year—the first such decline in the history of the SDF. The ratio of defense spending to gross national product was projected to be 0.95 percent in 1998.

The revised fiscal 1998 defense budget included ¥10.7 billion (US$92.48 million) for relocating some U.S. military facilities within Okinawa Prefecture, as approved by the Japan-U.S. Special Action Committee on Okinawa (SACO). Forty-four percent of the budget is allocated to personnel and provisions, 19 percent to equipment and materials, 18 percent to operational maintenance (including education and training), 11 percent to base security and support for U.S. forces in Japan, 4 percent to base and facilities maintenance, and 3 percent to research and development. (Defense expenditure figures do not include spending on the Coast Guard or pensions.)

The SDF has approximately 243,000 active-duty personnel. The Ground Self-Defense Force (GSDF) has 151,836 members, the Maritime Self-Defense Force (MSDF) has 43,842 members, the Air Self-Defense Force (ASDF) has 45,606 members, and the Joint Staff Council has 1,356 members (as of March 1998). In addition, the SDF has 49,273 reserves.

PROCUREMENT   Japan's defense procurement plan aims to achieve the force levels set forth in the new 1995 NDPO. Emphasis is placed on making the SDF streamlined, efficient, compact, and qualitatively improved.

Major equipment that Japan procured or started to procure in fiscal 1998 includes the following: the GSDF—19 type-90 tanks, 30 armored vehicles, six artillery (155 mm howitzer FH70), nine multiple-launch rocket systems (MLRS), one antitank helicopter (AH-1S), five multipurpose helicopters (UH-60JA), one transport helicopter (CH-47JA), two OH-1 helicopters, and eight surface-to-surface missiles (SSM-1); the MSDF—two 4,600-ton-class destroyers, one 2,700-ton-class submarine, one 510-ton-class minesweeper, one 8,900-ton-class transport ship, seven patrol helicopters (SH-60J), and two rescue helicopters (UH-60J); and the ASDF—nine fighter-support aircraft (F-2), two rescue helicopters (UH-60J), three search-and-rescue aircraft (U-125A), one multipurpose support aircraft (U-4), and nine intermediate-level jet trainers (T-4).

Japan procures about 90 percent of its equipment from domestic sources or licensed production. Its ban on arms exports limits the growth potential of its defense industry, which accounts for only about 0.6 percent of the total value of Japan's domestic industrial production.

Japan's military procurement system has been under critical review in the wake of a series of procurement scandals brought to light in the fall of 1998, which led to the resignation of the director-general of the Defense Agency in November, the arrest of officials on charges of breaches of trust and bribery, and a major reshuffling of ranking officials found to be involved in coverups. The widespread practice of granting private contracts rather than bidding competitively enabled some officials to treat certain companies favorably in return for jobs after their retirement. In November 1998, the Defense Agency announced drastic reform measures, including a reorganization of the procurement office and strengthened monitoring by a new organization, thus making procurement practices more transparent and competitive.

THEATER MISSILE DEFENSE AND RECONNAISSANCE SATELLITES
Given the recent proliferation of weapons of mass destruction and ballistic missiles that can deliver them, Japan and the United States have been conducting a joint study on ballistic missile defense for the past several years. In the April 1996 Japan-U.S. Joint Declaration on Security, the two countries made a commitment to continue to study ballistic missile defense. North Korea's missile test of August 1998 apparently prompted Japan's decision in September to proceed with upgraded research on theater missile defense (TMD) with the United States.

A low-level, or lower-tier, TMD system based on an advanced version of the U.S. Patriot missile appears to be a viable option for Japan in the near future. Tokyo reportedly has decided also to proceed with research on a higher-altitude, or upper-tier, system making use of its existing AEGIS vessels. However, given the cost and technical feasibility problems associated with upper-tier systems, as well as strong Chinese objections to Japan's acquisition of TMD systems, it is likely that Japan will postpone its decision on the actual development and deployment of upper-tier TMD systems until well into the future.

North Korea's missile test launch of August 1998 exposed Japan's inability to detect a North Korean missile launch and consequent total reliance on U.S. intelligence. This situation led to Japan's announcement on November 6 of its decision to launch four intelligence-gathering satellites by the year 2002. Two of these satellites are slated to collect radar signals, while the other two take high-resolution photos. A 1969 Diet resolution limiting Japan's use of space to peaceful purposes can be interpreted as denying Japan's acquisition of reconnaissance satellites for defense purposes, but Tokyo justified its decision by arguing that the satellites will be used for a variety of purposes, including defense, diplomacy, and crisis management during large-scale disasters. The estimated cost for the entire system is between ¥190 billion (US$1.64 billion) and ¥300 billion (US$2.59 billion).

U.S. BASES IN OKINAWA About 75 percent of U.S. bases in Japan are concentrated in Okinawa Prefecture, which accounts for only 0.6 percent of Japan's total land area. Since the final SACO report was released in December 1996, Tokyo and Washington have taken some measures to reduce and consolidate U.S. bases in Okinawa, while maintaining the capabilities and readiness of U.S. forces in Japan. However, efforts to return the U.S. Marine Corps' Futenma Air Station, which was the focal point of the SACO report, came to a halt owing to a disagreement between the central government and Okinawa Prefecture, as then Governor Ōta Masahide rejected the Tokyo plan to build an offshore heliport facility near Nago as an alternative to Futenma. Moreover, Ōta demanded that Futenma be relocated outside Okinawa Prefecture.

In the November 15, 1998, gubernatorial election in Okinawa Prefecture, Inamine Keiichi, a local business leader backed by the LDP, edged out Ōta. Two issues dominated the election campaign: U.S. base problems and the poor state of the local economy (at about 9 percent, Okinawa's unemployment rate is the highest in the country). Apparently, voters favored Inamine's economic policies and his conciliatory attitude toward the central government, which is likely to yield an increase in central government subsidies. On the base reduction issue, Inamine also opposed the government heliport plan, instead proposing the construction of a new airport in the northern part of the prefecture for shared use by civil aviation and the U.S. military over a period of 15 years. Thus, the prospects for base reductions in Okinawa remained uncertain at the end of 1998.

CONTRIBUTIONS TO REGIONAL AND GLOBAL SECURITY

THE JAPAN-U.S. ALLIANCE AND REGIONAL AND GLOBAL INSTITUTIONS   The Japan-U.S. alliance provides the foundation for Japan's broader contributions to regional and global security. As enumerated in the April 1996 Japan-U.S. Joint Declaration on Security, these cover a wide range of topics such as arms control and disarmament, the North Korean nuclear issue, the Middle East peace process, and peace implementation in the former Yugoslavia.

Japan has been playing an active part in regional institutions such as the Asia-Pacific Economic Cooperation (APEC) forum, ARF, and the Asia-Europe Meeting (ASEM). Along with Australia, Japan was instrumental in establishing APEC in 1989, and it has been keen to play a leading role in promoting trade and investment liberalization through this forum. Yet, Japan's ability to convincingly carry out this role has been marred by domestic political difficulties, which have impeded liberalization in certain sensitive sectors. At the APEC meeting in Kuala Lumpur in mid-November 1998, when the United States and other countries demanded that APEC economies pursue full participation in all nine fast-track sectors of the previously agreed upon Early Voluntary Sectoral Liberalization (EVSL) plan, domestic political considerations led to Japan's refusal to participate in tariff reductions for forestry and fishery products.

In view of the growing potential for instability and conflict on the Korean peninsula, the Obuchi government floated the idea of creating Six-Party Talks—involving China, Japan, North and South Korea, Russia, and the United States—as a new mechanism for building confidence. The Japanese government also strongly supported intensified trilateral security dialogues among Japan, South Korea, and the United States to deal with North Korea. Finally, Japan also has been active in regional track two mechanisms, including the Council for Security Cooperation in Asia Pacific, the Northeast Asia Cooperation Dialogue, and the Trilateral Forum on North Pacific Security.

At the global level, Japan has worked to strengthen nonproliferation and disarmament regimes such as the Comprehensive Test Ban

Treaty, the Nonproliferation Treaty, the Chemical Weapons Convention, and the Biological Weapons Convention. In September 1998, Japan ratified the antipersonnel land mines ban treaty. Japan's action on this treaty is particularly significant in view of the fact that the number of Asian signatories to the treaty is small, despite serious land-mine problems afflicting such countries as Cambodia.

PEACEKEEPING AND HUMANITARIAN OPERATIONS Japan has participated in UN peacekeeping and humanitarian operations since the enactment of the International Peace and Cooperation Law and the amended Disaster Relief Law in August 1992. In 1998, the SDF continued to take part in the UN Disengagement Observer Force in the Golan Heights. In November 1998, Japan dispatched 80 GSDF and 105 ASDF personnel to hurricane-stricken Honduras to provide medical and transport services, which marked the first SDF overseas operation under the 1992 legislation.

In June 1998, the Diet approved an amendment to the International Peace and Cooperation Law clarifying problems associated with the use of weapons and somewhat expanding the scope of Japan's participation in peacekeeping operations. The question of weapons use, which previously had been left to the judgment of individual personnel, is now left in principle to the discretion of the field commanding officer. The amended law has enabled Japan to participate not only in monitoring elections in foreign countries but also in humanitarian relief operations such as those undertaken by the United Nations High Commission for Refugees, even in a situation where no cease-fire is in place. The Japanese government sent personnel to monitor elections, under UN coordination and support, in Cambodia in July 1998 and in Bosnia-Herzegovina in September.

Nevertheless, Japan's participation in UN peacekeeping operations is still limited to logistic support assignments such as medical care, transportation, communications, and construction services. The assignments of core units of peacekeeping forces, such as monitoring disarmament as well as stationing and patrol in buffer zones, are "frozen" pending new legislation. The death in July 1998 of Akino Yutaka, killed in an ambush in Tajikistan while on duty as a civil affairs officer in a UN observer mission, tragically highlighted the challenge of securing the safety of unarmed UN personnel in dangerous environments.

ECONOMIC CONTRIBUTIONS   A majority of Japanese citizens believe that Japan should make significant "nonmilitary" contributions to the welfare and prosperity of the international community through Official Development Assistance (ODA). However, stringent financial conditions in Japan and the weaker yen in recent years have forced the Japanese government to fundamentally review its ODA policy. The fiscal 1998 ODA budget was reduced 10 percent from that of fiscal 1997, when ODA spending was about US$9.4 billion, or a 1.8 percent decrease from the previous year. Nevertheless, in 1998 Japan retained its position as the world's largest donor. The Council on ODA Reforms for the 21st Century, an advisory body to the foreign minister, in its final report issued in January 1998 called for qualitative improvement and enhanced transparency of ODA as well as a fundamental review of the 1992 ODA Charter.

8 Republic of Korea

The Security Environment

As the Republic of Korea entered 1999, public and government perceptions of the security environment continued to be shaped by three major and continuing concerns: the economic crisis, the situation in North Korea, and the larger politico-security environment in Northeast Asia. Although the country now has a more effective president, continued domestic political conflict affects debate on the above issues and complicates South Korean policy making.

ECONOMIC ISSUES   Whereas South Korea began 1998 in danger of imminent default on its foreign debt, government reserves grew rapidly during the year and the current account surplus reached an all-time annual high of about US$40 billion, compared with a deficit of US$8 billion the previous year. However, this reflected the collapse of internal demand more than it did an increase in exports, as low consumption and investment continued to plague the South Korean economy. Moreover, unemployment grew throughout the year, topping 7 percent by its end. Although a consensus developed around the need for significant structural reorganization of the *chaebol*-dominated private economy, it was only toward the end of the year that the *chaebol* finally announced significant efforts to pare down less efficient facilities. Also, the government made strides in facilitating foreign investment flows into South Korea, which reached almost US$9 billion in 1998 (half of which represented foreign purchases of South Korean business operations) and is expected to increase to about US$15 billion in 1999. The drop in production (gross national product fell 7 percent in 1998) has slowed, and there is a modest sense of optimism about the future.

Nevertheless, economic uncertainties remain. It is generally recognized that the recovery is likely to be slow, with even the most optimistic projections on the South Korean economy forecasting only a 2 percent increase in GNP in 1999, and unemployment could rise further as a result of company restructuring. Although pushed by government authorities, *chaebol* reform is not popular and faces opposition both from affected labor unions and from elements of the business community arguing that it will only weaken South Korean business to the benefit of foreigners. Also problematic is the economy's heavy dependence on external conditions. In this regard, South Korea's recovery could be abruptly halted by events completely outside domestic control, such as increased protectionism in the U.S. and European markets, global financial instabilities, or a hard landing for the skyrocketing New York stock market.

Domestic political competition also raises questions about South Korea's ability to continue on course with its economic recovery. The current government is based on a coalition of President Kim Dae Jung's National Congress for New Politics and Prime Minister Kim Jong Pil's United Liberal Democrats. Beginning as a minority government, the coalition became a majority as the result of 32 defections from the Grand National Party during 1998. However, tensions seem likely to rise within the coalition over a preelection deal under which Kim had promised to shift from a presidential to a parliamentary system in the year 2000, thereby transferring leadership to the prime minister. Backing away from this earlier pledge, however, the National Congress for New Politics more recently indicated that this shift should be delayed to facilitate further economic recovery. In addition, the party remains a potent force, as shown by its ability to slow legislation throughout 1998 with boycotts and demonstrations.

THE EXTERNAL ENVIRONMENT *Relations with the North.* South Korea's economic difficulties have had a significant impact on perceptions of and strategies toward the North. Whereas in 1995 considerable confidence existed in South Korea about its ability to handle the burdens of reunification should the North collapse, today South Koreans are almost exclusively preoccupied with the recovery of their own economy and show little or no willingness to accept the difficult additional burdens of bailing out the North's decrepit economy. At the same time, the common wisdom on North Korea's future has also changed. Previously, the North was widely regarded as being on the verge of collapse, but today majority thinking accepts the notion of North Korea's longer-term survival despite its current economic difficulties.

This change in assessment, in combination with the election to the presidency of Kim Dae Jung, induced the South Korean government to adopt a more realistic approach to unification, described as "peaceful coexistence." Kim's "Sunshine Policy" reflects his belief that Pyongyang will not seek improved relations with Seoul if faced with the prospect of a hostile takeover from the South. The three guiding principles of the Sunshine Policy are (1) the South will not tolerate armed provocation by the North, (2) the South will not seek to absorb the North, and (3) the South will promote inter-Korean reconciliation and cooperation.

Underlying the Sunshine Policy are Seoul's beliefs that the South can help open up the North and promote peaceful coexistence until unification, and that the separation of economics and politics will facilitate inter-Korean exchange and cooperation. A symbol of this separation was the landmark deal concluded between the Hyundai business group and Pyongyang under which Hyundai receives the right to conduct tourism to the Kumgang Mountains in return for large payments to the North Korean government.

To implement the Sunshine Policy, the South Korean government has (1) repledged its support for the light water reactors and continues to closely coordinate with other Korean Peninsula Energy Development Organization (KEDO) member states, (2) stated that it will cooperate with other countries in providing humanitarian food aid to the North and encouraging investment in the North's Rajin-Sunbong special economic district, (3) requested neighboring countries to improve their relations with the North in line with the improvement in inter-Korean relations, and (4) continued to coordinate with other countries to encourage the North's participation in various multilateral forums and in the Four-Party Talks between China, North and South Korea, and the United States.

The Sunshine Policy has not been immune to criticism, particularly as repeated North Korean provocations have caused South Koreans to question the policy's appropriateness and feasibility. Specifically, a series of highly visible infiltration incidents, North Korea's August 31 missile launch over Japanese territory, and the discovery of a large underground facility in the North by U.S. intelligence caused critics of government policy to wonder aloud whether North Korea did not in fact deserve to be treated as an implacable foe still bent on subverting the South, rather than as a legitimate cooperative partner. Conservatives in South Korea argue that a unilateral Sunshine Policy not requiring reciprocity from the North endangers the national security and, further, that it is naive and chimerical to expect any real policy change in the North as a result of the policy.

Despite these criticisms and the escalation of U.S.–North Korean tensions following the discovery of the underground facility, South Koreans generally are not alarmist regarding the North. Many South Koreans discount U.S. reports that the Keumjang-ri facilities are likely to house an underground reactor or reprocessing facilities. Moreover, while the United States appears to worry primarily about the dangers of nuclear proliferation, South Koreans are equally or even more concerned about Pyongyang's chemical and biological weapons.

Bilateral Relations. While the economy and North Korean provocations created uncertainties in South Korea's security outlook, trends in Seoul's bilateral relations with neighboring countries have been mostly positive.

During 1998, Kim visited both Japan and China with great success. Of particular note was the historic shift in South Korea's relations with Japan. Subsequent to Japan's official apology for the damage that Japanese colonial rule had caused in Korea, a South Korean–Japanese joint declaration issued on October 8 provided for cultural exchange and economic cooperation between the two countries. Moreover, a South Korean–Chinese declaration of partnership following later in the year indicated that Seoul can maintain cooperative relations simultaneously with Beijing and Tokyo.

Military cooperation with Japan, unthinkable until recently, will be reviewed in 1999 in light of the new Guidelines for U.S-Japan Defense Cooperation. More specifically, Seoul will pursue triangular military cooperation with Japan and the United States in such areas as the evacuation of noncombatants and feasibility studies for participating in theater missile defense. There is also a possibility of joint Japanese–South Korean training in minesweeping operations. As well, Seoul is pursuing more effective forms of information sharing on the North in its bilateral relations with neighboring countries.

In addition, 1998 saw positive developments in relations with the United States, a country that remains vitally important to South

Korean security and that has a major role to play in Northeast Asian peace and stability. U.S. policy toward the North began to shift as Washington gained experience in dealing with the North and as American analysts increasingly discounted prospects for a sudden North Korean collapse, a scenario that seemed more likely to U.S. observers two or three years ago. As a result, the United States has shifted from emphasizing a "soft landing" to advocating a policy of peaceful coexistence. This new U.S. perspective parallels Kim's Sunshine Policy and thus provides a basis for continuing intimate U.S.–South Korean cooperation. Nevertheless, continuing differences in their concrete assessments of the dangers from the North and how they should be practically handled present the South Korean and American governments with continuing challenges in coordinating their policies.

The only negative element in South Korea's relations with its neighbors in 1998 was a drastic deterioration in Russo–South Korean relations. Tensions rose after an exchange of spying charges between the two governments, largely the result of South Korea's diplomatic immaturity and clumsiness. Seoul's willingness to restore normalized relations with Moscow will depend heavily on Russia's ability to rejuvenate its economy.

DEFENSE POLICIES AND ISSUES

South Korean military forces consist of the army (599,702 personnel), the navy (74,368), and the air force (68,120). In addition, there are 37,000 U.S. military personnel stationed in South Korea, a number that could be augmented to 640,000 in the event of an emergency.

Because of the economic crisis, the government's efforts to enhance defense capabilities have undergone little significant change. Policies follow five basic guidelines: realization of a self-reliant defense posture, specialization of military personnel, modernization of weapons systems, rationalization of the overall operating system, and computerization of the national defense system. The financial crisis, however, brought severe stringencies. The annual defense budget for fiscal year 1998 was W13.90 trillion (US$11.57 billion at US$1 = W1,201), which amounted to 21 percent of revenue and about 3.1 percent of GNP in 1998. This was a slightly higher percentage of the national budget than the fiscal 1997 figure (20.2 percent), but actually a smaller percentage of the projected GNP (down from 3.3 percent in 1997). About 70 percent of the fiscal 1998 defense budget was spent on operations and maintenance, and 30 percent on force improvements. The government increased spending for force improvements 0.9 percent from the previous year, compensated for by a drop of 0.7 percent in spending on operations and maintenance. However, because of the sharp drop in the international value of the won since mid-1997 actual weapons procurements shrank despite the won-based increase in spending for force improvements.

Ongoing procurement projects in 1998 included long-range strike and three-dimensional high-speed mobile forces (including multiple-rocket launchers, the Hyunmu missile, and combat helicopters); maritime forces to control the sea; air supremacy capabilities (including the South Korean version of combat aircraft and precision missiles); and an independent, long-range information-gathering capability. However, 18 projects were canceled, postponed, or downsized for budgetary reasons, including those for enhanced surveillance. On the other hand, 16 projects were approved in April 1998 to increase defense capabilities, largely consisting of the establishment of new units or for research and development. These were projected to cost W210 billion (US$175 million), of which W120 billion (US$99 million) was to be expended in 1998.

Within its fiscal constraints, South Korea is continuing its medium- and long-term plans to develop high-quality military forces. Steps toward this goal include a simplification of the command system and increases in specialized personnel. In addition, efforts are being made to improve information systems and integrate the combat capabilities of all three armed services.

Because of the economic crisis, the future of defense spending and restructuring in South Korea remains uncertain. While the defense establishment hopes that its needs for modernization and restructuring will be met in light of the continuing security threat, the government needs to give priority to economic recovery. Consequently, any increases in the defense budget will be hotly debated.

CONTRIBUTIONS TO REGIONAL AND GLOBAL SECURITY

South Korea's principal contributions to regional and global security lie in its efforts to maintain stability and peace on the Korean peninsula. It also seeks to contribute to the building of an Asia Pacific regional order through its participation in multilateral security dialogues. At the global level, South Korea is a relatively new member of the United Nations and has been actively contributing to UN peace-keeping operations since 1993.

As described above, South Korean efforts on the Korean peninsula emphasize both engagement with the North through the Sunshine Policy and deterrence through the ROK–U.S. Mutual Defense Treaty and South Korea's own defense forces. Although the South no longer sees collapse in the North as a likely near-term scenario, it recognizes that the North's economic difficulties are a serious humanitarian problem and limit the Kim Jong Il regime's ability to engage in peaceful cooperation. Seoul is making substantial direct economic contributions to the economy of the North, including taking part in building light water reactors as part of the 1994 U.S.–North Korean Framework Agreement and granting permission to Hyundai to move ahead with the Kumgang Mountains tourism project. Further, the South Korean government provided North Korea with US$11 million in food assistance as well as technical and financial assistance to build a noodle factory and teach skills in harvesting corn. This kind of assistance is likely to increase in future years, regardless of the North's military adventures.

The South Korean government supports both governmental and track two bilateral, trilateral, and multilateral dialogues in the belief that economic and security cooperation ameliorates regional tensions, helps prevent another war on the Korean peninsula, and provides a favorable environment for peaceful reunification. Increasingly, it is understood that reunification cannot be achieved through South Korea's own efforts alone but requires support from other countries in the region.

Seoul is examining proposals such as that of the Japanese government for Six-Party Talks on the Korean peninsula. Indeed, it has already formulated its own proposal along these lines, the Northeast Asia Security Dialogue. In the meantime, South Koreans continue to participate in various private bilateral, trilateral, and multilateral dialogues relating to Korean issues, and discussions are taking place on various schemes for greater international dialogue. These include "two-plus-four" arrangements (North and South Korea plus the United States, Japan, China, and Russia) and "two-plus-two-plus-two" formulas (North and South Korea take the initiative, China and the United States participate as full partners, and Japan and Russia join as more junior partners).

In addition, South Koreans participate actively in such multilateral security dialogues as the intergovernmental ASEAN Regional Forum and two track two efforts—the Council for Security Cooperation in Asia Pacific and the Northeast Asia Cooperation Dialogue. Seoul seeks to induce Pyongyang to join these regional political and security arrangements. Further, South Korea also remains an active member in the Asia-Pacific Economic Cooperation forum, and in December 1998 while in Hanoi for the Association of Southeast Asian Nations (ASEAN) summit Kim proposed the establishment of an East Asian "Vision Group" for economic cooperation.

From the time South Korea joined the United Nations in 1991 (when North Korea also joined), South Koreans have regarded their country as belonging to the world community, with all the obligations that accompany this membership. Since October 1993, South Korea has sent some 1,350 personnel abroad to participate in UN peace-keeping operations in six locations, and despite its current economic difficulties the country expects to continue to contribute to UN operations. A special law to expedite South Korean contributions to peace-keeping operations has been proposed and may be taken up by the parliament again in 1999.

Military personnel exchanges and cooperation with ASEAN, Australia, Canada, China, France, Germany, Japan, the United Kingdom, and the United States are symbolic of South Korea's efforts to strengthen its understanding of regional and global issues. South Korea intends to further augment and diversify such exchanges and cooperation on both bilateral and multilateral levels.

9 Malaysia

THE SECURITY ENVIRONMENT

For Malaysia, 1998 was a year of trials. While continuing to grapple with the effects of the economic crisis afflicting the region, the country further suffered the political crisis brought about by the dismissal and subsequent arrest and trial of Deputy Prime Minister Anwar Ibrahim.

Given Malaysia's strong record of political stability and rapid economic growth, these two major and related developments together constitute perhaps the most serious challenge the country has ever faced. The task of steering the country simultaneously toward economic recovery and a resolution of the political crisis is made particularly complicated by the close nexus between economics and politics, and particularly precarious by the extent to which a wrong turn could affect domestic stability.

ECONOMIC CRISIS   Sixteen months after the start of the so-called contagion effect of the Thai baht crisis, initial optimism regarding Malaysia's quick economic recovery has tempered as the effects of the economic and financial turmoil have begun to be felt. Instead of the initially forecast 4 percent growth in gross national product for 1998, the government reported a contraction of 4.8 percent, the first drop since 1985. The causes include a weakened currency, increases in interest rates, a high level of private-sector debt, limited financial liquidity, and a plunge in the stock market and consequent decline in market capitalization.

The sectors of the economy that have been particularly badly hit by the crisis are construction, manufacturing, and services—especially financial institutions. There have also been significant direct effects on the citizenry: capital losses, higher interest rates, increased job insecurity, and a major decline in consumption.

The contraction of the real economy has produced rising unemployment: Total employment declined 2.7 percent in 1998, and unemployment, which was only 2.6 percent in 1997, is expected to reach 4.9 percent of the labor force, or 443,200 people, in 1999. Nevertheless, the level of unemployment in Malaysia is still low by comparison with the levels in Indonesia and Thailand, where the rates were 15 percent and 7 percent, respectively, in 1998.

When the crisis hit, the Malaysian government initially followed the advice of the International Monetary Fund (IMF), which prescribed strict monetary and financial management via high interest rates and cuts in government spending, but not an IMF bailout. However, when the government saw that the IMF's austerity measures were merely causing difficulties to multiply, it changed course. New measures to revitalize the economy included easing monetary policy and providing fiscal stimulus. In addition, the government established two new agencies to help the banking sector: an asset management company known as Danaharta, and Danamodal, whose mission is to recapitalize the banking system. Finally, in September 1998 foreign exchange controls were introduced to protect the ringgit from volatile international short-term capital flows.

Easier monetary policy, lower interest rates, and capital controls have increased liquidity. However, the government has maintained a flexible approach and remains committed to the principles of the market mechanism and liberalization.

POLITICAL CRISIS   *The Prelude.*   Interpretations abound as to how and when the political crisis began. Some point to the economic crisis and the aforementioned reversal of economic strategies as the basic reasons for the falling-out between Prime Minister Mahathir bin Mohamad and Deputy Prime Minister Anwar Ibrahim. Indeed, there did appear to be sharp differences in policy approaches and styles between the two. Anwar, who was also finance minister, favored the IMF approach to economic recovery, cutting back expenditures and imposing a credit squeeze. Mahathir, on the other hand, argued that unregulated currency trading was a major cause of the region's financial crisis. Believing that the fundamentals of the Malaysian economy were strong—though not strong enough to counter the power of the international currency traders—the prime minister preferred expansionary policies aimed at stimulating the economy. The differences between the two men became more pronounced when the deputy prime minister appeared reluctant to endorse rescue plans favored by the government for certain large corporations hit by the financial crisis.

Other Factors? Other observers, however, claim that more serious reasons were behind Anwar's dismissal. During the June 1998 General Assembly of the ruling United Malays National Organization (UMNO), the head of the UMNO youth wing and some members who were close to Anwar raised the issues of corruption, cronyism, and nepotism. This was seen as a thinly veiled attack on Mahathir's leadership and an attempt on Anwar's part to wrest power from the prime minister—despite the fact that, as deputy, Anwar was already next in line to succeed Mahathir. The prime minister effectively blunted the attack by revealing that other people, including Anwar's family and friends, had also benefited from the government's privatization programs.

Only a month before the UMNO General Assembly, the political crisis in Indonesia came to a head with the resignation of President Suharto. Some members of Malaysia's opposition parties have drawn parallels between Suharto and Mahathir. Although the events in Indonesia bear little resemblance to the situation in Malaysia, similar calls for reform were heard in both countries.

Finally, during the June meeting a mysterious book was circulated to party delegates, entitled *50 Reasons Why Anwar Cannot Become Prime Minister*. The book chronicled Anwar's alleged sexual improprieties and corruption. Anwar had been sufficiently concerned about the book to obtain a court injunction prohibiting the distributor from releasing either the book or its contents, but it appeared at the General Assembly nevertheless.

The Charges. On September 2, Mahathir dismissed Anwar from his posts as deputy prime minister and finance minister on the grounds of immoral conduct. The government claimed to have convincing evidence of Anwar's involvement in immoral activities. Shortly thereafter, the UMNO Supreme Council (the party's highest body) expelled Anwar from the UMNO. Then, on September 20 Anwar was arrested, initially under the Internal Security Act (ISA), on five charges of corruption and five charges of sodomy.

Anwar contended that his sacking was politically motivated. From the time of his dismissal until his arrest, he held a series of meetings—at his home as well as at selected sites in Kuala Lumpur and in other states—to rally support. During this period, Anwar launched the "Reformasi" (reform) movement calling for democratic reforms and an end to cronyism.

The Anwar saga involved a number of unprecedented events in Malaysian politics, which may have a profound effect on the country's longer-term political development. Anwar became a focal point for political dissent, with street demonstrations in the capital almost every weekend demanding reforms and the resignation of the prime minister. Although participant numbers dwindled from a high of perhaps 30,000 before Anwar's arrest to only hundreds toward the end of the year, the demonstrations seemed to take on a life of their own.

Opposition and nongovernmental organization (NGO) groups also echoed the demands of the Reformasi movement. One of these is the Malaysian People's Movement for Justice (GERAK, Gerakan Keadilan Rakyat Malaysia), launched on September 27 and comprising the three opposition parties (the ethnic-Chinese-based Democratic Action Party [DAP], the Islamic fundamentalist Islamic Party of Malaysia [PAS], and the Malaysian People's Party) and 11 NGOs. The other principal group is the Coalition for People's Democracy (GAGASAN, Gagasan Demokratik Rakyat), also an NGO, which seeks the repeal of the ISA. (The ISA, inherited from the colonial period, allows the government to detain a person indefinitely without trial if he/she is considered a threat to national security.)

The impact of these groups in mobilizing opposition to the government remains to be seen. Some commentators have pointed out that an alliance between the ethnic-Chinese-based DAP and the Islamic PAS is not viable and can only be sustained as long as both are able to gain political mileage from the immediate political crisis.

Anwar's trial began in early November and was expected to last into the first part of 1999. Whatever the outcome, this affair has altered the once tranquil politics of the country. What stands out most prominently is not the political dissent but, more importantly, the unprecedented manner of expressing this dissent—through street demonstrations. With certain groups calling on the government to hold an early election (not required before 2000), some doubt exists as to whether UMNO and government leaders can maintain political support in the face of mounting discontent.

Impact on National Security. The demonstrations in Kuala Lumpur over the Anwar affair do not pose an immediate security threat; except for one incident in which three people were reportedly injured, the demonstrations have been peaceful. However, if the political crisis continues it will adversely affect the recovery of the Malaysian economy. As in the rest of the region, restoring confidence is critical to Malaysia's economic recovery. Unfortunately, though, Anwar's dismissal and trial have brought severe criticism from the foreign media and from some foreign political leaders, thereby exacerbating negative perceptions of the country and its prospects.

On the other hand, if the government's strategies succeed in turning around the economy, then overall confidence and political support may be restored and the protests dissipate. The government's proposed budget for 1999 was designed to promote this outcome, projecting a return to a positive 1 percent growth rate. Furthermore, in his budget address the prime minister reported that the imposition of foreign exchange controls had for the moment resolved the problem of liquidity and led to the return of some local capital that had fled the country at the height of the financial crisis. However, it is too soon to definitively conclude that Malaysia—or the Mahathir government, for that matter—is out of the woods.

REGIONAL DEVELOPMENTS   Certain developments in Malaysia's relations with other countries in the region during 1998 also affected the country's security environment. Most important, Malaysia's relations with Singapore underwent a number of strains. Specific events included the Singapore government's demand that Malaysia move its customs, immigration, and quarantine facilities from Tanjong Pagar in downtown Singapore to Woodlands near the border; Singapore's refusal to allow people from peninsular Malaysia to withdraw their savings from Singapore's Central Provident Fund (the national pension system); and negative comments in Singaporean Senior Minister Lee Kuan Yew's memoirs regarding some former Malaysian leaders.

Despite domestic calls for the Malaysian government to respond decisively to these developments, so far the two governments have performed a delicate diplomatic balancing act in managing them. Mahathir and Singaporean Prime Minister Goh Chok Tong met in Kuala Lumpur in November and agreed to set aside differences and work on improving bilateral relations. Accordingly, Goh offered to assist Malaysia in overcoming its financial problems by helping it to raise funds in Singapore, while Mahathir agreed to further examine the issue of meeting Singapore's future water requirements (in line with an agreement reached in principle in February 1998 but not yet signed on continued water supply to Singapore beyond 2061). Malaysia also relaxed restrictions that it had imposed earlier on Singaporean military aircraft entering Malaysian air space.

In response to Indonesian President B. J. Habibie's and Filipino President Joseph Estrada's public expressions of sympathy for Anwar and concern about his treatment, the Malaysian government dismissively characterized the comments as interference in its domestic affairs. This reaction was even stronger to the two presidents' separate meetings with Anwar's daughter, Nurul Izza, on Indonesia's Batam Island and in Manila, respectively. At one point, it was conjectured that the two presidents might boycott the Asia-Pacific Economic Cooperation (APEC) summit meeting hosted by Malaysia in mid-November; however, both Habibie and Estrada ultimately attended.

The economic and political crises in Indonesia also bear on the internal security of Malaysia, particularly as the bulk of foreign workers in Malaysia are from Indonesia—approximately one million. Since the economic downturn, the Malaysian government has embarked on a program to repatriate foreign workers. However, with unemployment and inflation in Indonesia soaring, a strong possibility exists of a further influx of illegal migrants, particularly from those areas of Indonesia closest to Malaysia.

Moreover, the political unrest in Indonesia, including demonstrations by students, labor unions, and NGOs, has had a visible effect in Malaysia, as illustrated by the adoption of the originally Indonesian slogan "Reformasi" as the name of the political reform movement in Malaysia. The shape and extent of this influence remain indeterminate, but its ultimate impact could be considerable.

MAJOR POWERS   Malaysia's relations with the major powers of the Asia Pacific region present a mixed picture. On the one hand, the Malaysian government has welcomed and appreciated the financial support offered by China and Japan to the Southeast Asian countries affected by the economic crisis, especially Japan's US$30 billion package announced on September 30 and discussed at the summit meeting of the Association of Southeast Asian Nations (ASEAN) in Hanoi in December. On the other hand, Malaysian leaders, including Mahathir, have been outspokenly resentful of their country's treatment by both the U.S. government and American business interests. Specifically, they have accused international financial "manipulators," personified by American George Soros, of instigating the regional financial/economic crisis and harboring quasicolonial ambitions to gain control of Malaysia's economy. Moreover, Malaysian leaders bitterly resented public statements made by U.S. Vice President Al Gore to an international business group on the eve of the November APEC summit in Kuala Lumpur expressing support for the Malaysian political protest and reform movement. These developments cast a chill over Malaysian-U.S. relations that may last for some time to come.

DEFENSE POLICIES AND ISSUES

Malaysia's defense policy is based on two premises: national resilience and conventional deterrence. Although there are no perceived immediate external threats to the country, the Malaysian government is concerned about the potential for conflict over disputed claims in the South China Sea as well as about other external developments that could have repercussions on the security of the country.

Owing to the current economic crisis, Malaysia's budget for national security (which includes the defense forces) has been cut. In the 1998 budget, expenditure on security was projected to decline 20 percent, to US$1.39 billion from US$1.74 billion in 1997. The defense subsector was expected to absorb an even larger cut, of nearly 25 percent, and a number of major defense expenditures were deferred.

The government has put on hold plans to purchase six CN-235-220 tactical transport aircraft. In addition, it has scaled back the US$1.3 billion program to acquire 27 modern patrol vessels, only six of which are now to be built by a German shipbuilding consortium, at least until the Malaysian economy recovers. These will be the New Generation Patrol Vessels.

Citing difficulties caused by the economic crisis, Malaysia opted out of the 1998 military exercises organized under the Five Power Defense Arrangements (FPDA) with Australia, New Zealand, Singapore, and the United Kingdom. As well, in early October Malaysia canceled its yearly defense talks with the Philippines. It has been speculated that Malaysia's withdrawal from the FPDA exercises was due to strained relations with Singapore and that its cancellation of defense talks with the Philippines was in reaction to Estrada's public support for Anwar.

Finally, during the year Malaysia's defense minister announced an overall review of national defense policy, which will include a review of military exercises with other nations, to be completed by the middle of 1999.

CONTRIBUTIONS TO REGIONAL AND GLOBAL SECURITY

In spite of its current problems, Malaysia remains active in ASEAN. Concurring on the acceleration of the timetable for an ASEAN Free Trade Area and other steps outlined in the statement "Bold Measures" released at the December ASEAN summit, Malaysia also advocated taking concrete actions to better protect the ASEAN economies from the kinds of external financial pressures that led to the 1997–1998 economic crisis. In this regard, the Malaysian government has been at the forefront of those calling for a new international financial architecture to provide a means of regulating currency trading and speculation. In the regional context, moreover, Malaysia has strongly supported the Manila Framework for Enhanced Asian Regional Cooperation to Promote Financial Stability.

To enable ASEAN economies to better cope with such problems as credit tightening and currency rate volatility, Malaysia also proposed to its neighbors that local currencies be used for intra-ASEAN trade, on a voluntary basis. This proposal received support from other ASEAN states, with the result that bilateral agreements were being negotiated at the end of 1998 between Malaysia and Indonesia, the Philippines, and Thailand.

Finally, Malaysia continued to support the expansion of ASEAN to include all ten Southeast Asian countries by favoring the admission of Cambodia at the December ASEAN summit. Although the admission of Cambodia was postponed pending the consolidation of the new coalition government in Cambodia, Malaysia remains hopeful that the ASEAN-10 goal will be achieved in 1999.

Malaysia also remains committed to regional security consultations through the ASEAN Regional Forum (ARF) as well as other regional confidence- and peace-building efforts. Strongly supporting ASEAN's continued role as the leading party in ARF, the Malaysian government has resisted suggestions that the coordinating role be rotated among all members. As part of ARF's activities, in 1998 Malaysia and Australia together organized a Seminar on Production of Defense Policy Documents, held in Canberra from August 31 to September 3. Malaysia will also cochair, with Canada and Japan, ARF's Peace Training Course in Tokyo in March 1999.

The annual APEC ministerial and summit meetings, hosted by Kuala Lumpur in mid-November, proved both less productive and more controversial than the Malaysian government had hoped. Progress on the Early Voluntary Sectoral Liberalization plan was effectively stymied by Japan's refusal to agree to inclusion of the forestry and fisheries sectors. More important at the time, however, was that the actual proceedings of the summit were largely overshadowed at least in the public perception by issues relating to the dismissal, jailing, and trial of Anwar. Gore's premeeting statement supporting the Reformasi movement elicited a very strong response from both the Malaysian government and many private Malaysian individuals, as well as criticism from officials and business representatives from other countries attending the meetings. Despite the Malaysian government's efforts to achieve a successful outcome, as well as the issuance of positive official declarations by the ministerial and leadership meetings pledging continued support for both the concept and objectives of regional cooperation, the Kuala Lumpur meetings failed to attain significant progress in either economic cooperation or political cohesion within APEC, making its future course somewhat uncertain.

At the global level, in 1998 Malaysia was elected to the UN Security Council for a two-year membership in 1999–2000. Malaysia has long been active in UN-sponsored activities, including peacekeeping operations starting from the Congo mission in 1963 and continuing through missions in Namibia, Cambodia, Somalia, and Bosnia-Herzegovina. Since 1993, however, Malaysia has steadily reduced the size of its UN contingent, and in July 1998 it was forced to temporarily demobilize its last peacekeeping contingent owing to the economic crisis. The resumption of participation in such multilateral operations will have to await improvement in the country's economic circumstances.

10 New Zealand

THE SECURITY ENVIRONMENT

New Zealand's perceptions of security in Asia Pacific changed dramatically in 1998. Concerns with economic security now occupy center stage: Alongside a general consensus that New Zealand faces a prolonged downturn run fears that what started as an Asian crisis could become a global recession.

The general security enjoyed by the region in recent years has been possible in part because governments in the region have been able to deliver economic benefits to the majority of their populations. Now that this is no longer the case, especially in Indonesia, internal unrest can be expected to increase. Whether this will in turn undermine the security of the whole region is a question that draws contrasting opinions from analysts and government officials. On the other hand, analysts and decision makers generally agree that the Asian economic crisis has curbed defense spending in most states, which is considered to be a positive development.

While the New Zealand government views the role of the United States as crucial to the region's prosperity and security, analysts debate this point. Some argue that there are worrying signs that the U.S. economy is slowing, which will reduce its capacity to absorb goods and services produced elsewhere in the region. This in turn will slow economic recovery in East Asia as well as New Zealand. Others point to the accordionlike character of the U.S. economy and warn of the dangers of overly relying on the American economy as the market of last resort.

The capacities of China and Japan to handle the economic crisis are generally viewed as critical to the future economic prospects of the region. The successful visit by U.S. President Bill Clinton to Beijing in June–July 1998 is generally regarded in New Zealand as an important step in the development of one of the region's most important bilateral relationships.

The nuclear tests by India and Pakistan in May 1998 were generally regarded as destabilizing by both the New Zealand government and independent commentators, and vigorously condemned. New Zealand withdrew its high commissioner to New Delhi. Domestic dynamics were generally viewed as the source of India's tests, but the general consensus was that the nuclear tests had the potential to set off an arms race in South Asia.

CONCERNS   The government and mainstream commentators are divided on their assessments of the extent to which negative influences flowing out of the economic crisis may create an unstable security environment. The government and some (nonmainstream) commentators stress the risk that illegal migration may inflame cross-border tensions and test the internal unity of the Association of Southeast Asian Nations (ASEAN). Also, this line of opinion notes that domestic isolationist impulses may be unscrupulously cultivated for political gain in some states of the region. Finally, states suffering severe economic downturn might lose confidence in current economic and political structures to such an extent that they decide to withdraw their cooperation or involvement, thereby leading to a breakdown in regional dialogue and a more volatile security environment.

These concerns are not universally shared among mainstream commentators, however, who suggest that regional cooperation processes have remained largely unaffected by the crisis and that relations between states in the region have not changed measurably. The potential flash points that existed prior to the onset of the economic crisis—the Korean peninsula, the South China Sea, and the Taiwan Strait—remain, but the economic crisis has not negatively affected these sensitive areas. Although the dynamics underlying North Korea's launch of a missile that overflew Japan will require sensitive handling, this incident does not appear to signal a new round of tension on the Korean peninsula. The visit by the Taiwanese senior envoy, Koo Chen-fu, to China to meet with President Jiang Zemin was interpreted in New Zealand as a small but important development toward mutual respect between China and Taiwan. Significantly, the visit implies that deeper underlying trends in relations between China and Taiwan have not been affected by the economic crisis. Finally, clashes in the South China Sea between China and the Philippines also illustrate that deep-seated tensions there will continue to need careful management.

RESPONSE TO THE ECONOMIC CRISIS   The global economic crisis slowed New Zealand's economic growth rate to 0.5 percent for 1998; however, a sense of optimism is increasing that the worst of the economic crisis is over. New Zealand's response to the crisis has been flexible. Government spending has remained relatively constant, aside from a blanket 1 percent drop in spending spread evenly over all government departments. New Zealand has sought to compensate for the decline in demand for its goods in East Asia by switching markets, with some success: While it has been a struggle to find new markets for some products, especially wood, pulp, and fish, new export opportunities have arisen for dairy and meat products and aluminum in Europe. Positively, the decline in the value of the New Zealand dollar has increased export competitiveness and also makes New Zealand an attractive destination for tourists whose domestic currencies, especially North American and European, remain strong.

DEFENSE POLICIES AND ISSUES

DEFENSE SPENDING AND FORCE STRUCTURE   New Zealand defense spending remained constant in 1998. Several defense modernization projects specified in the 1997 defense white paper were approved by the government in November 1998. These projects include the acquisition of 28 nearly new U.S. F-16 multirole fighters once destined for Pakistan (on a lease-to-buy basis), light armored vehicles (in a joint buy with Australia), reconnaissance vehicles and medium-range antiarmor defense systems, as well as the completion of the modification of the Military Support Ship. All acquisitions will be fully covered by current New Zealand Defense Force budgets.

Antidefense sentiment, however, continues to affect the modernization of the New Zealand Defense Force. Domestic political considerations, for example, caused the National Party government to defer until the year 2000 a decision on the controversial proposal to acquire a third Australia–New Zealand Army Corps (ANZAC) frigate. The acquisition of both a third frigate and the F-16s is opposed by the opposition Labour Party and its Alliance Party ally; the Labour Party has actually stated that it might consider selling the F-16s should it win government in the 1999 election.

While a few mainstream commentators oppose high-tech capital acquisitions, general support comes from most analysts and newspaper editors for the purchase of a third modern frigate and the F-16s. Polls conducted by the Labour Party and a TV news station found high levels of public opposition (76–81 percent) to the proposal to acquire a third ANZAC frigate. However, many question whether these polls, mainly based on sampling in those urban areas where opposition to defense spending is highest, accurately reflect overall national sentiment.

The current public debate over defense acquisitions reflects the re-emergence of insularity among left-wing activists and politicians. In the debate over frigates and fighters, the peace movement and the Labour Party have advocated the disarmament of the Royal New Zealand Navy and the Royal New Zealand Air Force and the adoption of an essentially isolationist approach, moving away from the concept of collective defense of the country's external interests and toward a focus on the Southwest Pacific and New Zealand. This view is championed in a report of the Parliamentary Select Committee for Foreign Affairs, Defense and Trade, expected to be released early in 1999. This new isolationism is vigorously challenged by most mainstream commentators.

Under the North Atlantic Treaty Organization (NATO) definition of defense spending, New Zealand allocates 1.2 percent of its gross domestic product, or NZ$1.177 billion (US$620.88 million at NZ$1.00 = US$0.53), to defense. The New Zealand Defense Force is staffed by 9,550 active service personnel and approximately 6,900 reserves.

DOCTRINE   The New Zealand Defense Force's operational doctrine is an adaptation of doctrines of Australia, Canada, the United Kingdom, and the United States. This doctrine is consistent with NATO defense doctrine, which now underpins most United Nations peace-keeping operations, and also is similar to those of Malaysia and Singapore.

The Royal New Zealand Army continues to examine the implications of the technological Revolution in Military Affairs and other changes in the international environment through what is called the AD 2015 process. This process, which models Royal New Zealand

Army doctrine, force structure, and capability options based on realistic future employment scenarios, seeks to provide a blueprint for the "army after next" for use in the second decade of the 21st century. The Royal New Zealand Navy and Royal New Zealand Air Force force structure development processes have adopted similar methodologies.

DEFENSE RELATIONS WITH AUSTRALIA   New Zealand's defense relationship with Australia is close and enduring, and formalized in the Closer Defense Relations (CDR) agreement. Both countries work together to harmonize this defense relationship, sharing perspectives on strategic issues and seeking streamlined defense acquisitions and force structure-capability mixes. Following New Zealand's suspension from ANZUS military exercises by the United States (after Wellington unilaterally banned visits by nuclear-armed and nuclear-powered military ships and aircraft in 1984), CDR exercises have played a crucial role in sustaining New Zealand Defense Force capacity. However, New Zealand's postponement of its decision about whether or not to acquire a third ANZAC frigate from Australia again raised doubts in Canberra about Wellington's willingness to pull its weight in the defense relationship. Australia's reaction to the postponement of the decision was controlled and understated, as Australian doubts are partially offset by New Zealand's decision to acquire F-16 multirole fighters (which fill a niche not covered by the Australian Defense Force) and to join with Australia in the acquisition of light armored vehicles. Nevertheless, should New Zealand renege on its decision to acquire F-16s and should it ultimately not purchase a third frigate, the wider Australia–New Zealand relationship will almost certainly be undermined.

Defense cooperation with Australia in 1998 included close cooperation on the implementation of the Bougainville Peace Process, the deployment of a New Zealand special forces troop to the Persian Gulf in February 1998 as part of an Australia SAS squadron, trans-Tasman visits by defense ministers and senior officers, and routine exercises. In addition, the combined ANZAC special forces unit provided the search-and-rescue component of the multilateral force assembled in the Persian Gulf for operations against Iraq until June 1998.

NEW ZEALAND AND THE UNITED STATES   New Zealand's high-level diplomatic relations with the United States continue to improve. One sign of this warming between Wellington and Washington was

Clinton's agreement to participate in a state visit following his participation in the 1999 Asia-Pacific Economic Cooperation (APEC) forum in Auckland. Another factor helping to deepen the relationship is the shared commitment of both states to the furtherance of trade liberalization as well as to human rights.

Despite the fact that few prospects exist for any change to Wellington's nonnuclear status (which has now achieved icon status domestically), New Zealand–U.S. defense relations are also improving. In 1998, New Zealand supported the U.S.-led coalition that provided the forces which underpinned United Nations diplomacy with Iraq in February. Following Clinton's discussion of the situation with Prime Minister Jenny Shipley in a private phone call, New Zealand provided two P-3 Orion maritime surveillance aircraft and a detachment of special forces for the coalition that formed in the Persian Gulf in February 1998. Moreover, the visit of U.S. Secretary of State Madeleine Albright on August 1 signaled a further warming of bilateral relations, and New Zealand's decision to acquire some of the ex-Pakistani air force F-16s embargoed by the United States helped Washington mend fences with Islamabad. When U.S. Pacific Commander-in-Chief (CINCPAC) Admiral Joseph Prueher visited Auckland in September 1998, the New Zealand government provided him a list of 32 areas for increasing defense links between the two countries. Finally, New Zealand strongly supported the U.S.-British air campaign against Iraq in December 1998.

CONTRIBUTIONS TO REGIONAL AND GLOBAL SECURITY

New Zealand expressed firm support for the work of the United Nations Special Commission (UNSCOM) after Iraq halted the commission's visits to sites suspected of storing weapons of mass destruction in January–February 1998 and again in August and November–December. New Zealand also expressed strong support for the U.S. and British determination to underpin diplomacy with force on this issue. Public support for the New Zealand government's decision to provide military assistance (see the previous discussion of New Zealand and the United States) to the U.S.-led multilateral coalition in the Persian Gulf in early 1998 was evenly divided.

New Zealand contributed four observers to participate in the

UN-coordinated Joint International Observer Group during the Cambodian elections in July 1998.

THE BOUGAINVILLE PEACE PROCESS   New Zealand's role in the peace process in Bougainville (discussed in more detail in the chapter on Papua New Guinea) represented a major contribution to the security of the Southwest Pacific in 1998. The Lincoln Agreement, signed near Christchurch in January 1998, formalized the cease-fire on Bougainville and paved the way for UN participation. New Zealand welcomed the United Nation's decision to establish a small political office on the island.

The peace process moved from truce monitoring to peace monitoring in May 1998, and Australia's role in the process increased significantly at that time when New Zealand handed command of the military element to Australia. New Zealand is contributing 30 military personnel to the Australian-led Peace Monitoring Group.

DEFENSE COOPERATION WITH MALAYSIA AND SINGAPORE   New Zealand's defense relations with Malaysia and Singapore remain close and were reinforced by the September 1998 visit of Minister of Defense Max Bradford to both countries. With New Zealand excluded from ANZUS exercises involving the United States and Australia, the annual military exercises under the Five Power Defense Arrangements (FPDA) linking Australia, New Zealand, and the United Kingdom with Malaysia and Singapore are the largest such program for New Zealand. Malaysia's withdrawal from participation in the 1998 FPDA exercises, citing financial reasons, was a disappointment to New Zealand, and Malaysia's decision to resume participation in the 1999 exercises was highly welcomed.

DEFENSE ASSISTANCE   New Zealand's Defense Mutual Assistance Program provides military training and other assistance to the Cook Islands, Fiji, Indonesia, Malaysia, Niue, Papua New Guinea, the Philippines, Samoa, Singapore, the Solomon Islands, Thailand, Tonga, and Vanuatu. This essentially cooperative program is coordinated with counterpart defense assistance programs in Australia and the United States, and a wide range of training assistance is provided. The emphasis is on promoting good governance and human capital development through leadership, staff, resource management, officer promotion, and technical courses. In addition to the 370 personnel from Southeast Asian and South Pacific countries that study in New Zealand annually, each year 13 New Zealand Defense Force teams deploy to Southeast Asia and 45 to the South Pacific. New Zealand military instructors are on long-term attachments in several South Pacific countries.

In July 1998, New Zealand provided emergency assistance in the form of a military medical team and transport aircraft to Papua New Guinea following a devastating tidal wave.

REGIONAL COOPERATION AND DIALOGUE   New Zealand will chair the annual APEC ministerial and heads of government meetings in 1999. New Zealand takes the position that all countries and economies of Asia Pacific should "hold their nerve," maintaining gains made toward trade liberalization and investigating new paths toward further liberalization that are attuned to regional circumstances.

New Zealand remained fully committed to and engaged in the ASEAN Regional Forum (ARF) process at the track one and track two levels and supports work on the development of preventative diplomacy within ARF. The 5th Meeting of the Comprehensive and Cooperative Security Working Group of the track two Council for Security Cooperation in Asia Pacific was held in Wellington in July. The meeting focused on regional cooperation in a climate of economic turbulence.

HUMAN RIGHTS   New Zealand voted for the statute developed at the 1998 Rome conference establishing a standing International Criminal Court in The Hague.

ARMS CONTROL   New Zealand supported the actions of the United Nations to ensure the elimination of Iraqi stockpiles of weapons of mass destruction and urged the government of Iraq to cooperate with UNSCOM. New Zealand takes the position that full compliance with the United Nations on the part of Iraq must be a precondition to the lifting of sanctions.

New Zealand has worked within the Conference on Disarmament for the speedy conclusion of negotiations for a Fissile Material Cut-off Treaty. New Zealand joined with Brazil, Egypt, Ireland, Mexico, Slovenia, South Africa, and Sweden in June 1998 in a call for the elimination of atomic weapons and all other major weapons adaptable to mass destruction.

PEACEKEEPING   The New Zealand contribution to the Bougainville Truce Monitoring Force peaked at approximately 500 personnel and represented New Zealand's largest contribution of military personnel and resources since the Vietnam War. The contingent included a frigate, a dive support team and ship, transport aircraft and helicopters, and a ground element including the truce command team, engineers, and transport, medical, and other support personnel.

Fourteen defense force personnel were stationed in Baghdad with UNSCOM (and were withdrawn in December 1998), three officers are posted to UN headquarters in New York, seven observers are with the UN Observer Mission in the former Yugoslavia, two advisers are part of the UN Mozambique Demining Operation, two support staff work with the Unexploded Ordnance Program Laos, two mine action staff are in Cambodia, 17 personnel are with the UN Angola Verification Mission, two staff are with the UN Observer Mission in Sierra Leone, and seven staff officers work in the NATO Stabilization Force (SFOR) in Bosnia along with 20 artillery personnel and 20 armored corps soldiers working with British units in the SFOR.

11 Papua New Guinea

THE SECURITY ENVIRONMENT

EXTERNAL Papua New Guinea enjoys a relatively benign external security environment. A 1996 defense white paper observed that Papua New Guinea is geographically located in one of the least troubled areas of the world, although it acknowledged the country's vulnerability to intrusions into its air and maritime space (particularly by foreign fishing vessels) and to trafficking in arms and drugs.

In past years, the existence of the Melanesian separatist movement, Organisasi Papua Merdeka (OPM, the Free Papua Movement), in the neighboring Indonesian province of Irian Jaya has been a source of tension in relations between Papua New Guinea and Indonesia. OPM freedom fighters have sometimes sought refuge in the dense jungle on Papua New Guinea's side of the border and occasionally have been pursued across the border by the Indonesian military. Also, in periods of military crackdown in Irian Jaya large numbers of Irianese have crossed the border into Papua New Guinea seeking sanctuary. Following a major influx of Irianese into Papua New Guinea in 1984, the Papua New Guinean government, assisted by the United Nations High Commission for Refugees, resettled a large number of these refugees in East Awin, in Papua New Guinea's Gulf Province. Two years later, Papua New Guinea and Indonesia signed a Treaty of Mutual Respect, Friendship and Cooperation, which acknowledged their shared security concerns and elaborated arrangements for border management and liaison.

Since 1986, relations between Papua New Guinea and Indonesia have improved. In the wake of the political upheaval in Indonesia in

May 1998, there has been some support in Papua New Guinea for the renewed demands of West Papuan nationalists for self-determination. However, Papua New Guinean Prime Minister Bill Skate—who in June became the first foreign head of state to visit Indonesia's newly installed President B. J. Habibie—has reaffirmed his government's support for Indonesian sovereignty over Irian Jaya. The two national leaders also signed a memorandum of understanding establishing a Joint Commission on Bilateral Cooperation, through which senior ministers will meet regularly to discuss a range of bilateral and international issues of mutual interest including defense and security, trade and investment, and agricultural and human resource development. At the same time, the Papua New Guinean government has granted residency status to some 1,200 Indonesian border crossers and their families now living in East Awin.

At the height of the Bougainville rebellion (see below), relations between Papua New Guinea and its eastern neighbor, the Solomon Islands, were troubled as members of the Bougainville Revolutionary Army (BRA) ferried personnel and supplies across the narrow strait separating southern Bougainville from the western islands of the Solomons. In a series of incidents, Papua New Guinea Defense Force (PNGDF) troops exchanged fire with members of the Solomon Islands Police Field Force, raided a Solomon Islands village, and claimed sovereignty over a small island on the Solomons side of the border. With changes of government in both the Solomon Islands and Papua New Guinea and with progress toward peace on Bougainville, relations between the two countries have improved substantially, although in late 1998 the Solomon Islands presented the Papua New Guinean government with a demand for K7 million (US$3 million at K1.00 = US$0.43) in compensation for damages suffered during the Bougainville conflict.

INTERNAL   Papua New Guinea is a small country, fragmented by geographical and ethnolinguistic divisions. Its population of around four million speaks some 800 languages, and even at the national level politics tends to be heavily influenced by parochialism and personal loyalties. Nevertheless, its essentially Westminster-style parliamentary system has produced regular elections since independence in 1975, and all changes of government have been constitutional and without incident. Accordingly, Papua New Guinea is one of the relatively few countries in Asia Pacific with an unbroken record of democratically elected government.

While noting the absence of external threats, the 1996 defense white paper expressed "major concern" over Papua New Guinea's internal security situation, specifically referring to increased problems of law and order, the escalation of land compensation disputes, and the possibility of "uncontrolled ethnic and secessionist movements" similar to the Bougainville insurgency. Although other potential sources of secessionist threats are not readily identifiable, the Bougainville problem has been a major preoccupation of the past several Papua New Guinean governments.

Progress toward Peace on Bougainville. For over a decade, Papua New Guinea has suffered from the separatist rebellion on the eastern island of Bougainville in North Solomons Province. The conflict originated in a dispute over landowners' demands against Bougainville Copper, the company operating the vast gold and copper mine at Panguna, and the national government, which holds equity in the mine. Shortly after the dispute broke out, police and PNGDF personnel were deployed to Bougainville and the situation then escalated into a separatist armed rebellion, which neither political negotiation nor military action was able to contain.

Following the breakdown in 1997 of peace talks and a failed military operation in which PNGDF hostages were taken by the BRA, and on the eve of national elections, the Papua New Guinean government secretly hired international military consultant Sandline International to move against the leadership of the BRA and eventually recapture the Panguna mine site. However, in March 1997 the PNGDF commander, Brigadier General Jerry Singirok, publicly denounced the Sandline contract, ordered the detention and deportation of Sandline personnel, and called for the resignations of then Prime Minister Sir Julius Chan, the deputy prime minister, and the defense minister. All three eventually agreed to step aside pending the outcome of an inquiry into the Sandline affair. In the ensuing election, both Chan and the defense minister were defeated. Before being removed from office, however, Chan sacked Singirok and appointed in his stead the hardline former commander on Bougainville, Colonel Leo Nuia (who in 1996 had been decommissioned by Singirok). Singirok was eventually charged with sedition, and several of the officers associated with his "quasi coup" and subsequent incidents were charged with mutiny. (These incidents included placing then Brigadier General Nuia under house arrest and forcibly releasing some of the implicated officers' colleagues from police custody.)

Chan's successor as prime minister, Bill Skate, had been a supporter of Singirok's actions in March 1997. Taking advantage of the improved political climate on Bougainville resulting from the PNGDF commander's rejection of Sandline, Skate supported a New Zealand–led initiative to revive peace negotiations. A truce was reached through talks held in New Zealand in July and October 1997 and in Australia in November, after which a 250-strong regional Truce Monitoring Group (TMG) comprising soldiers and civilians from Australia, Fiji, New Zealand, Tonga, and Vanuatu established a presence on Bougainville to assist in the peace process.

In January 1998, representatives of the Papua New Guinean government, the government-backed Bougainville Transitional Government (BTG), the (anti-BRA) Bougainville Resistance, the rebel Bougainville Interim Government (BIG), and the BRA, as well as Bougainville community leaders, came together at Lincoln University near Christchurch, New Zealand. The outcome of this meeting was the Lincoln Agreement on Peace, Security and Development on Bougainville, which provides a basis for continuing consultations and negotiations. The meeting also agreed on a cease-fire, which came into effect at the end of April 1998, at which time the TMG was replaced by a regional Peace Monitoring Group (PMG), command of which shifted from New Zealand to Australia. The United Nations was also asked to send an observer mission, which arrived in September. The Papua New Guinean government subsequently agreed to withdraw its troops from Bougainville and to establish the mine site township of Arawa as a demilitarized neutral zone. A democratically elected Bougainville Reconciliation Government is to be established, replacing the BTG and BIG.

Although the peace has at times looked fragile, the process of negotiation, reconciliation, and reconstruction at the national, provincial, and community levels continued throughout 1998. An end to the rebellion now seems finally to be in sight, although many Bougainvilleans still see independence as their ultimate goal—an option that the national government continues to rule out.

Law, Order, and State Capacity. Localized, generally clan-based conflicts (or "tribal fighting") and the criminal activities of so-called *raskol* gangs have been on the increase since the early 1970s. Increasing lawlessness resulted in the declaration of a state of emergency in five highlands provinces as early as 1979. Corruption, intimidation, and violence have since spread to national and provincial politics.

The 1997 national election campaign was marked by widespread demands for reform and an end to corruption. Notwithstanding this, the coalition government that emerged after the 1997 elections was tainted by allegations of vote buying and by its association with key figures in the Sandline deal. In late 1997, videotapes screened on Australian television showed Skate (a self-confessed former *raskol*) claiming to be a godfather of the *raskol* gangs in Papua New Guinea's capital, Port Moresby. Further videotapes shown in early 1998 implicated a senior government minister, Fr Robert Lak, theretofore considered to be a man of high moral profile, in a sex scandal.

Such incidents, combined with continuing fiscal problems and allegations (by the National Security Advisory Committee among others) of nepotism and administrative inefficiency, have done little to build popular confidence in the state apparatus. Further, declining standards and morale in both the PNGDF and the Royal Papua New Guinea Constabulary only exacerbate the problem.

DEFENSE POLICIES AND ISSUES

Although the primary constitutional function of the PNGDF is the defense of Papua New Guinea, the defense force has had little role to play in external security. Indeed, it has been generally accepted, both at independence and currently, that if Papua New Guinea were attacked its security forces could do little more than mount a holding operation until help arrived from Australia or possibly other countries. A Joint Declaration of Principles signed by the prime ministers of Papua New Guinea and Australia in 1987 makes provision for consultation on matters of common security interest and states: "In the event of external armed attack threatening the national sovereignty of either country, such consultation would be conducted for the purpose of each government deciding what measures should be taken, jointly or separately, in relation to that attack." Australia has provided assistance to the PNGDF through its Defense Cooperation Program.

However, Papua New Guinean defense officials and senior PNGDF officers have repeatedly expressed a desire to reduce their dependence on Australian military assistance, consistent with the "Look North" emphasis of Papua New Guinea's foreign policy of "selective engagement." The PNGDF has also signed status of forces agreements or memoranda of understanding with Indonesia, Israel, Malaysia, New

Zealand, and the United States. During the prime minister's visit to Indonesia in June 1998, the defense minister signed a memorandum of understanding that, he said, would enhance relations between the PNGDF and the Indonesian Armed Forces. As a result of the visit, Papua New Guinea is to obtain aircraft maintenance, training, and uniforms from Indonesia.

In the absence of a major external threat, the PNGDF's role in external security has consisted principally of patrolling its western borders (essentially to deny access to the OPM) and its eastern borders (to prevent the movement of Bougainville rebels between Bougainville and the Solomon Islands), and policing the waters of its 200-mile Exclusive Economic Zone against illegal fishing.

Since the early 1980s, however, the PNGDF has been called upon increasingly to assist the civil authorities in maintaining law and order. In 1991, it was formally stated that Papua New Guinea would give highest priority to internal security needs and that Australian assistance would be geared to supporting the PNGDF and the Royal Papua New Guinea Constabulary in this objective. The new emphasis on the PNGDF's role in internal security took on new significance with the onset of the Bougainville crisis in 1988 and the subsequent commitment of troops on Bougainville.

There has been a general acknowledgment for some years that the state of equipment, training, and discipline within the PNGDF has been deteriorating since the 1970s. In recent years, notwithstanding persistent over-budget spending by the Defense Department (partly as a result of the Bougainville campaign), the PNGDF has on a number of occasions been unable to pay its creditors, meet salaries and allowances due to PNGDF personnel, or cover the basic costs of the day-to-day provisioning of troops. A ten-year program to reorganize the force structure, increase force size, and replace major equipment was drawn up in 1988 but never implemented.

The 1996 defense white paper, submitted to the National Parliament in 1997, outlined a new *"Banis* [perimeter defense] strategy." The focus of the *Banis* strategy is on managing the country's borders, preserving its natural resources, and monitoring and policing its territory. Five major components of the strategy were identified: (1) rationalization of the PNGDF force structure into a small, versatile, mobile force; (2) expansion of its relations with neighboring countries; (3) decentralization, to give the PNGDF a strategic presence in each of the country's four administrative regions; (4) strengthening the capability of the force to deal with internal security, in part through closer cooperation with the Royal Papua New Guinea Constabulary; and (5) greater emphasis on nation building and development through a variety of measures, including a revitalized Defense Civic Action Program in conjunction with provincial governments. In November 1998, it was announced that, in accordance with the white paper, a new PNGDF engineers base was to be established in the Western Highlands, and that the PNGDF would undergo "a change of culture," with greater emphasis on civic action. Apart from that, however, little progress has been made toward the implementation of the 1996 white paper objectives, and morale within the force remains low.

Defense force size at the end of 1998 stood at about 4,600, with numbers projected to decline as some 600 personnel reach retirement age in 1999. Budget estimates for 1999 also envisage a small reduction in defense spending, from K86 million to K80 million (US$34 million), which represents 0.9 percent of gross national product.

Toward the end of 1998, Skate announced to much general surprise that Singirok was to be brought back to replace Nuia as commander of the PNGDF. Singirok's reappointment was welcomed on Bougainville but greeted with mixed feelings within the defense force, which has become factionalized in the aftermath of the Sandline episode and Singirok's earlier dismissal. A group of former PNGDF commanders have called on Singirok to stand aside pending the outcome of the sedition trial (set to begin in January 1999). The newly reappointed commander has promised to effect "a massive clean-out of colonels" in the defense force and to instill discipline back once again in the force. But some commentators have seen Singirok's reinstatement as a move to bolster Skate's political position in the event of a parliamentary vote of no confidence, and in November unsubstantiated (and insubstantial) rumors of an imminent military coup were circulating in Port Moresby. The Skate government would have been vulnerable to a no-confidence vote in January 1999, but in early December it adjourned Parliament until July 1999.

CONTRIBUTIONS TO REGIONAL AND GLOBAL SECURITY

Papua New Guinea plays an active role in the Pacific Islands region as a member of the South Pacific Forum (and its Regional Security Committee) and as a leading force in the Melanesian Spearhead

Group. Papua New Guinean secretary-general of the Forum Secretariat, Noel Levi (formerly foreign minister of Papua New Guinea), has played a prominent role in the formulation of an action plan for economic reforms endorsed in 1998 by Forum leaders, in drawing international attention to the economic and physical vulnerability of small island states, and in arguing the case for regional preventive diplomacy.

The 1996 defense white paper supported the idea of collective security arrangements, including the formation of a regional peacekeeping force. It also recommended the establishment of defense relations with Fiji, Tonga, and members of the Melanesian Spearhead Group as a first step toward regional security cooperation. The experience of the regional TMG/PMG on Bougainville has been seen by some as evidence of the value of such an arrangement.

In addition to its Pacific Islands ties, Papua New Guinea is also geographically linked to Southeast Asia. It is a signatory to the ASEAN Treaty of Amity and Cooperation as well as a participant in the Asia-Pacific Economic Cooperation forum and the ASEAN Regional Forum. During his visit to Indonesia, Skate undertook to support Indonesia's bid to become a dialogue partner of the South Pacific Forum, and in return Indonesia offered to support any request by Papua New Guinea to become a permanent associate member of the Association of Southeast Asian Nations (ASEAN).

Internationally, Papua New Guinea has made clear its opposition to nuclear testing, in South Asia as in the Pacific, and its support of human rights in and beyond the region. Its capacity to play an international role, however, suffered a setback late in the year when, as a result of expenditure cuts in the 1999 budget, it was revealed that Papua New Guinea is to close 14 of its 21 overseas missions and cut its foreign affairs staffing by 50 percent.

If the various parties involved in the peace process on Bougainville are able to bring that conflict to an end, a major source of instability in the region will be removed. But if Papua New Guinea is to make a larger contribution to regional and global security, it must first overcome its internal problems of law and order and strengthen the capabilities of its security forces.

12 Philippines

THE SECURITY ENVIRONMENT

Like most Asia Pacific states, the Philippines entered 1999 after enduring a volatile environment in 1998. On the political side, the country
weathered an important leadership transition, emerging with fundamental policies unchanged. The regional economic crisis shattered the
Philippines' aspiration to reach newly industrializing country status
and forced Filipinos to think more carefully about the best strategy for
development. The overall external security environment was stable,
but a number of specific foreign policy problems and security issues
arose, the most serious of which was another round of tensions with
China over the Spratly Islands.

DOMESTIC POLITICS   After strong public opposition to attempts by
supporters of President Fidel Ramos to amend the Constitution to allow him a further term, a national election was held on May 11, 1998,
and Ramos made a gracious exit. The peaceful transition of power
was a further step toward the consolidation of democratic processes
in the Philippines.

The elections also raised the profile of the poorer sector of the society. Former Vice President Joseph Estrada, who led a field of eight
candidates with almost 36 percent of the vote, campaigned as a cham-
pion of the poor and received almost 80 percent of his votes from the
so-called mass vote. Accordingly, Estrada was dubbed "President for
the Masses."

Estrada was also known as someone who could balance contending
political camps and thus who might dilute political tensions. However,

such a characteristic can also be a weakness, and indeed Estrada quickly encountered problems getting his cabinet to work together. Another early problem for Estrada was the return of a number of cronies of discredited former President Ferdinand Marcos to prominent political and economic positions.

Another outcome of the 1998 election was some small but potentially significant changes in the composition of the political elite. For example, many new members of the House of Representatives came from the younger generation. Further, a new "party list" electoral system added 52 seats to the House of Representatives for sectoral groups and small political parties, which in the past had been overwhelmed by the influence of the big traditional political parties representing the landed elite. However, the extent to which such sectoral groups and small parties will be able to advance a programmatic agenda remains to be seen.

THE ECONOMY   The Philippines sustained a dynamic business environment up until the end of Ramos' term; indeed, the Philippine economy was among those regional economies least affected by the Asian economic crisis. Gross national product managed to grow through the third quarter of the year, although it shrank 0.5 percent for 1998 as a whole. Further, the International Monetary Fund (IMF) declared the Philippine banking system to be sound, and exports grew 18.8 percent in the first half of 1998.

In contrast to the relative political stability of 1998, however, the volatility of Asian currencies introduced serious uncertainties to the Philippine economy. As Estrada took over, the Philippines was experiencing nearly double-digit inflation, high interest and unemployment rates, low productivity growth, a diminishing growth rate, and a large budget deficit. Agricultural production was also falling (owing more to drought than the regional economic crisis), which was a major contributor to the slowdown of GNP growth.

In his state of the nation address, Estrada gave priority to revitalizing agriculture, which requires genuine agrarian reform. However, the resistance of the landed elite remains a stumbling block. In addition, some experts argue that the focus of economic policy should be industrialization.

Most seriously, the Estrada administration appears to lack a clear national economic agenda and specific strategies to revitalize the private sector, despite a stated commitment to this objective. Many observers fear that the government's inability to act decisively may lead to a further decline of the economy and a consequent disenchantment with the government on the part of the poor.

INTERNAL SECURITY   Another element of continuity between the Ramos and Estrada administrations was the effort to bring the communist and Muslim rebel movements into mainstream politics. In January 1998, the Ramos government and the communist rebels announced a human rights accord, a significant step in the peace process. The Armed Forces of the Philippines (AFP) and the National Program for Unification and Development launched the *Balik-Baril* (Return of Arms) program, which resulted in the return of 196 communists and 525 secessionist rebels, who surrendered 150 and 366 firearms, respectively. Under the Estrada administration, peace talks continued, although with a change in the composition of the government's negotiating panel.

However, in Mindanao, where 1997 had seen promising developments including a reconciliation agreement with the Moro National Liberation Front (MNLF) and a cease-fire agreement with the Moro Islamic Liberation Front (MILF), peace remains elusive. Holdout factions of both the MNLF and the MILF, plus the Abu Sayaf Group (ASG), are still following a strategy of violence.

Though some members of the MNLF are undergoing training for integration into the AFP, some 10,000 MNLF rebels continue to mount armed resistance in the south. Further, the planned 1998 referendum on regional autonomy for nine Mindanao provinces not yet included in the Autonomous Region in Muslim Mindanao was postponed, with some fearing that it might be canceled altogether. Likewise, huge logistical problems must be overcome to conduct elections in March 1999 in the existing Autonomous Region, a situation which may also lead to their postponement until the latter part of the year. These problems, in turn, may have implications for the success of the Southern Philippines Council for Peace and Development and for the overall peace effort with the MNLF.

The July 1997 cease-fire agreement between the government and the MILF was followed in November by an agreement on implementing guidelines and ground rules. However, talks stalled over the terms of repositioning troops in Central Mindanao, and both the government and the MILF forces continued to strengthen their capabilities.

As 1999 began, hostilities dramatically intensified, resulting in significant casualties among both noncombatants and combatants, as well as the dislocation of residents of affected areas. Potentially exacerbating the situation, the National Democratic Front of the Philippines announced that it would join forces with the MILF. While Estrada pledged to continue the peace negotiations, he has also insisted that his government is ready to retaliate against any lawlessness. But in the meantime, governmental recognition of the camps and territories held by the MILF is tantamount to recognition of the MILF's belligerency and to toleration of continuing violence within their areas of control.

The ASG, with only approximately 1,000 members, has been involved in a variety of criminal and terrorist activities including kidnappings, robberies, assassinations, extortion of wealthy businessmen and prominent personalities, arson, and massacres of civilians. The ASG is believed to have formalized its organizational structure, realigned its operational activities, and increased its capability to carry out acts of terrorism and violence. Due to its relatively small size and essentially criminal orientation, the Estrada administration has not explored peace negotiations with the ASG.

In addition to trying to end the communist and secessionist struggles, the Ramos administration had also stressed combating organized crime. The Estrada administration has given an even higher priority to this effort, placing the Department of the Interior and Local Government directly under the president's supervision, creating an anticrime commission, and reorganizing the police force.

FOREIGN POLICY AND EXTERNAL SECURITY   In spite of initial fears that Estrada's lack of exposure and ability in foreign affairs and his inward-looking development strategy might undermine the active foreign policy launched under Ramos, the political transition did not alter Philippine foreign policy goals or enthusiasm for multilateral cooperation. An important indication of continuity in foreign policy was the reappointment of Domingo Siazon as foreign secretary.

Estrada defined his administration's foreign policy objectives as follows:

• Strengthening of bilateral security arrangements, particularly with the United States, Association of Southeast Asian Nations (ASEAN) countries, and other Asian nations;

- Pursuit of confidence building and security cooperation with the Philippines' multilateral security partners in the ASEAN Regional Forum (ARF) and in the United Nations;
- Cooperation with the international community in addressing the regionwide financial and economic crisis and in finding peaceful solutions to threats to international peace;
- Closer links with other nations in combating international crimes and in addressing issues of nuclear proliferation, transborder pollution, women and children, indigenous peoples, and human rights; and
- Global cooperation in promoting the rights and welfare of migrants and initiatives on other migration issues.

The final issue above has particular salience for the Philippines because of the large number of Filipino workers overseas, including in the Middle East.

The United States. Philippine-U.S. relations have reemerged as a public issue. During the Ramos presidency, domestic political considerations discouraged efforts to renew close ties with the United States. Even so, negotiations were held on military exercises and a Status of Forces Agreement (SOFA), on which agreement was concluded, although the Ramos government did not push for its ratification by the Senate. The Estrada administration, however, most likely out of a desire to improve Philippine defense capabilities, publicized the contents of the SOFA, renamed as the RP-U.S. Visiting Forces Agreement (VFA), and sought Senate ratification.

The VFA provides general guidelines for "treatment of the U.S. armed forces and defense personnel who will be temporarily visiting the Philippines to take part in the activities covered by the Mutual Defense Treaty." It is intended to facilitate the entry and exit of U.S. military personnel and to establish a procedure for handling criminal cases against members of the American forces.

The VFA aroused strong emotions, with the nationalist camp especially aggravated by Estrada's apparent reversal of his previous opposition (when a senator) to the American bases. To such criticism, Estrada's response focused on the idea that as a senator he had been most concerned with Philippine sovereignty, while as president he was responsible for Philippine security. Specifically, he stated "Until we develop a credible military deterrent, we must depend on the goodwill of our neighbors, on our treaty commitments with the United States, and on the skills of our diplomats in conveying to everyone that we want only peace, stability, and a shared sense of prosperity."

Government officials cited a variety of reasons for seeking closer defense ties with the United States, including enhanced military preparedness, interoperability with allied forces, easing the impact of the financial crisis on military procurement, and deterrence. Others argued that the Philippines, like any other Southeast Asian country wanting to benefit from the security presence of the United States in the Asia Pacific, had to make a contribution to maintaining order in the region.

The debate over the VFA gave the previously weakened nationalist and leftist movements renewed energy. Their arguments focused on the entry of nuclear weapons and the dumping of nuclear waste, the exploitation of women and children, the spread of AIDS, issues of immunity and jurisdiction over crimes committed by American forces, and the derogation of national sovereignty. They also warned that the stationing of forces would lead to the reestablishment of U.S. military bases in the Philippines.

As 1999 began, the government was still engaged in negotiations with the United States and the legislature was studying the various arguments surrounding the agreement. Although the Senate was divided over the VFA, the renewed problems with China in the Spratly Islands could lead to ratification. Meanwhile, in August 1998 American and Philippine forces held annual military exercises provided for under the Mutual Defense Treaty, with particular emphasis on search-and-rescue training and civilian-military operations.

China. Philippine-China relations were calm through most of the year. High-level consultations between Manila and Beijing and diplomatic assurances from China allayed concerns about Chinese intentions in the South China Sea. In addition, because the Philippine military lacked the capability to carry out close surveillance, it was unaware of some developments in the area.

This atmosphere changed abruptly in late October when the Philippine military discovered that China had been building concrete structures on the contested Panganiban (Mischief) Reef. The Philippine defense establishment interpreted this development as representing an escalation of the Chinese presence in the Spratlys, and Estrada accordingly instructed the armed forces to intensify surveillance around the Spratlys. The Department of Foreign Affairs, counseling caution in dealing with China, recommended reliance on diplomatic means to prevent a further expansion of the Chinese presence, the position

Estrada ultimately adopted. Indeed, the relevant factor in his decision was that the Philippines lacked the naval capability to enforce its claims on the Spratlys. Moreover, in a period of economic turmoil a cash-strapped government understandably does not want to choose between bread and weapons.

ASEAN. There has long been a consensus in ASEAN that members should refrain from interfering in each other's domestic affairs—a consensus that has been slowly eroding. During the 1998 ASEAN Ministerial Meeting in Manila, Thailand, supported by the Philippines, argued for the need for "flexible engagement." Indonesia and Malaysia opposed the concept, however, and it was put aside.

The question of intervention among ASEAN members arose once again following the ouster of Malaysian Deputy Prime Minister Anwar Ibrahim. Estrada, openly sympathetic toward Anwar, suggested that he might not attend the November Asia-Pacific Economic Cooperation (APEC) meeting in Kuala Lumpur, thus angering Malaysian Prime Minister Mahathir bin Mohamad. Estrada reconsidered, however, and in the end attended the Kuala Lumpur meeting. For this altercation, the domestic media criticized Estrada for erratic and impulsive foreign policy making.

Estrada's willingness to advocate such positions appealed to the proponents of greater openness and democracy in the region. It also underlined differences within ASEAN and the fact that ASEAN's younger leaders are more open to the idea of constructive intervention, a term initially proposed by Anwar himself. However, if the rift between Malaysia and the Philippines worsens, it could affect other aspects of their relations, such as the number of Filipino workers allowed in Malaysia (now an important source of revenue for the Philippines).

Finally, the Philippine government and public expressed deep concern over the chaotic political transition in Indonesia, with human rights advocates and ethnic Chinese Filipinos rallying against the persecution of ethnic Chinese Indonesians. While the Philippine government fears the possible repercussions of political instability in its huge neighbor, economic constraints render the Philippines ultimately incapable of doing much in this situation beyond providing moral support. In theory, ASEAN could play a more active role, but it too has been weakened by its member states' current domestic problems.

DEFENSE POLICY AND ISSUES

RESTRUCTURING After tedious negotiations with the Philippine Congress, the government in 1997 launched a major military restructuring program, the main elements of which were reorganization, streamlining of manpower, and development of reserves. Several offices and units were deactivated and new ones created at the general headquarters and service levels. In addition, some units and missions were absorbed by other units. As of June 1998, at least 33 units and offices had been restructured.

According to the International Institute for Strategic Studies, in 1998–1999 the AFP comprised 117,800 active-duty military personnel (up from 110,000 the previous year): 74,500 in the army (up from 70,000), 25,900 in the navy and Coast Guard (up from 24,000), and 17,400 in the air force (up from 16,000). The increase in army personnel partly reflects the inclusion of the MNLF.

SUPPORT SYSTEMS AND PROCUREMENT To support the restructuring program, the AFP also started improving its bases and support systems, human resources, and doctrines. Similarly, a program to modernize military equipment and technology was launched in April 1998 with two major procurements—a navy offshore patrol vessel and an air force multirole fighter. Other acquisitions being prepared or under review included 105 mm howitzer and APC M103 upgrades, an assault rifle, an air surveillance radar, and long-range patrol aircraft. Assuming office in the midst of the financial crisis, Estrada quickly put force modernization projects on hold. However, the escalation of tensions with China over Mischief Reef has prompted a reconsideration of this decision.

REGIONAL OUTREACH The financial crisis did not, however, prompt a holdup of Philippine regional networking efforts aimed at confidence building. In August 1998, the new Philippine defense secretary visited his ASEAN counterparts in Brunei, Singapore, and Thailand. Furthermore, the Department of National Defense concluded cooperative agreements with Indonesia for combined training and exercises, information exchange, and interoperability in operations and logistics. The department also continued to implement other international commitments such as the RP-Indonesia Border Agreements, in addition to taking part in defense-related activities with Australia, France, Malaysia, Singapore, South Korea, and the United Kingdom. However, a military exercise with Malaysia was canceled due to the situation involving Anwar.

CONTRIBUTIONS TO GLOBAL AND REGIONAL SECURITY

GLOBAL CONTRIBUTIONS   The Philippine government recognizes the importance of international organizations and forums to its security and sustainable development objectives. In its final year, the Ramos administration was particularly active in consolidating the country's place in the international community.

The Philippines supports the strengthening of the UN and the Reform Package presented by UN Secretary General Kofi Annan in 1997. Also in late 1997, the Philippine government signed the UN Convention on the Prohibition of the Use, Stockpiling, Production and Transfer of Anti-Personnel Mines and Their Destruction, although the Philippine Senate is still considering the ratification of the treaty. As well, the Senate confirmed the Philippines' commitment to the advancement of international humanitarian law by ratifying the Revised Protocol II (Prohibitions or Restrictions on the Use of Mines, Booby Traps and Other Devices) and Additional Protocol IV (Protocol on Laser Blinding Weapons) of the Unhumane Weapons Convention. Finally, in peacekeeping activities the Philippines maintained a contingent in Iraq, which was a contribution both to the UN and to the Middle East peace process.

REGIONAL CONTRIBUTIONS   Despite the economic crisis, the Philippines continues to support the strengthening of regional economic and political cooperation arrangements, reflecting the government's belief that they provide the best foundation for long-term regional stability.

The Philippines considers ASEAN to be a major pillar of its foreign policy. Accordingly, it has supported the ASEAN Free Trade Area and ASEAN Vision 2020, a joint statement by ASEAN leaders. The Philippines also favors the expeditious integration of new ASEAN members. Consistent with this position and to revitalize bilateral relations with new members, then President Ramos visited Laos and Myanmar in late 1997, the first ASEAN head of state to travel to the two countries after their admission.

In addition, the Philippines hosted the 1998 ASEAN Ministerial Meeting, which resulted in the signing of the second protocol of the Treaty of Amity and Cooperation, as well as a Joint Declaration for a Drug-Free ASEAN. Also, in July 1998 the Philippine government hosted the Fifth ASEAN Regional Forum. In March 1997, it had co-chaired with China the ARF Intersessional Support Group on Confidence Building Measures (CBMs) in Beijing, which reached a consensus on a number of CBMs to be undertaken by ARF countries. In this context, the Philippines proposed several additional nonmilitary CBMs for discussion.

Moreover, the Philippine government has undertaken numerous regional activities reflecting its concern over organized crime. In December 1997, Manila held the ASEAN Conference on Transnational Crime. Among the measures proposed at this conference was the establishment of an ASEAN Center for Transnational Crime, which will promote intelligence sharing, harmonization of policies, and coordination of operations. Toward the same end, the Philippines initiated several development cooperation projects with its ASEAN dialogue partners, such as a campaign against drug addiction among ASEAN youth.

Outside the ARF framework, the Asia Regional Ministerial Meeting on Transnational Crime in Manila in March 1998 adopted the Manila Declaration on the Prevention and Control of Transnational Crime, which expressed the region's concern over increasing organized crime and supported the strengthening of domestic institutions as well as regional and global cooperation to combat transnational crime. Following the ministerial meeting, the Philippine government and the Council for Security Cooperation in Asia Pacific (CSCAP) Philippines also cosponsored a track two CSCAP Working Group Meeting on Transnational Crime.

Finally, the Philippines has been actively involved in the Asia-Europe Meeting (ASEM) dialogue process. Along with South Korea, the EU Presidency, and the European Commission, it has been tasked to draw up a program to promote trade opportunities between Asia and Europe, which is to include the reduction of nontariff barriers. The Estrada administration pledged to continue these projects and also to work on the implementation of the ASEM Trade Facilitation Action Plan and the Investment Promotion Action Plan.

BILATERAL RELATIONS   Complementing its multilateral efforts, the Philippines also seeks closer bilateral ties, particularly with the other

ASEAN states. In 1998, bilateral meetings were held with Vietnam on several concerns and with Malaysia on the protection of the environment in the South China Sea. As well, agreements were signed with Laos and Myanmar on anti–drug trafficking, trade and development, agriculture and forestry, and culture and health. Finally, prior to Anwar's arrest frequent high-level contacts also took place between Malaysian and Philippine officials.

Bilateral relations with countries in Northeast Asia have also expanded, particularly economic ties with Hong Kong, Japan, and South Korea. In addition, exchanges with Canada, Australia, and Russia have produced a large number of new agreements on trade, investment, education, and crime prevention.

13 Russia

THE SECURITY ENVIRONMENT

DOMESTIC CRISIS   In 1998, Russia entered its first major crisis of the postcommunist era, effectively ending a phase that started in 1991. This is above all a comprehensive crisis of Russian reform, highlighting the issue of Russia's postimperial identity. Liberalism is in retreat in most spheres, muddling continues, and the bottom is not yet in sight.

Owing to a combination of domestic and external factors, including high budget deficits, declining oil prices, and economic fallout from the Asian crisis, Russia's finances collapsed in August 1998. While the stock market crashed, the ruble was first devalued and later allowed to float, losing two-thirds of its value against the U.S. dollar. The state has de facto defaulted on its domestic and foreign debt. With an international bailout unlikely, the prospects are for continued high inflation.

Russia's international standing has suffered enormously as a result, and its true geo-economic position has been revealed as relatively insignificant. Having inherited in 1991 roughly half of the former Soviet Union's economic might, it lost some 50 percent of this in the following seven years. At the exchange rate before the August 1998 devaluation, Russia's gross domestic product equaled only US$440 billion. Russia is the first major country since the end of World War II to face the prospect of a default on its external sovereign debt, now US$155 billion (including debts assumed from the former Soviet republics). Consequently, debt restructuring has taken center stage in Russia's relations with the West.

While the failed August putsch of 1991 marked the beginning of

149

President Boris Yeltsin's ascendancy, the 1998 August financial crisis signaled the end of his effective rule. In March 1998, Yeltsin dismissed his longtime Prime Minister Viktor Chernomyrdin and, after winning a battle of wills with the lower house of parliament (State Duma), replaced him with the virtually unknown Sergei Kiriyenko. Four months later, however, when Yeltsin dismissed Kiriyenko and attempted to reinstall Chernomyrdin, the political environment had drastically changed: The parliament confidently rejected Chernomyrdin, and Yeltsin, virtually isolated, had to back down. As a result, he nominated Foreign Minister Yevgeny Primakov as the head of government, yielding him virtually full authority over the day-to-day running of the country. In the last months of 1998, Yeltsin was seen as being in semiretirement, with Primakov increasingly performing as deputy, or acting, president.

Meanwhile, political pressure on Yeltsin did not stop. Impeachment procedures in the parliament have continued, with every episode of ill health leading to loud calls for his resignation. There was a growing likelihood that new presidential elections would be held sooner than the scheduled July 2000 date. Meanwhile, parliamentary elections are due in December 1999.

In the government reshuffles of 1998, several top officials responsible for foreign and security policy lost their jobs, including Security Council Secretary Andrei Kokoshin, Interior Minister Anatoly Kulikov, Federal Security Service Director Nikolay Kovalyov, and Federal Border Service Chief Andrei Nikolayev. The Defense Council was merged with the Security Council. Defense Minister Igor Sergeyev and Chief of the General Staff Anatoly Kvashnin, both appointed in 1997, continued in office. Primakov was succeeded as foreign minister by his former deputy, Igor Ivanov.

Surprisingly to many, Russia's internal security during the year was only marginally affected by social discontent directed at the government. Discontent manifested itself largely in nonviolent and orderly forms, such as temporary blockades of railways (the Trans-Siberian railroad and the Russian Far East region were severely hit by this kind of protest). At the same time, however, across Russia corruption and criminality reached unprecedented levels, most dramatically evidenced by the assassination in St. Petersburg in November of leading democratic parliamentarian Galina Starovoitova.

The crisis has further loosened the bonds tying the peripheral provinces to the federal center, with the specter of confederation frequently

invoked. Many regional leaders introduced policies widely at vari-
ance with the federal Constitution, from declaring a regional state of
emergency to planning a regional currency, and some have even developed what may be called proto-foreign policies. The election of former
General Alexander Lebed as governor of Krasnoyarsk sent a powerful and disturbing signal to Moscow, as some were ready to see him
as the leader of all Siberia in a struggle against Moscow's oppressive
domination. In the Northern Caucasus region, continuing internal
instability, disputes with Moscow, and widespread violence in Chech-
nya were mirrored on a smaller scale in other nearby republics. Responding to these trends, Primakov identified separatism as a major
threat to Russia's security.

While the Russian military was seriously affected by these trends,
few signs of organized military discontent were evident. The opposition Movement in Defense of the Army, the Defense Industry and
Military Science has virtually crumbled since the July assassination
of its controversial and highly active leader, General Lev Rokhlin.
Regionalization of the Russian Armed Forces is still a remote threat,
although Lebed's offer to feed strategic forces personnel in the Krasnoyarsk territory when centralized supplies were interrupted acted as
an effective warning signal that this threat cannot be completely excluded.

FOREIGN POLICY IMPLICATIONS   In foreign policy, Primakov's approach is similar to that of Russia's foreign minister after the Crimean
War debacle, Prince Gorchakov—concentrating effort on fundamental goals as the country goes through a period of external weakness
and painful domestic reform. Thus, Primakov focuses on keeping
Russia whole and on maintaining some influence in areas near its borders, while requesting debt restructuring from and avoiding confrontation with Washington and other Western countries. At the same
time, he preserves long-term objectives by insisting on Russia's continuing great-power status, advocating multipolarity in international
relations, and refusing to accept unilateral American world leadership.

The notion of Russia as one of the world's great powers is a far
cry from the current reality, which places it at best only among the
regional powers. The erstwhile empire suffers under a crushing debt
burden. In Europe, it faces further eastward expansion of Western institutions such as the North Atlantic Treaty Organization (NATO)
and the European Union. Following the anticipated admission to

NATO in early 1999 of the Czech Republic, Hungary, and Poland, the very sensitive issue of the Baltic States' membership in NATO will become more prominent. Another area of discord between Moscow and the West is the situation in Kosovo, where Russia has adamantly opposed the use of force by NATO without a UN Security Council resolution, which Russia can block.

Given these circumstances, the implementation of the 1997 Russia-NATO Founding Act of Mutual Relations, Cooperation and Security did not result in any significant improvement in relations. The Permanent Joint Council established by the act serves as a useful point of contact but not yet as a true interaction mechanism. Russia did take part in several Partnership for Peace exercises in 1998, including Sea Breeze in the Black Sea (which it had boycotted in 1997), but military-to-military contacts were overshadowed by political tensions. Mutual irritation over the Balkans is exacerbated by disagreement over how to deal with Iraq. Moscow refuses to endorse any military action against Baghdad, a stance which has earned it a reputation as Iraq's protector. Russian officials, however, prefer to view their position as oriented toward war prevention.

Russia's influence within the post-Soviet Commonwealth of Independent States (CIS) has further waned. Several newly independent states have formed associations that exclude Russia. One example is GUAM, which brings together Georgia, Ukraine, Azerbaijan, and Moldova. Of these, Ukraine, formerly the second largest Soviet republic after Russia, has tried to enhance its role in Moldova, the Caucasus, and Central Asia. In the Caucasus/Caspian region, Moscow's influence is being eroded by the combined efforts of the West, the Islamic world, and some of its nominal partners in the CIS. Armenia remains Russia's only real ally in the region. Relations with Georgia have become increasingly tense, and those with Azerbaijan have not improved. Having had to partially withdraw its border troops from Georgia, Moscow now relies on its peacekeepers in Abkhazia as the sole means of exerting some influence there.

In Central Asia, Russia reached agreement with Kazakhstan on the Caspian, resolving issues of compensation for base rights, including the Baikonur space and missile launch center. Russia also showed willingness to treat Uzbekistan, the region's most powerful state, as a more equal partner. This was undoubtedly facilitated by the two states' shared view of the Afghan Taliban movement as a potential source of danger. To oppose potentially aggressive Taliban behavior toward neighboring countries, Moscow in 1998 entered into a de facto alliance with Uzbekistan, with Tajikistan as a junior partner.

CIS-wide military cooperation remained modest and the 1992 Tashkent Collective Security Treaty largely dormant during the year. Joint air defense was the only area of practical cooperation, with exercises in Astrakhan on the lower Volga including units from Russia, Belarus, Kazakhstan, and Kyrgyzstan. Armenia expressed its desire to join future exercises. Moscow officials blame the lack of closer military cooperation with other CIS countries on Western, in particular American, efforts to isolate Russia strategically.

U.S. criticisms notwithstanding, Russia continued its nuclear energy cooperation with Iran, vowing to complete the construction of the Bushehr nuclear power station. Moscow condemned the Indian and Pakistani nuclear tests but refused to impose sanctions on the two countries. As a result, Russian arms and technology transfers to India were not affected.

RELATIONS WITH ASIA PACIFIC STATES   In 1998, despite its overwhelming domestic problems Russia significantly expanded its political contacts with Asia Pacific countries. In November, it was officially admitted to the Asia-Pacific Economic Cooperation (APEC) forum and participated in the APEC summit in Malaysia. Although less than 10 percent of its trade is with Asia Pacific countries, and despite the Asian economic crisis, Russia's strategic and economic interests in the region remain important. The future of resource-rich yet grossly underdeveloped and underpopulated Siberia and the Russian Far East is a growing, though still underappreciated, concern in Russia, given that Russia could benefit from exploitation of the area's vast energy resources. Finally, roughly 50 percent of Russia's total arms trade is with China and India (US$1,055 million and US$505 million, respectively, in 1996).

China continued to be the main focus of Russia's policy in the region. Numerous high-level contacts took place between the two countries, with President Jiang Zemin in November 1998 and Prime Minister Li Peng in February 1998 paying visits to Moscow, and the Russian premier, the foreign and defense ministers, and the secretary of the Security Council traveling to Beijing. The two governments pledged to maintain the same rate of high-level contacts in the future. Further, in 1998 a hot line between the two countries' leaders became operational.

Political engagement notwithstanding, Sino-Russian commercial contacts continued to stagnate, at approximately US$6 billion a year in total trade, which represented only 4.6 percent of Russia's exports and 1.9 percent of its imports. Arms and nuclear contracts accounted for a major portion of Russian exports. The Komsomolsk-on-the-Amur aircraft plant continued to supply components for China's new F-11 (an indigenous version of the Su-27), and negotiations were in progress for the sale to China of Su-30 aircraft, which Russia also sells to India. In addition, Russia offered China the option of buying the Su-33. In contrast, Russia's attempts to win a share of China's civil aviation market have been far less successful. Currently, Moscow pins its greatest hopes on energy projects that would entail supplying China—and potentially the whole of Northeast Asia—with Russian natural gas. The Russian company Gazprom wants to repeat in Asia its remarkable success in becoming a principal gas supplier to much of Europe. Still, these plans are far from implementation and funding is not assured.

While bilateral relations are officially described as excellent, some Russian observers believe that China will pursue a policy of restraint for the next five to seven years and then become more assertive. They see China as a major economic and military power, expanding its influence primarily toward the south and southeast. Russians were much impressed with the marked improvement in Sino-U.S. relations symbolized by President Bill Clinton's trip to China. Some commentators even characterized the visit as the opening of a new chapter in international relations, with Beijing emerging as Moscow's successor in the Big Two arrangement with Washington. Russians, however, do not wholly rule out a Sino-U.S. confrontation in the long term, and they clearly want to stay out of this.

Relations with Japan, revitalized in 1997 at Tokyo's initiative, were further consolidated at the informal summit at Kawana in April 1998. At that meeting, the Japanese side reportedly presented a plan to solve the Kuril Islands (Northern Territories) issue by drawing the borderline north of the disputed islands while allowing flexibility on the modalities of the actual handover of the territories. For their part, the Russians continued to emphasize joint economic exploitation of the area, without the transfer of sovereignty. Despite these differences, in addition to the resignation of Prime Minister Hashimoto Ryūtarō and the waning of Yeltsin's authority, work on the peace treaty between the two countries continued. Japan also disbursed

US$800 million of its promised US$1.5 billion in financial aid to Russia.

During the November visit of Prime Minister Obuchi Keizō, the first official visit to Moscow by a Japanese prime minister in 25 years, it was agreed to establish two joint subcommissions—one on the border issue and another on economic cooperation in the area of the Kuril Islands. Outright cession of territory remains anathema to most of the Russian political class, and Moscow has been trying quietly to recast the peace treaty as an accord on "peace and friendship" to avoid a definite solution to the territorial problem. Yuri Luzhkov, mayor of Moscow and a leading presidential contender, has decided to patronize the Kuril Islands issue in much the same way as he does the Crimean issue.

Economic exchanges between Russia and Japan remain fairly insignificant, accounting for 3.6 percent of Russia's exports and 1.4 percent of imports.

Russia's relations with South Korea have long been essentially stagnant. Although a spy scandal in mid-1998 strained diplomatic relations for two months, these have now normalized. Pointing to the lack of progress in the Four-Party Talks, Moscow continued to press for inclusion in these discussions. South Korea has not become a source of large-scale investment and advanced technology to Russia, as some Russians had hoped in the early 1990s. Former Soviet Union and Russian debts are now being repaid partially through arms sales, an arrangement that elicits some opposition from the United States. While Moscow's shipments of Ka-32 helicopters (around 25 delivered so far, with 30 more to follow) are not problematic as far as Washington is concerned, the S-300 air defense system is regarded as a competitor of the American Patriot.

With North Korea, Moscow has long lost any leverage. Russian officials expressed concern after both the North Korean missile launch on August 31 and the discovery of a small unauthorized shipment of secondhand helicopters to Pyongyang in October.

The Asian crisis has destroyed Russian hopes of expanding its arms sales, at least in the short term, to member countries of the Association of Southeast Asian Nations (ASEAN), in particular to Indonesia, which some Russian arms dealers had regarded as a potentially large customer. Be that as it may, Moscow has made a concerted effort to revive economic, political, and military links with Vietnam. Among other things, the Russians have proposed to build Vietnam's first oil refinery. In May, the president of Vietnam came to Russia, followed by visits to Hanoi by both Russia's defense minister and chief of the General Staff. Russia plans to sell Vietnam 24 Su-27s and several naval craft. Despite financial problems, the Russian navy believes it is important to maintain the Cam Ranh Bay supply facility, and accordingly negotiations are continuing to extend the lease beyond 2000.

Relations with India, Moscow's traditional friend in Asia, have remained cordial, as highlighted by Primakov's visit to New Delhi at the end of the year. Arms transfers continue to play a major role in the relationship, with much of India's weapons and equipment being of Soviet origin. Russia hopes to win big Indian contracts for weapons modernization.

Worth noting is the fact that, in contrast to its stance on NATO enlargement in Europe, Russia takes virtually no issue with the U.S. presence in Asia. For instance, there is no call for the dismantling of America's cold war–era treaties with Japan and South Korea. Sergeyev's criticism of U.S.-Japanese efforts in the field of missile defense are best viewed in the context of Russia's relations with China, where Sergeyev was visiting when he made the criticism, and as related to Moscow's long-standing aversion to the U.S. ballistic missile defense program. In the longer term, Russian defense analysts regard the U.S. presence both as a counterweight to potential Chinese regional domination and as a guarantee against Japan's rejection of its modest post–World War II strategic role.

DEFENSE POLICIES AND ISSUES

NEW CONCEPTS   In December 1997, the long-awaited National Security Concept was formally approved in Russia. The document enunciating this concept concludes that the main threats to the nation now and in the foreseeable future lie in the domestic political, economic, social, and cultural spheres, and deems the risk of a large-scale war to be minimal. The general security environment in reality, however, is anything but risk-free. Regional and local conflicts of medium and low intensity are believed to present the main military threat, principally along Russia's southern periphery. Military conflict with a major power is not ruled out but appears very remote. Still, Russian security policy and force missions remain vaguely defined.

In the summer of 1998, however, a full-scale military concept was announced, stipulating that the chief mission of the Ministry of Defense (MOD) and its subordinate armed forces is national defense and protection of the country's borders. According to this more detailed formulation, the 237,000-strong Interior Troops of the Ministry of the Interior (MOI) are to deal with domestic unrest, the Federal Border Service (FBS, also numbering some 200,000) is responsible for border control, and the Federal Security Service is to fight terrorism, smuggling, espionage, and political extremism. The General Staff of the Armed Forces has acquired a coordinating function, but its wider ambition of assuming de facto control over all military forces has been expressly denied for fear of vesting too much power in one agency. The Duma, meanwhile, has been preparing a bill on comprehensive civilian control over the country's military forces.

Over the coming decade, many of the currently militarized agencies, such as the FBS and the Emergency Ministry (ex-Civil Defense), are to be civilianized. By 2005, the MOI Interior Troops are to constitute the Federal Guard.

The territorial organization of Russia's military forces will be further trimmed. In place of eight military districts (MDs), six strategic commands are to be established: Northwestern (Northern MD); Western (Moscow MD); Southwestern (North Caucasus MD); Central Asian (Volga and Urals MD, to be merged); Siberian (Siberian and Trans-Baikal MD, to be merged); and Far Eastern (Far East MD, which will also include the Republic of Sakha, formerly part of the Trans-Baikal MD). These strategic command headquarters will be responsible for all troops, that is, MOD, MOI, FBS, and others, in their respective territories.

Following the 1997 integration of the Military Space Forces and the Anti-Missile Defense into an expanded, 100,000-strong Strategic Rocket Force (SRF), the Air Force and the Air Defense were merged under a new Air Force (210,000 officers and men). Plans are to continue this streamlining initiative and by 2001 to have a classic three-service structure, thereby abolishing the SRF. However, a proposal supported by the MOD, the government, and some Duma members to centralize all nuclear assets under a Joint Command of the Strategic Nuclear Forces has met with opposition from the Air Force and the Navy as well as come under severe criticism from political figures such as Lebed.

With the combat-readiness of the Russian military at an all-time low, the formation of a few ready units has become a priority for the high command. An avowed goal is to maintain ten divisions at 80 percent strength, including three motorized rifle divisions, three airborne divisions, one peacekeeping division, and four motorized rifle brigades, with understrength units to be phased out. In general, further radical cuts in armed forces personnel will be necessary to increase readiness. By early 1999, the authorized strength of the MOD forces was to be reduced to 1.2 million personnel, with no immediate plans for further cuts. On paper, 400,000 soldiers and sailors were to be discharged, but in reality the measure affected only 150,000 to 200,000, including 80,000 commissioned officers and 500 generals. The MOD has the dual problem of releasing unneeded but unwilling to leave officers and of keeping those who are needed but currently unwilling to renew their contracts.

DEFENSE BUDGET Meeting defense requirements with the available resources remains impossible for Moscow. At best, momentary expediency rather than organized restructuring drives resource allocation. For example, in 1998 the MOD received only roughly 30 percent of the funds allocated to it under the federal budget.

As in the past, actual defense expenditure in Russia remains conjectural. The publication *Military Balance 1998/99*, from the International Institute for Strategic Studies, puts the total expenditure at US$64 billion for 1997, which would make Russia the world's second largest spender. Russian sources, by contrast, use a figure of US$10 billion, at the predevaluation exchange rate. What is certain, however, is that spending is being reduced from year to year and now constitutes perhaps 3 percent of the nation's gross domestic product. From 1992 through 1997, the total reduction in spending amounted to 60 percent, with a further 40 percent cut in 1998 alone. As a result, Russia now spends only 27 percent of the 1992 level on operation and maintenance of the armed forces, 10 percent of the 1992 level on research and development, and a mere 7 percent on procurement. In an attempt to cut expenses, the joint use of resources is being encouraged, and the standardization of weaponry and equipment has again been proposed though not implemented. Although modernization of hardware remains the order of the day, with rearmament not expected to begin before 2005, there still remains the problem of too many parallel armies in existence in Russia, such as the 237,000 MOI troops and the 420,000-strong MOD ground forces.

The professional and moral degradation of the Russian military has accelerated and is a serious concern. Bearing witness to this deplorable state of affairs is an unprecedented series of violent fatal incidents in all the armed services, including the nuclear forces, that occurred in 1998.

NUCLEAR POLICY AND FORCE DEVELOPMENT Russian politicians and military officials routinely stress the deterrence role of nuclear weapons. This can be interpreted as an attempt at self-reassurance during the current period of extreme conventional weakness. In any case, most actual and potential threats to Russia can hardly be managed by nuclear deterrence.

Officially described as 90 percent combat-ready, Russia's nuclear forces (6,250 strategic nuclear warheads at mid-1998) are aging. Deputy Prime Minister Yuri Maslyukov spoke during the year of the need to produce 35–45 ballistic missiles annually to offset "retirement losses." Actual production, however, remains in single digits. Moreover, in October 1998 the Russian nuclear program suffered a setback when a Topol-M missile malfunctioned during a test launch. Clearly, then, Russia may well lose much of its nuclear potential in the medium to long term; even now, it could be decisively overwhelmed by the United States, with China becoming Russia's nuclear equal.

Within the Russian nuclear triad, the role of sea-based systems is growing and will eventually match that of land-based systems. At the same time, the role of the airborne component, never especially prominent, is dwindling.

The only real alternative to Russian unilateral nuclear disarmament is ever-deeper strategic arms reductions. There is no longer any question that Russia will live up to the 1991 Strategic Arms Reduction Treaty 1 (START-1) levels. Even the much lower START-2 ceilings can be maintained for ten years at most, after which Russia will be down to a few hundred nuclear warheads. Ironically, the 1993 START-2 treaty, presented to the Duma for ratification in 1995, remains unratified, thereby blocking the way to agreement on deeper mutual reductions. As of the fall of 1998, as many as two-thirds of the Duma members opposed ratification. To breach this legislative impasse, a compromise is conceivable, requiring the government to assure a certain level of spending on Russia's nuclear forces and spelling out contingencies under which Russia could withdraw from the treaty.

CONVENTIONAL FORCES DEVELOPMENT   The chief mission of Russian conventional forces is to defeat an enemy in a local conflict. Currently, however, such forces are too poorly trained, ill-equipped, and weakly commanded to convincingly accomplish this task. Despite several widely publicized naval, air, and air defense exercises, training levels remain low. A case in point, the best Russian combat aircraft pilots fly just 80 to 90 hours a year. Furthermore, conventional force armaments are aging fast: It is believed that by 2000 only 10 percent of Russian arsenals will be composed of modern weapons, and by 2005 about 5 percent. In particular, strategically mobile assets are pathetically inadequate, considering the vastness of the country.

Although Russian defense scientists acknowledge the need to develop new high-technology defense systems, in practice Russia's defense industry has been contracting chaotically. The government has said that of the 1,700 military industrial enterprises, only around 700 may get state defense orders in the future. Sociopolitical concerns, however, are likely to prevent the government from taking such radical action. The planned privatization of military industrial enterprises never took off. At the same time, however, arms exports, which once sustained important parts of the defense industry, have been dropping—to US$2.5 billion in 1997, Russia's worst performance since 1993.

CONTRIBUTIONS TO GLOBAL AND REGIONAL SECURITY

GLOBAL ARMS CONTROL   As mentioned previously, Russia has yet to ratify the START-2 treaty; similarly, the Comprehensive Test Ban Treaty remains tabled. The ratification of the former, when it comes, would open the way to a START-3 treaty and thereby potentially lead to even deeper reductions of U.S. and Russian strategic nuclear weapons.

EUROPE AND FORMER SOVIET TERRITORY   In addition to the continued participation of a 1,400-man Russian brigade in the NATO Stabilization Force in Bosnia-Herzegovina, Russia pledged to take part in the 2,000-man verification force in Kosovo of the Organization for Security and Cooperation in Europe (OSCE). As well, Moscow actively pursued a political settlement of the Kosovo problem, both within the Contact Group and in bilateral contacts with Serbia.

Having reduced the size of its peacekeeping element in Moldova to about 500 men, Russia, along with the OSCE and Ukraine, continued diplomatic efforts to facilitate a political solution to the conflict between Chisinau and Tiraspol. Despite such efforts, in 1998 a solution appeared just as remote as in previous years.

Russia's peacekeeping role in Abkhazia remained as controversial as ever, with both Tbilisi and Sukhumi accusing Moscow of aiding the other side, especially during the flare-up of fighting in the area in May 1998. Toward the end of 1998, the risk of war between Georgia and the breakaway Republic of Abkhazia had palpably increased, with Russian peacekeepers frequently targeted in terrorist attacks.

Following the 1997 Moscow accord ending the five-year-old civil war in Tajikistan, a modicum of progress was achieved toward integrating the former Tajik opposition into Tajikistan's existing political and military structures. However, fragmentation of the country continued, with new warlords appearing in various areas. The overall security situation remained extremely precarious, as highlighted by the murder of members of a UN observer mission there.

THE MIDDLE EAST   Despite its nominal cosponsor role, Moscow kept a very low profile in efforts to break the deadlock in Israeli-Palestinian relations; it was conspicuously absent from the October Wye talks. In Iraq's ongoing conflict with the United Nations, Russia consistently championed political solutions in an effort to prevent the use of military force against Iraq.

EAST ASIA   Pursuant to its 1997 accord with China, Russia in 1998 implemented a set of measures to reduce its military presence in the Chinese border area. Accordingly, approximately 300 units there were phased out. In addition, the Russian military engaged in joint peace-keeping exercises with U.S. forces near Vladivostok in August 1998 and a search-and-rescue exercise with the Japanese navy in the Sea of Japan. Finally, Moscow continued to expand its contacts with ASEAN countries, taking part in the ASEAN Regional Forum meeting in Manila and holding talks at the deputy foreign minister level in Moscow in mid-1998.

14 Singapore

The Security Environment

The past year and a half has been a period of "domestic stability, external turbulence" for Singapore, and the next few years promise to be a further and fundamental test of Singapore's viability under such conditions.

Trends in the strategic environment at the beginning of 1999 were probably the least favorable to the city-state since it attained independence on separation from Malaysia in 1965. Unlike some Southeast Asian countries, Singapore does not face domestic political or security threats; indeed, the Hong Kong–based Political and Economic Risk Consultancy in its 1998 report described Singapore as the "most stable country in Asia." The less sanguine security outlook stems rather from changes in the external environment, underscoring the small city-state's essential vulnerability.

THE EXTERNAL ENVIRONMENT: DETERIORATION   Three principal developments have contributed to the more uncertain security outlook: the Asian economic crisis, which has led to political crises in Indonesia and Malaysia; a parallel deterioration in Singapore's relations with both of these neighboring states; and the erosion of cohesion within the Association of Southeast Asian Nations (ASEAN).

Economic Crisis and Political Instability. The economic crisis has made a number of Asian countries not only significantly poorer but also politically less stable. A vicious cycle of economic, social, and political crises is most evident in Indonesia, where the collapse of the Suharto regime has led to a state of semianarchy. This is troubling to

162

Singapore not only because Indonesia is an important economic partner but also out of concern that an unstable Indonesia might not continue the benign and responsible foreign policy of the Suharto government. (This three-decade-old policy contrasted sharply with that of the preceding Sukarno regime, which in the early years of the 1960s conducted an armed confrontation with Malaysia, of which Singapore was then a component state.)

In Malaysia, the economic crisis engendered a tense political rivalry and fundamental disagreement between Prime Minister Mahathir bin Mohamad and then Deputy Prime Minister Anwar Ibrahim over which macroeconomic policies the country should adopt. This in turn precipitated a serious falling-out between Mahathir and Anwar, with Anwar's detention in September 1998 and his subsequent trial leading to political violence, which is quite unusual in Malaysia. Instability in Malaysia, one of Singapore's most important economic partners, is also clearly not in Singapore's interest.

Uncertain Relations to the South and North. Paralleling the domestic instability of its two close neighbors, Singapore's bilateral relations with both countries became markedly more problematic in 1998. Despite Singapore's offer early on in the crisis of a standby credit line of US$5 billion to Indonesia and its willingness to provide humanitarian food aid, new Indonesian President B. J. Habibie was only scornful of the city-state. Habibie was quoted as stating that Singapore is only "a little red dot" in Southeast Asia and that he considered Germany, Japan, and the United States to be friendlier countries than Singapore. It is possible that these comments were precipitated by Singaporean Senior Minister Lee Kuan Yew's earlier suggestion that the international business community might question the suitability of then Vice President Habibie to ascend to the presidency.

On top of this, Singapore's relations with Malaysia during the year became even more difficult than those with Indonesia. Kuala Lumpur's displeasure with the city-state went beyond rhetoric as it adopted a series of actions that threatened to unravel the two countries' intimate relationship. In September 1998, Malaysia unilaterally withdrew its permission for the Republic of Singapore Air Force (RSAF) to use Malaysian airspace, traditionally available under agreements providing for six months notification of cancellation. The reason given for Malaysia's decision was the RSAF's frequent violations of the terms of the agreement, an allegation that Singapore emphatically denied.

Kuala Lumpur also refused to participate in the 1998 annual

exercises of the 27-year-old Five Power Defense Arrangements (FPDA) comprising Australia, Malaysia, New Zealand, Singapore, and the United Kingdom, ostensibly because of financial pressures caused by the economic crisis. However, many analysts believe that the actual reason for Malaysia's nonparticipation was the strained relations between Kuala Lumpur and Singapore.

In the economic field, Kuala Lumpur forced the closure of CLOB (Central Limit Order Book), a facility where Malaysian shares were traded in Singapore. Malaysia's rationale for the closure was that CLOB stymied the growth of the domestic Malaysian stock exchange. About 90 percent of the 197,000 CLOB account holders were Singaporeans, and the impending closure led to panicked selling by and severe losses for many of them. As part of its response to the economic crisis, Kuala Lumpur also introduced capital controls on the ringgit, the Malaysian currency. Although not necessarily targeted at Singapore, this move followed earlier criticisms from Malaysia that Singapore was being "unfriendly" and that very high interest rates offered by Singaporean banks for ringgit deposits had encouraged Malaysian capital to leave the country and thus hurt the Malaysian economy.

The Malaysian government also refused to relocate its customs, immigration, and quarantine (CIQ) facilities to Singapore's new Woodlands border checkpoint. (By a quirk of history, the Malaysian CIQ facilities have been located near the heart of Singapore rather than at the border with Johore state.) Finally, Malaysia displayed reluctance to commit to extending into the next century agreements to supply Singapore with water.

In addition, popular hostility in Malaysia toward Singapore was demonstrated when crowds in Kuala Lumpur booed the Singaporean contingent at the opening ceremony of the 16th Commonwealth Games (ironically, in this case, known as the "friendly games"). Singapore's was the only team booed at the ceremony.

Underpinning these issues between Kuala Lumpur and Singapore are the burden of history—Singapore's uncomfortable merger with and later dramatic separation from Malaysia—and fundamentally differing conceptions of an ideal polity (Malaysia's Malay dominance versus Singapore's multiethnic equality). The old historical wounds were reopened when Lee published his memoirs, which included a discussion of Singapore's stormy period as part of Malaysia. Although Lee's memoirs have no official status as history in Singapore, they deeply offended the Malaysian leadership because in them Lee blamed certain top Malaysian politicians for the 1964 ethnic riots in Singapore and the subsequent expulsion of Singapore from Malaysia.

In November 1998, the prime ministers of Singapore and Malaysia met in an attempt to improve relations. Among the issues discussed were Singapore's financial assistance and loans to Malaysia, permission for the RSAF to use Malaysian airspace for emergency rescue operations, and water supply to Singapore. Malaysian officials stated after the meeting that ties with Singapore had been improved, specifying that they had requested assistance from Singapore in raising billion-dollar loans and suggesting that the water issue could be resolved favorably for Singapore. Moreover, Malaysia reaffirmed its intention to participate in the FPDA exercises in 1999. However, barely a month after the meeting Mahathir announced that Malaysia no longer needed a US$4 billion loan from Singapore because a Japanese loan to Malaysia would suffice. The real reason for Mahathir's turnabout was not clear, although there was speculation that Kuala Lumpur was not truly comfortable with a "money-for-water" deal between the two neighbors. Another possible explanation is that, due to basic Malaysian suspicions of Singaporean intentions, some Malaysian leaders were reluctant to risk financial dependence on Singapore.

While Singapore would welcome any thawing of the frosty relations with its northern neighbor, many Singaporeans feel that perhaps the apparent softening recently in Malaysian attitudes toward Singapore only reflects momentary expedience on Malaysia's part. It came at a time of sharp international criticism of Mahathir's treatment of Anwar in political detention, and when Malaysia was seeking financial assistance from Singapore. Although the top leaderships of both countries have sought to normalize relations, inevitably the bad feelings will not dissipate overnight. The current heavy atmosphere obviously is not conducive to ASEAN cohesion.

Erosion of ASEAN Solidarity. A strong ASEAN is good for a small state such as Singapore because by acting collectively small states can enhance their individual clout in international affairs. In addition, a cohesive ASEAN helps to buffer bilateral tensions between member states and thus contributes to regional order. Unfortunately, the domestic political struggle between Mahathir and Anwar has spilled over to Malaysia's bilateral relations with both Indonesia and the Philippines owing to Anwar's strong personal relationships with presidents Habibie and Joseph Estrada. Both presidents publicly expressed concern about Anwar's treatment as a political detainee, which was construed by Malaysia's top leadership as interference in their country's domestic politics.

Indeed, the general question of whether or not member countries should be able to comment on each other's domestic politics—termed "flexible engagement"—has become an issue within ASEAN. Thailand and the Philippines support the flexible engagement concept, while other ASEAN countries including Singapore believe that this practice could undermine ASEAN solidarity.

MAJOR POWER RELATIONS   While Singapore's relations with its immediate neighbors are marked by uncertainties, its relations with the United States, Japan, and China are excellent and thus remain bright spots in its security outlook. The government of Singapore believes that a stable U.S.-Japan-China triangular relationship is important for regional security, and has actively sought to strengthen its bilateral relations with all three.

Prime Minister Goh Chok Tong met with U.S. President Bill Clinton in Washington in September 1998 and subsequently described the bilateral relationship as entering into "summer," in contrast with his earlier description of Singaporean-Malaysian relations as "wintry." To facilitate a continued U.S. military presence in Southeast Asia with the goal of underpinning regional stability, in November Singaporean Deputy Prime Minister and Minister for Defense Tony Tan and U.S. Secretary of Defense William Cohen signed an Addendum to the 1990 bilateral Memorandum of Understanding, under which the city-state will provide berthing facilities for U.S. navy ships, including aircraft carriers, from the time the first phase of its new Changi Naval Base is completed in the year 2000.

In May 1998, then Japanese Foreign Minister Obuchi Keizō gave a speech in Singapore on Japan's relations with the region toward the new millennium. In that speech, Obuchi presented details of Japan's US$42 billion assistance package for the Asian economies most affected by the financial crisis. In the same month, Singapore gave permission for Japanese military transport planes to be positioned in the city-state in case of the need to evacuate Japanese nationals endangered by rioting in Jakarta. Among other exchanges of visits by other officials, in December Tan met in Japan with officials from the Defense Agency. He also visited the Maritime Self-Defense Force base at Yokosuka and the Air Self-Defense Force Control Operation Command

Center at Fuchu. These exchanges underscored progress in defense ties between Singapore and Japan.

Singapore's relations with China continue to be underpinned by strong economic and cultural ties. In October, Tan visited China at the invitation of the vice chairman of China's Central Military Commission, General Chi Haotian, who is also state councilor and defense minister. The following month, Chi visited Singapore and held extensive discussions with Tan on international and regional developments as well as bilateral matters. Chi also delivered a major public speech in Singapore, the first such address in Southeast Asia in recent years by a top Chinese defense official.

ADDRESSING REGIONAL UNCERTAINTIES   In addition to active diplomacy, deep financial reserves and national cohesion—plus a strong Singapore Armed Forces (SAF)—are complementary approaches used by the Singaporean government to ensure the country's viability.

Singapore has estimated national reserves of at least S$120 billion (US$72.7 billion at US$1 = S$1.65), which can be used if necessary to stimulate the economy and to minimize unemployment during periods of economic downturn or turbulence. Singapore also has the financial capacity to build expensive desalination plants to reduce its dependence on imports of water, a strategic necessity; construction will begin on a billion-dollar pilot desalination plant by the year 2000, and three plants are slated to be in operation by 2011.

The Singaporean government has called on its citizens to remain calm and resilient in the face of external economic and political pressures. Responding to the very low (or possibly negative) economic growth in 1998, it has also asked Singaporeans to make sacrifices individually to surmount the crisis collectively, specifically in the form of 15 percent wage cuts across the board effective from January 1999 and lasting for at least two years. The cuts include a 10 percent reduction in employers' contributions to the Central Provident Fund, Singapore's national pension system. Wage cuts are intended to help restore Singapore's international competitiveness, which has been eroded by high wages.

To strengthen national cohesion, the government has sponsored national history exhibitions targeted especially at the younger generation. By portraying Singapore's acute vulnerability and struggle for success, such exhibitions teach the young not to take economic progress and national unity for granted.

Goh has urged Singaporeans to learn from the bout of bilateral bickering in 1998. His basic argument: "Be aware that things get [sic] terribly wrong suddenly. Don't assume economic growth will continue forever, [that] strong ties will be a permanent feature. So be prepared for sudden turns of events." The government hopes that the current external problems will propel Singaporeans to rally around the flag and that young people doing national service under Singapore's conscription system will take their training even more seriously.

DEFENSE POLICIES AND ISSUES

DEFENSE SPENDING   With its strong financial reserves, Singapore has not been forced to cut back on defense spending. In fiscal year 1998, the defense budget will amount to 4.6 percent of gross domestic product, up from 4.4 percent in fiscal 1997 but still well below the 6 percent of GDP that the government has said it is prepared to commit. Defense spending in fiscal 1998 is projected at S$7.26 billion (US$4.4 billion), or 26.69 percent of the total budget. Of this, operating expenditure (salaries, maintenance, and equipment) is slated to be S$6.49 billion (US$3.9 billion), and development expenditure (development of new camps and renovation of old camps) is set at S$775 million (US$470 million). The philosophy behind sustained defense spending is that long-term, steady investment rather than variable spending based on current economic growth will ensure the SAF's constant readiness in the event of unpredictable developments in the region.

A STRONG AND CREDIBLE SAF   Unlike some armed forces in the region, the SAF performs no domestic policing or administrative functions and can therefore focus single-mindedly on its mission of external defense. The SAF's main constraints are a lack of land and airspace for training, as well as a small manpower base (a standing force of only 50,000 soldiers, including both regulars and full-time conscripts, in addition to 250,000 reserves, or Operationally Ready National Servicemen). To compensate for these constraints, the SAF seeks training facilities in other friendly countries, uses high technology in training, focuses on advanced weapons systems, and is developing its own defense industry.

In October 1998, Tan officially opened the new S$60 million (US$36 million) Defense Science Organization (DSO) National Laboratories in Marina Hill, near the Science Park. The DSO National Laboratories are expected to play a pivotal role in maintaining the SAF's strategic edge through research and development on weapons systems and other advanced capabilities. According to press reports, in addition to studying and developing electronic warfare systems and chemical weapons, the DSO modifies purchased systems.

The SAF also makes extensive use of computer simulation in its air traffic control, air force, armored units, and navy training programs to compensate for its limited training space. For this purpose, the new Simulation System for Land Battles (SIMLAB) was commissioned in July 1998 at the SAF War Games Center.

In 1998, the defense chiefs of Indonesia and Singapore officially opened joint air force facilities in Pekan Baru, Sumatra. Also in 1998, the RSAF obtained an arrangement to train at Cazaux Air Base in France, where there will be 200 RSAF personnel to fly or service 20 A4-SU Super Skyhawks. In addition, a new F-16 detachment is in New Mexico for training. Finally, an agreement with South Africa provides for SAF military facilities in that country.

To modernize its forces, the SAF has embarked on a number of weapons acquisitions and upgrading programs. By October 1998, ten of a total purchase of 18 F-16 C/D Fighting Falcons arrived in Singapore, with the rest to be delivered shortly at regular intervals. These planes are advanced multirole fighters that are fully operable under all weather conditions, day or night. The defense minister has also announced that the RSAF plans to buy a new-generation fighter aircraft over the next five to six years, with the French Rafale, the European Union's Eurofighter, the Russian SU-30, and the next generation of the American F-15 under consideration. In addition, the RSAF is considering acquiring attack helicopters: Candidates include the South African Rooivalk, the French Tiger fighter helicopter, and the U.S.-made Apache. Also, the RSAF has adopted a new FPS 117 radar system that will enhance detection capability. It is also closely monitoring pilotless aircraft technology.

The Republic of Singapore Navy (RSN) has continued its upgrading program. In April 1998, Singapore and Sweden signed an agreement covering the provision of Swedish facilities and personnel to support RSN submarine training. In August, two new patrol vessels, the *RSS Freedom* and the *RSS Independence,* were commissioned, the first major warships designed and built in Singapore. In addition, the first two locally built Landing Ships have been launched and two more are to be completed by 2001.

The army in 1998 unveiled a Light Strike Vehicle to be added to the arsenals of its guard and infantry units. The Australian-made, dune-buggy-like vehicle is light enough to be helicopter-portable, can travel at 110 km/hr, and is mountable with an antitank missile system, 40 mm auto grenade launchers, or a general purpose machine gun. The army has also unveiled the Bionix, an armored personnel carrier designed and built in Singapore.

The combination of indigenous high-tech development, access to external technology, and extensive training arrangements abroad ensures the SAF's place at the cutting edge of defense technology in the region. Further, cooperation with multiple foreign partners allows Singapore to avoid dependence on only a few countries for military technology and training grounds.

CONTRIBUTIONS TO REGIONAL AND GLOBAL SECURITY

Singapore's strong support of the United Nations and the international rule of law reflects the belief that these institutions benefit the community of nations, especially small states. Taking part in UN peace-keeping operations is one means by which Singapore supports the United Nations; Singapore is currently participating in the UN Observer Mission in Kuwait. Other contributions include active participation in the FPDA, in addition to the provision of berthing facilities to the U.S. navy to underpin the strategic balance in the Asia Pacific region.

Singapore also strongly supports multilateral regional processes such as the ASEAN Regional Forum (ARF) to enhance confidence building and transparency. In April 1998, Singapore's Institute of Defense and Strategic Studies hosted an international conference entitled "The Future of the ARF." Singapore's national committee of the Council for Security Cooperation in Asia Pacific participates actively in track two activities, while the Singapore Institute of International Affairs, a nongovernmental organization, takes part in other bilateral and multilateral activities, including ASEAN-ISIS (Institutes for Strategic and International Studies) events.

15 Thailand

THE ECONOMIC CRISIS   The Chuan Leekpai government took office in November 1997 amid high expectations of its ability to solve Thailand's most serious economic crisis in decades. By mid-1998, however, the government's popularity was suffering as the crisis steadily worsened and the unemployment rate rapidly increased. In addition, the International Monetary Fund (IMF) bailout had become by then a divisive issue in Thai society, with the IMF and the surge of foreign businessmen into the Thai economy seen by some as the end of the Thai nation.

Some leading Thai businessmen were particularly concerned about the dominant role of foreigners in the financial sector. However, the fiercest opposition to the IMF and to the current government came from social activists, university academics, and leaders of farmers' groups. These groups believe that the crisis originated in the Western-derived strategy of economic development, which had largely benefited a small group of people at the expense of the rural masses. Consistent with this interpretation, some argued for a policy of economic self-sufficiency focusing on building up the agricultural sector to foster the people's independence.

This debate has not (yet) seriously threatened the government. On the contrary, the democratic change of government at the start of the economic crisis demonstrated the strengthening of the "institutionalization of democracy" that has been taking place over the past decade. Be that as it may, the stability of the Chuan government still could be jeopardized by the wave of corruption cases that caused two ministers to resign in 1998.

INTERNAL SECURITY   The three main security concerns in 1998 were the impact of the economic crisis, drug problems, and terrorism in the south.

Economic Insecurity. The number of Thais now living below the official poverty line is estimated at 7 to 8 million. Given that Thailand has only a minimal social welfare system, it is remarkable that the country has avoided widespread social turmoil. This perhaps is due to the fact that Thais still maintain relatively strong traditional family networks.

Nevertheless, the impact of the economic difficulties has been grave. For the first time in many years, unemployment among white-collar workers is high. This aspect of the crisis alone has left a deep psychological impact on many of those who had once been considered the new upwardly mobile urban middle class. As for unskilled workers, the government has encouraged those who have suffered from the higher cost of living and lowered incomes to return to farming. However, many such unskilled workers gave up their land to come to the city during the economic boom and therefore have no choice now but to rely on work in the industrial sector.

Drugs. Thailand has continued to be a major transit route for drugs from the Golden Triangle region of Myanmar, Laos, and Thailand, which is the source of more than half of the world's opium and heroin. In recent years, Thailand has also become a consumer country. Surveys indicate that during the economic crisis drug addiction has increased about 30 percent. Moreover, the economic slump has driven many drug users to become dealers, as well.

In June 1998, at the special United Nations General Assembly session on drugs Thailand and five of its neighbors—Cambodia, China, Laos, Myanmar, and Vietnam—endorsed action plans addressing precursor chemicals, amphetamine-type stimulants, judicial cooperation, money laundering, elimination of illicit crops and alternative development, and demand reduction. These six countries also announced their intention to create, by 2008, a zone free of illicit drug production, trafficking, and use.

South Thailand Insurgency. Early in 1998, several leaders of separatist movements in South Thailand were arrested. An important factor in these arrests was the cooperation of Malaysia, where members of the movements had taken shelter or received training, and where some had dual citizenship. The prime minister of Thailand acknowledged indebtedness to Malaysia for helping to tackle the problem. The Thai government also granted amnesty to those members of any movement who gave up armed resistance, with the result that some 50 turned themselves in.

However, terrorism in the south continued to pose a serious security problem—46 armed terrorist attacks took place in the five border provinces during the first quarter of 1998 alone. Underlying unresolved issues include demands for fair treatment by the Muslim community.

SOUTHEAST ASIA   *Myanmar.* Relations with Myanmar remain of great concern for the Thai government. Incidents along the border have taken place regularly since early 1997, when Myanmar government forces decimated the rebel movements located in the area. Subsequent attempts by Yangon to wipe out the remaining Karen rebels have occasionally spilled over into Thai territory. In addition, because a number of refugee camps along the border shelter anti-Yangon Karens they have become assault targets by pro-Yangon Karen forces (15 major incidents occurred during the first eight months of 1998). After the Myanmar government denied responsibility for such incidents, the Thai army in March 1998 declared that it would use military means to counter the incursions. The Thai foreign minister also suggested that the intrusions be discussed at the annual Association of Southeast Asian Nations (ASEAN) Ministerial Meeting.

Other outstanding issues between Thailand and Myanmar included a territorial dispute, which continued to spark armed confrontations. In late 1997, the two countries agreed to demarcate the entire 2,401-kilometer border shared between them, but only 58 kilometers have been demarcated to date and no major progress was made in 1998.

In addition, as of early 1998 Thailand was sheltering some 100,000 displaced persons from Myanmar. After criticism by Western governments over a series of cross-border attacks on Thai refugee camps, the Thai government agreed to assistance from the United Nations High Commission for Refugees. Moreover, following the rapid increase in local unemployment the presence of nearly a million illegal workers from Myanmar became a major concern for the Thai government. Regulations issued in January 1998 aimed at sending back at least 300,000 of these illegal workers within six months and the rest by

1999. However, this effort received minimal cooperation from the Yangon government.

Laos. The Hmong minorities who use Thai territory as a base for anti-Vientiane activities continued to be a source of friction between the Lao and Thai governments. Thai authorities maintain that it is difficult to track down the 200 or so Hmong rebels, many of whom mingle with over 20,000 refugees at a camp in Saraburi Province.

Of the 1,810-kilometer border shared between Thailand and Laos, 261 kilometers have been demarcated to date. Demarcation problems have occurred mostly on the Mekong River, where the task is complicated by changing water courses and a territorial dispute over an island in the middle of the river. However, Thai authorities are optimistic that demarcation can be completed by 2003, in line with an agreement between Thailand and Laos reached in November 1998 to make their common border problem-free by that date.

Vietnam. In October 1998, President Tran Duc Luong became the first Vietnamese president to visit Thailand since diplomatic relations were established in 1976, thus marking a new high point in Thai-Vietnamese relations. During the visit, agreements were reached on cooperation in rice pricing and narcotics traffic. The two sides also agreed to step up efforts to develop the so-called East-West Corridor, a subregional transportation and industrial route linking Thailand's east coast to Danang in Vietnam via central Laos. Also, the Vietnamese side praised the Thai government for suppressing a group of mostly overseas-based anti-Vietnamese government forces in Thailand before the presidential visit. Finally, before the presidential visit, in December 1997, Thailand had ratified an agreement on maritime demarcation in the Gulf of Thailand between Thailand and Vietnam.

Malaysia. In April 1998, Thailand and Malaysia signed their first agreement on gas supply from the Joint Development Area (JDA) in the Gulf of Thailand, under an arrangement on joint development of hydrocarbon resources in the JDA made 23 years before. The two countries expressed the hope that their cooperation, within the framework of the Indonesia-Malaysia-Thailand Growth Triangle, would further encourage interdependence of the regional economies and bring more investment to the area.

THE LARGE POWERS   Economics is the major factor in Thailand's relationships with the large powers.

China. For Thai leaders, China has played a crucial role in alleviating and containing Thailand's and the region's economic troubles. China provided financial assistance via the IMF to Thailand in late 1997, and more importantly, the Chinese leaders gave repeated assurances in 1998 that there would be no devaluation of their currency, thereby sparing the Thai and other regional economies the cost that such a devaluation would incur.

Thailand and China have enjoyed a cordial relationship since the two countries formed an unofficial alliance against Vietnam's occupation of Cambodia during the 1980s. Over the years, the relationship has been strengthened and cooperation has expanded. In February 1998, during a visit by China's deputy foreign minister to Bangkok, the two countries agreed to draw up a cooperation plan for the 21st century, a first for China. The plan, expected to be completed by the end of the year, provides for regular exchange visits of officials, an annual meeting between high-ranking officials of the two foreign ministries, and cooperation in areas such as security and defense, trade and investment, culture, and the environment.

During a visit to China in June 1998 by then Thai Army Commander-in-Chief General Chetta Thanajaro, Thailand and China agreed to launch a 12-year military cooperation program (1998–2010). Under the program, Thai army officers will study Chinese language, tradition, and culture with the Chinese army, followed by a year at the Chinese defense college and then seven years as military attachés at the Thai Embassy in Beijing. In addition, China offered the sale of weapons to the Thai army at reduced prices, plus free spare parts.

The United States. Public attitudes toward the United States in Thailand are currently rather negative. Many Thais feel that their country, as an old ally, should have received more immediate attention and assistance than it did from the United States in the economic crisis. The general perception in Thailand is that the United States paid attention to the crisis only once it had spread to Indonesia.

In contrast to public attitudes, Thai-American military relations remained good. The Thai government and air force were particularly grateful for the United States' willingness to accept cancellation of Thailand's purchase of a squadron of U.S.-built F/A-18 fighter jets, which Thailand could no longer afford as a result of the crisis. The United States also agreed to a Thai military request to cover four-fifths of the cost of the 1998 Cobra Gold naval and marine exercise. In addition, the U.S. government gave Thailand 100 million baht (US$2.7 million at US$1 = B36.65) for scholarships for Thai military officers to study in the United States.

Japan. Thai leaders fully expected that Japan, the country's leading economic partner over the past two decades, would play a major role in aiding Thailand's economic recovery. However, Japan's ability to fulfill its expected role has been greatly constrained by its own recession and financial fiasco.

Nevertheless, Japan was the major donor to the IMF fund for Thailand and also provided other bilateral and multilateral assistance, including emergency aid to help fund social and human resources development programs as well as cooperation in the fields of trade and technology. In addition, Japan provided financial aid for the construction of a second Thai-Lao bridge across the Mekong River. Moreover, at a Japan-ASEAN forum meeting in May 1998 it was agreed that Tokyo would utilize a special US$20 million "solidarity fund" for manpower development, poverty alleviation, and regional ASEAN projects. Then, on September 30, Japan announced the US$30 billion Miyazawa Plan for Asia, which the Thai government viewed as a sign of Tokyo's serious intent to improve the Thai and other regional economies.

DEFENSE POLICIES AND ISSUES

DEFENSE POLICIES AND SPENDING   Thailand's 1997 defense white paper identified land and sea boundary disputes as one of the country's immediate security problems. Other concerns included the internal problems of neighboring countries that directly affect Thai security through illegal entry, cross-border smuggling, and illegal trade in weapons and drugs. To deal with these threats, the white paper endorsed a significant arms buildup and force modernization, with a particular emphasis on strengthening air and naval capabilities.

The sudden collapse of the Thai economy had a profound impact on the armed forces. In addition to being forced to cancel various new weapons and equipment purchases, the armed forces have found that it is now too expensive to utilize and maintain some of the modern weapons and equipment already in their inventory.

As part of its response to the crisis, the government significantly reduced the defense budget. After several cuts, the 1998 budget was finally set at 81 billion baht (US$2.2 billion), about 28 percent less than the initial request from the ministry. According to the armed forces, about half of the final budget was to be spent on general administrative costs (with the bulk going to officials' salaries) and the rest on investment costs, including debt payments and the procurement of new spare parts (mostly paid for in U.S. dollars). The defense budget for 1999 currently stands at 77.2 billion baht (US$2.1 billion), down 4.6 percent from the final 1998 budget. This is approximately 9.7 percent of the government's total 1999 budget and 1.32 percent of the country's gross domestic product.

ADJUSTING TO AUSTERITY   Budget cuts and the weakening of the baht prompted Thailand's defense commander in January 1998 to outline three immediate measures: (1) a halt to all weapons procurement, with investment spending limited mostly to payments on previously incurred debt; (2) a cutback in general administrative costs, including a halt in recruitment and accelerated implementation of existing early-retirement plans; and (3) a continuation of the armed forces' emergency assistance work, especially flood and drought relief.

The first measure was the most sharply felt and difficult to fulfill. During the early part of 1998, the baht at times was worth less than half of its former value against the U.S. dollar, thus doubling the real value of the armed forces' foreign debts, which were mostly denominated in dollars. Under this pressure, the armed forces were obliged to arrange the postponement of most of 1998's installment payments of 21.4 billion baht (US$584 million). In addition, they halted 83.2 billion baht (US$2.3 billion) in procurement projects. By office and service branch, the following projects were affected: Office of the Permanent Secretary for Defense—military satellite system and new office building; Office of the Supreme Command—housing and communications development; Army—tanks, trucks, M16-A2 assault rifles, light armored vehicles, general-use helicopters, repair of 100 Bell helicopters, and upgrade of Scorpion tanks; Navy—offshore patrol boats, surveillance radar and missiles, and two submarines; Air Force—training aircraft, eight F/A-18 fighter jets, and medium transport aircraft.

Thailand's military leaders assess that a halt in weapons and equipment procurement will not cause a significant short-term degradation of national security, given that most countries in the region are experiencing similar difficulties. In any case, they estimate that Thailand will not face any major threats in the next five to 10 years. However, continued austerity measures could jeopardize national security in the long term as the country will continue to face various cross-border problems and potential conflicts with neighboring countries, especially territorial and natural resources disputes.

RESTRUCTURING THE ARMED FORCES   In late 1997, Prime Minister Chuan became the second civilian leader in Thailand's history to concurrently hold the post of defense minister. At that time, he declared that the main thrust of his defense policy was to effect structural changes to make the armed forces politically neutral, more professional, and more transparent, as well as increasingly responsive to changes in economic conditions. Despite widely held doubts at the time that Chuan would be able to exert control over military affairs, given the historical lack of a tradition of civilian control over the military, the prime minister vigorously pursued his restructuring plan for the armed forces, the major elements of which are the following:

- Restructuring of the chain of command within the ministry. In accordance with a 1997 plan approved by the previous government, in May Chuan set up a study committee headed by a trusted military advisor. The committee's proposal (not finalized as of the end of 1998) is expected to increase the power of the permanent secretary for defense in policy formulation and administration— including budgets and weapons procurement. The rationale for this is that the ministry needs to consolidate policy responsibilities, which previously were distributed among the three service commanders.
- Reduction in the number of senior officers. The present number of generals (1,859) is much higher than that in other countries' armed forces and thus excessively expensive. Accordingly, the number of generals will be reduced annually by 25 percent. In addition, the promotion period from colonel to general will be lengthened, from the current 1–2 years to 3–5 years.
- Increased transparency of the armed forces' economic activities. This part of the plan empowers the Treasury Department to look into the armed forces' secret funds. Also to be subjected to public scrutiny for the first time are the armed forces' lucrative commercial ventures, which include contracts, budgets, and related matters regarding media outlets operated by the military (Channel 5 TV and the 128 radio station). Finally, the armed forces were

instructed to survey and reclassify their land use. Currently, the military holds more than 5.3 million *rai* (approximately 2.12 million acres) of public land, or almost half of all public land. They will be allowed to retain land only for military installations and training grounds, being required to return the rest to the Treasury Department.

The current structure and power of the armed forces are largely the legacy of the military's dominant role in politics during most of the post–World War II period. It is not surprising, then, that not all military leaders eagerly embraced Chuan's plan, and it still remains to be seen how far Chuan and his team can go with it. The proposed restructuring received a lukewarm response from some military leaders, including the supreme commander, and the military has not yet cooperated in opening up its commercial finances on the grounds that this step could jeopardize national security.

Be that as it may, the growing democratization of Thai society (most strikingly demonstrated in the May 1992 uprising against the military prime minister) and the democratic principles undergirding the present Constitution, plus the current economic crisis, give considerable leverage to the advocates of reform. As a result, the military will find it more difficult than in the past to oppose efforts aimed at greater transparency, accountability, and adjustment.

In the annual military reshuffle in October 1998, General Surayuth Julanont was appointed as commander-in-chief of the Royal Thai Army. At the time of his appointment, Surayuth declared that he would support Chuan's policy of structural changes and would keep the army out of politics. Unlike his predecessors, he subsequently resigned from the Senate and has since refrained from commenting on political affairs. However, Surayuth's authority within the armed forces remains uncertain because he came from the traditionally less powerful post of army advisor and received the appointment only because he was Chuan's personal choice.

CONTRIBUTIONS TO REGIONAL AND GLOBAL SECURITY

REGIONAL SECURITY   In 1998, Thailand played a key role in bringing national reconciliation to Cambodia. When fighting again spilled over into Thai territory and drove a number of Cambodian refugees into Thailand during the early part of the year, Thai leaders initiated a series of meetings seeking a political solution to the conflict between Cambodian government troops and opposition alliance forces. Efforts by Thailand and ASEAN ultimately brought about the July general election in Cambodia.

Fifteen Thai observers joined the UN-coordinated Joint International Observer Group monitoring the election. Although the international monitoring team declared its satisfaction with the election, which the ruling party won by a narrow majority, the opposition parties accused the government of using fraud and intimidation. By early September, Cambodia was again on the brink of civil war as massive opposition-led antigovernment demonstrations turned violent.

These events prompted Thailand's deputy foreign minister to visit Phnom Penh, where he met with Cambodia's King Sihanouk and the three main party leaders. The Thai Foreign Ministry also offered Bangkok as a venue for talks between the conflicting parties, as had been suggested by the king. In addition to a general desire to bring peace to the Cambodian factions, Thailand's actions were linked to Cambodia's anticipated admission to ASEAN.

"Flexible Engagement." Prior to the annual ASEAN Ministerial Meeting in July, Foreign Minister Surin Pitsuwan proposed a concept he termed "flexible engagement," which calls on ASEAN to end its strict adherence to the long-standing principle of mutual noninterference regarding the internal affairs of other member states and recommends more flexibility for individual members to express their views on internal developments that affect the association as a whole. Although such a proposal was not new, this was the first time it had been officially put before ASEAN.

The primary impetus for the proposal was Thai policymakers' perception, based heavily on their recent experience with the spillover into Thailand of conflicts within Myanmar, that the internal affairs of any one country are increasingly affecting other countries and in many cases are beyond one individual member's ability to resolve. Also, the Thai government felt that, because societies in the region are becoming more pluralistic as a result of rapid socioeconomic changes, ASEAN should be empowered to tackle such issues as human rights and political participation that affect regional, as well as individual nations', stability.

The proposal, which gained support from the Philippines but encountered fierce opposition from Myanmar and Indonesia, was in any case well publicized and generated much discussion among member states. ASEAN ultimately adopted an "enhanced interaction" approach, whereby members will have expanded opportunities for consultation on issues affecting individual members and the region as a whole.

EXPANDED GLOBAL RELATIONS   Thailand became an observer of the Organization of American States (OAS) in September 1998 and of the Organization of Islamic Countries (OIC) in October. It is hoped that participation in the OAS will enable Thailand to forge closer cooperation with American states on economic, political, and transnational issues such as drug control and human rights. Regarding Islamic countries, Thailand hopes that participation in the OIC ideally will enhance mutual understanding and contribute to the Thai government's attempts to solve problems concerning the Thai Muslim community in South Thailand.

16 United States

The Security Environment

The U.S. government entered 1999 with a reaffirmed basic assessment of the security situation in, and corresponding security policies for, the Asia Pacific region. At the same time, some fundamental underlying dilemmas for U.S. policy in the region were reinforced by an eventful year and growing medium-term uncertainties.

The Asia Pacific region continues to be overshadowed in overall American policy making by the United States' global responsibilities, including a preoccupation with crises in the Middle East and the former Yugoslavia, as well as the continuing conundrum of the former Soviet Union. In East Asia, the financial-economic crisis was a major focus of concern, and its potential implications for regional security were recognized by those charged with American policy in this region. However, security relations with China and Japan, and the continuing uncertainty of the situation on the Korean peninsula, were seen as having more direct and urgent significance for U.S. defense and security planning. Also, the nuclear explosions by India and Pakistan in May focused renewed U.S. attention on the security problems of South Asia as well as on the broader issue of the proliferation of nuclear and other weapons of mass destruction.

OFFICIAL ASSESSMENTS   The major official U.S. analysis of the security environment in the Asia Pacific region during 1998 was the fourth in the East Asian Strategy Report (EASR) series, entitled *The United States Security Strategy for the East Asia-Pacific Region*, released on November 23. The EASR analysis is informed by a mostly

182

positive assessment of the regional security environment. After acknowledging that "areas of uncertainty remain and new challenges have emerged in the region," it states: "In spite of these challenges . . . we still see a region mostly at peace, where interests converge and the reservoir of political will to deal with new challenges runs deep." It also explicitly denies any significant changes in the U.S. approach: "This . . . report is not being issued because of a change in our security strategy. Our priorities remain constant. . . ."

The EASR analysis also emphasizes the strengthening of traditional elements of American policy in the region: the 100,000-troop forward presence, the alliance network, cooperation with friendly states and engagement with former or potential adversaries, efforts to prevent and counter the proliferation of weapons of mass destruction, and so on. This heavy emphasis on continuity despite significant developments in the region, including the deep economic crisis and the South Asian nuclear tests, led some observers to criticize the report as short on both strategic analysis and vision.

U.S.–ASIA PACIFIC RELATIONS   The economic crisis was the major and defining concern in the Asia Pacific region throughout 1998. By the year-end, encouraging steps had been taken in all of the affected economies to remedy the underlying structural problems behind the crisis, but the human toll was continuing to rise and the ability of governments—even with international assistance—to respond to the needs of the victims of the economic crisis varied widely. The combination of present suffering and dashed expectations was in turn putting greater pressure on governments throughout the region; the potential for violence remained high, particularly in countries such as Indonesia and Malaysia where the economic crisis was coupled with political crisis and pressures for regime change or other reforms.

Although the United States had been slow to respond to the first symptoms of the crisis in mid-1997, regarding it as a "glitch" (in President Bill Clinton's term) in the road rather than a major problem, and did not participate in the original International Monetary Fund (IMF) bailout package for Thailand, the American assessment and approach changed dramatically in the latter months of 1997 as the crisis expanded within Southeast and then Northeast Asia. The United States participated in all subsequent IMF agreements in the region, and throughout 1998 American regional policymakers devoted substantial attention to the economic, humanitarian, and political elements of the crisis. The most senior U.S. officials, including the president, vice president, and numerous cabinet members, traveled to the region during the year to discuss these and other issues.

U.S. economic growth was not significantly reduced as a result of the Asian economic crisis in 1998, as some had feared (and as some analysts still predict for 1999). Healthy growth was sustained throughout the year (3.9 percent GNP growth for the full year, and an astonishing 5.6 percent annual rate in the fourth quarter). At the same time, inflation remained low—the consumer price index rose only 1 percent for the year. However, the U.S. international trade deficit rose substantially, exceeding US$250 billion in trade in goods for 1998 (US$168.6 billion trade deficit overall, more than 50 percent above the level of 1997). Trade with Asia was one of the factors in the rise of the deficit, partly due to reduced U.S. exports to the affected Asian economies but more importantly because of rising imports into the United States from those economies as part of their response to the crisis. On the positive side, the U.S. deficit reflected the U.S. role as the principal foundation of Asia's economic recovery; on the negative side, the deficit stimulated demands by some affected industries (steel, agriculture) for protective governmental actions.

The most serious worry among U.S. policymakers concerning the Asian economic crisis was that it would worsen or spread, or that new developments would trigger a fresh round of currency devaluations and reductions in economic activity, possibly leading to widening violence or even a general breakdown of law and order in some countries. By the year-end, these worst-case scenarios had not occurred, but the concerns remained. Although recognizing that the primary solutions to the crisis lay in nonsecurity measures, American security policymakers and regional commanders both supported a forthcoming U.S. policy in assisting the affected countries and prepared to support more direct disaster relief efforts, if necessary. (Actual operations conducted in the region during the period were limited to a few instances of natural disasters.)

Interestingly, despite strongly critical media commentary in the region the domestic political scandal involving Clinton that so preoccupied American attention during 1998 did not seem to affect Asian confidence in the fundamental strengths or regional role of the United States. Similarly, Vice President Al Gore's November statement in Kuala Lumpur praising the efforts of political reformers opposed to Malaysian Prime Minister Mahathir bin Mohamad, which triggered angry reactions in Malaysia and elsewhere, had no immediately detectable wider repercussions on U.S. relations with other states in the region. Clearly, neither episode improved the standing of the United States in the region, but in both cases the underlying importance of the U.S. role presumably served to cushion any lasting negative impact.

CHINA AND JAPAN   China continued to occupy a prominent position in U.S. relations with the region in 1998, including in the security field. The major event of 1998 in Sino-U.S. relations was the visit of Clinton to China in June–July, reciprocating the state visit of Chinese President Jiang Zemin to the United States in October–November of 1997. The Clinton visit completed and symbolized the establishment of a new modus vivendi in relations between the two countries. More specifically, it provided a formal American acknowledgment of the prime importance of China to the region's future and demonstrated the U.S. commitment to a policy of "comprehensive engagement" with China in security and other fields (a careful formulation that paralleled but slightly differed from the more assertive Chinese phrase, "constructive strategic partnership").

For the Americans, the highlight of the Clinton visit was the acknowledgment by the Chinese side (chiefly through an unprecedented live television press conference by the two leaders) that American concerns over the state of human rights in China would have a legitimate and lasting role in the bilateral dialogue. For the Chinese, the major gain was the public recitation by Clinton in Shanghai of the "three no's" in U.S. Taiwan policy (no Taiwan independence, no "one Taiwan–one China" policy, and no Taiwan participation in international forums of sovereign states). This formal statement by the president initially created some controversy in American China policy circles but was generally interpreted as part of the broader deal allowing more open discussion of human rights issues.

U.S.-Chinese defense relations also continued to expand. The first formal defense consultations between the two countries took place in December 1997, and Secretary of Defense William Cohen visited China in January 1998. Lower-level contacts consisted of ship visits by U.S. naval ships to Chinese ports (as well as continued visits to post-reversion Hong Kong) and exchanges of visits by military and civilian defense personnel, including travel by numerous Chinese military officers to the United States.

The Clinton visit and the growing network of other contacts notwithstanding, by the end of 1998 issues had again emerged that could test the new modus vivendi in U.S.-Chinese relations in 1999. The "Cox Report," a Congressional study alleging that China had acquired militarily sensitive technology through commercial satellite contracts, was angrily rejected by the Chinese government. In addition, the harsh Chinese reaction to proposed U.S.-Japanese cooperation on theater missile defense (TMD) signaled a new area of disagreement. On Taiwan, following the Clinton visit both State Department and Pentagon spokesmen reverted to the more standard American formulation that this was an issue for China and Taiwan to settle, and that the United States' primary concern was that any settlement be peaceful. Finally, on the Chinese side of the human rights–"three no's" trade-off a series of arrests and trials of human rights activists in China at the year-end triggered renewed U.S. criticism of China's practices and intentions on human rights. This raised the possibility of further Congressional actions on China, an eventuality made more likely by the continued growth of the U.S. trade deficit with China— US$55 billion in 1998 (according to U.S. figures) and projected to reach US$70 billion in 1999. (At the same time, however, the two governments continued to try to work out an arrangement under which China might enter the World Trade Organization.)

Economic issues were uppermost in U.S. relations with Japan during 1998, most importantly the question of what Japan would or could do to revive its own economy and thereby contribute to the region's recovery from the financial-economic crisis. Also, continuing differences over trade policy were highlighted by Japan's inability to make concessions in the forestry and fisheries sectors, which effectively blocked progress on the Asia-Pacific Economic Cooperation (APEC) sectoral liberalization agenda. Finally, the huge U.S. trade deficit with Japan—some US$64 billion in 1998—remained a politically sensitive issue in the United States.

The major security issues in U.S.-Japan relations concerned three interrelated subjects: China, the Korean peninsula, and Okinawa. Clinton's praise of China's responsible role in the Asian financial crisis, which contrasted with continuing American criticism of Japan for failing to take the lead in responding to the crisis, caused discomfort in Japan. Also, the fact that Clinton did not stop in Japan on his way to or from China was seen by many in Japan as a calculated signal that the U.S.-Chinese relationship is independent of and not necessarily subordinate to the U.S. security relationship with Japan. This concern was only partially alleviated by Clinton's visit to Japan at the end of the year.

Uncertainties about the future dynamics of the U.S.-Japan-China trilateral relationship were also highlighted by continuing Chinese criticism of the September 1998 Guidelines for U.S.-Japan Defense Co-operation, compounded by the strongly negative Chinese reaction to U.S.-Japanese cooperation on TMD. In both cases, China's primary concern was the possible implications of these arrangements for contingencies involving Taiwan.

Developments in 1998 reinforced mutual U.S. and Japanese concerns over the unpredictability and potential threat of the North Korean regime. North Korea displayed persistent intransigence in various dialogues and negotiations despite the dire state of its economy. In addition, new questions were raised about North Korea's compliance with the 1994 nuclear Framework Agreement by the discovery of new underground facilities possibly related to the nuclear program. Most dramatically, the August 1998 launch by the North Koreans of a three-stage missile that overflew Japan demonstrated the wider security threat potentially posed by the North—and reversed previous Japanese caution about working with the United States on TMD.

Practical issues in U.S.-Japanese security cooperation again centered around the thorny issue of U.S. facilities, particularly those on Okinawa. Efforts by the Special Action Committee on Okinawa, formed in 1995, to seek ways to reduce the irritants caused by these facilities ran into a major obstacle when a proposal to relocate the key U.S. Marine Corps' Futenma Air Station in Okinawa was rejected by the local government. At the year-end, no clear alternative or solution was in sight. This problem underlined the difficulties of sustaining an effective U.S. force presence in Japan over the long term, especially during periods of relatively weak central governments in Tokyo.

POLICY DILEMMAS   The U.S. response to the Asian financial-economic crisis illustrated a continuing dilemma in American policy in this region. U.S. support for efforts by international financial institutions (the IMF, the World Bank, the Asian Development Bank, etc.) to help the nations of the region deal with the crisis was undermined by the reluctant and belated approval by the U.S. Congress of a US$18 billion U.S. contribution to a desperately needed funding replenishment for the IMF. Of note here is the fact that ultimate Congressional approval of IMF funding in October was stimulated more by the spread of the financial crisis to Russia and then Latin America (Brazil) than by concern over the needs of the East Asian countries where the crisis originated. Moreover, continuing Congressional refusal to grant the administration so-called fast-track authority for the negotiation of new trade agreements limits the ability of the United States to pursue further trade liberalization as part of a longer-term economic recovery and growth-promotion policy.

A different policy dilemma was reflected in the Indonesian crisis. Here, U.S. policy seemed torn between a desire that the economic crisis and the political transition made possible by the resignation of Indonesian President Suharto in May lead to fundamental reforms including greater democratization, and the fear that economic hardships and pressures for change could unleash deep-seated ethnic animosities and produce a general breakdown of law and order. The U.S. security community has long regarded the Indonesian Armed Forces (ABRI, Angkatan Bersenjata Republik Indonesia) as the ultimate guarantor of political stability in the country. However, U.S. relations with ABRI were complicated in 1998 by a series of revelations of military involvement in human rights violations over many years, as well as by the disclosure of a program of military exercises (not fully reported to the U.S. Congress and seemingly incompatible with Congressional restrictions on security assistance to Indonesia) between elite American military units and those Indonesian special forces that were at the center of many of the atrocity allegations.

Finally, the nuclear tests by India and Pakistan, which triggered the imposition of sanctions restricting U.S. assistance to and economic relations with both countries, revived wider debates over the effectiveness of sanctions policies versus the relative merits of unilateral and multilateral approaches to problem areas. After six months of intense dialogue with both governments, public commitments by India and Pakistan to adhere to the Comprehensive Test Ban Treaty by September 1999, and the resumption of long-suspended bilateral talks on the Jammu and Kashmir problem, Clinton (with Congressional support) on November 6 partially lifted the sanctions. Despite these positive steps, however, the fundamental issues remain far from solution.

DEFENSE POLICIES AND ISSUES

The November 1998 EASR series report reconfirmed the basic U.S. policy of continued engagement in the Asia Pacific region, including the commitment to maintain 100,000 forward-deployed troops as well as the major U.S. alliances and other military cooperation arrangements. This policy is seen as consistent with the U.S. global security strategy of maintaining a stable international environment, sustaining current force readiness, and improving capabilities to deal with future contingencies. The 1997 Quadrennial Defense Review (QDR) summarized this strategy as one of "shape, respond and prepare."

As in previous years, the principal difficulty faced by American military planners in 1998—in both the Asia Pacific region and worldwide—was how to meet these multiple objectives within the constraints of severe resource limitations. The recent national political objective of eliminating the budget deficit, as well as competing domestic needs, have produced several years of both absolute and relative cuts in the defense budget: defense spending fell from 6.5 percent of gross national product in 1985 to 3.2 percent in 1997. The number of active-duty military personnel correspondingly declined some 35 percent during the 1990s, with the fiscal year 1999 budget projecting a further modest reduction, to 1.40 million from 1.43 million in fiscal 1998 and 1.45 million in fiscal 1997.

Military procurement, particularly the development and acquisition of new equipment and weapons systems, has suffered even greater cuts than those to personnel levels, falling nearly 70 percent from fiscal 1985, to US$42 billion in fiscal 1998. Procurement—including new advanced-technology systems to take the armed forces into the next century—was identified as a major problem area in the 1997 QDR, which recommended a funding increase to US$60 billion annually and, assuming that defense budgets would remain constant, proposed to generate savings through further personnel reductions and more military base closures.

That was the story through 1997. The nature of the budget debate changed in 1998, however, as the eighth straight year of U.S. economic expansion made possible the first balanced federal budget in decades and undergirded projections of growing future surpluses. Not surprisingly, the prospect of budget surpluses engendered a mounting chorus of complaints from the military and the defense committees of

Congress about the impact of previous budget cuts and revenue short-falls on readiness, personnel morale and retention, and research and procurement programs. At a series of Congressional hearings during the year, armed service chiefs and the secretary of defense acknowl-edged these problems and discussed the steps necessary to deal with them.

This changed fiscal atmosphere produced an agreement between the administration and Congress to increase the fiscal 1999 defense budget by US$9 billion over the previously established increase ceil-ing of US$250 billion, as well as an administration pledge of a further US$10 billion increase in fiscal 2000, subsequently raised to US$12 billion in the president's budget proposal released in early 1999. This prompted Cohen's announcement that the QDR procurement target of US$60 billion would now be reached by fiscal 2001.

Nevertheless, the future of defense spending and the defense struc-ture remains subject to an ongoing political process. Congress' refusal to approve the administration's 1998 request for two further rounds of base closures in order to reallocate resources to readiness and pro-curement needs, as well as the approval by Congress of funding for several weapons programs opposed by the administration, illustrated the continuing tug of war between domestic political considerations and the defense establishment's perception of its priority needs.

CONTRIBUTIONS TO GLOBAL AND REGIONAL SECURITY

GLOBAL The decade-old debate in American society, particularly within the Congress, continues over the appropriate U.S. role in se-curity operations around the globe in the post–cold war era. In 1998 as in 1997, this debate centered principally around Iraq and prob-lems in the former Yugoslavia. The proponents of active projection of American military power include both internationalists and those observers concerned with specific regions or situations. Critics of the activist approach range from neo-isolationists and others who priori-tize domestic considerations to those who argue that a given situation does not engage fundamental American interests.

The Clinton administration has maintained the fundamentally internationalist position that American global interests necessitate American global engagement. However, administration policy also stipulates that U.S. military forces should be used only selectively and for well-defined, limited purposes, ideally in conjunction with other states and with the support of the broader international community. Specific decisions involving the use of force during 1998 varied. In Iraq, the intensive mobilization of forces in response to Saddam Hussein's defiance of the United Nations weapons inspection regime early in the year was followed by a more restrained response to further challenges in early November, which finally yielded to the short but intensive series of bombings and missile attacks in December. Terrorist bombings of the American embassies in Kenya and Tanzania in August triggered swift retaliatory missile strikes against the Osama bin Laden organization in Afghanistan and Sudan. In the former Yugoslavia, North Atlantic Treaty Organization airpower was mobilized but ultimately not used in the Kosovo crisis of October, and was mobilized again as 1999 began. In the Asia Pacific region, the one development during 1998 that might have triggered the mobilization of armed force—the discovery of North Korean underground construction possibly violating the 1994 nuclear agreement—was handled through diplomatic channels without the overt threat of the use of force.

REGIONAL   *East Asia—Forward Deployment.* As noted above, the U.S. commitment to maintain roughly 100,000 military personnel in Asia Pacific was reaffirmed in the November 1998 EASR document. Although the fiscal 1999 defense budget projected a reduction of some 35,000 military personnel worldwide, the prospect of increases in defense spending for both personnel and equipment relieved some of the strains that had prompted criticism of the 1997 QDR. In both declaratory policy and resource allocation, the United States at the beginning of 1999 was standing behind its commitment to retain existing force levels in the Asia Pacific region for the indefinite future. Furthermore, none of the emerging candidates for the U.S. presidency in the year 2000 has challenged the underlying commitment of the United States to global or regional engagement.

That much said, it is worth noting that the 100,000-troop figure is largely symbolic, reflecting neither concrete threat assessments nor alternative means of projecting power into the region. Future developments, including eventual Korean reunification and/or increased opposition in Japan to foreign troop presence, could over time lead to changes in the number of U.S. troops deployed in the region without necessarily implying a change in the fundamental willingness or ability of the United States to respond effectively to regional contingencies.

Bilateral Dialogues. Intense dialogue is necessary to maintain the network of American alliances and other security cooperation arrangements in the region. This involves major allies such as Australia, Japan, and South Korea; other treaty allies including the Philippines and Thailand; and numerous other countries with which the United States has specific arrangements without formal alliances. In this final category, for example, in 1998 the United States concluded an agreement with the Singaporean government under which deep-draft American naval vessels will have access to a new Singaporean port facility.

Such arrangements often involve delicate domestic political issues and therefore can easily be delayed or derailed. For example, in 1998 a status of forces agreement negotiated with the Philippines was still unratified by that government at year-end. Also, as noted above, U.S. and Japanese efforts to find an alternative to the Futenma Air Station in Okinawa remain unresolved.

The United States also seeks constructive dialogue with countries such as China, North Korea, and Vietnam, with which relations have been strained or conflictive. Progress made during 1998 with China was noteworthy, though numerous difficult issues remain. As well, the normalization of U.S.-Vietnamese relations is proceeding steadily if not rapidly. By contrast, the dialogue with North Korea probably suffered a net setback during the year.

Multilateral and "Minilateral" Processes. Support for multilateral approaches to security remains another important element in American regional as well as global security policy, although U.S. policymakers emphasize that multilateral processes are complementary to, rather than alternatives for, the alliance network and other bilateral arrangements. For example, the United States looks to multilateral mechanisms to play a primary role in countering the proliferation of weapons of mass destruction. Global instruments geared to this end include the Comprehensive Test Ban Treaty, the nuclear exporters control group, and the Chemical Weapons Convention. In Asia Pacific, the ASEAN Regional Forum (ARF) is the primary regional security forum.

As in the past, there are instances where other interests conflict with U.S. support for multilateral initiatives. For example, the U.S. refusal to sign the UN convention banning antipersonnel land mines completed in late 1997—despite the fact that it supported the objective and had participated intensively in negotiating the convention—reflected the importance of mines to the defense of South Korea against the North. U.S. officials argued that these mines could not be removed until alternative systems were developed in keeping with the treaty, which would take some time. However, the United States was unable to win agreement to a formal exception on the Korean situation in the convention.

A recent addition to the lexicon of Asia Pacific multilateral diplomacy is "minilaterals," referring to small multilateral groups and forums such as the Four-Party Talks involving the United States, China, and the two Koreas. U.S. policy supports the use of such smaller groups to deal with subregional and other issues involving a limited number of parties.

Finally, the United States endorses various bilateral and "minilateral" dialogue processes in which it is not directly involved. These include the talks on the South China Sea sponsored by the Association of Southeast Asian Nations (ASEAN); the renewed though still halting and embryonic contacts between mainland China and Taiwan; a series of bilateral processes in Northeast Asia involving China, Russia, and Japan; and (more prominent since the 1998 nuclear tests) the dialogue between India and Pakistan. Although it does not expect quick or dramatic progress in these forums, Washington believes they can help both ease immediate tensions and develop longer-term approaches to resolving problems.

Comprehensive Security, Cooperation, and Transparency. U.S. security policy is devoting increased attention and priority to nontraditional security issues such as terrorism, drug trafficking, natural resource problems, and various environmental and health-related concerns. The U.S. government believes that these problems, which affect the Asia Pacific region as they do other regions around the globe, require transnational cooperative solutions.

Finally, the U.S. government believes that increased transparency is one of the keys to dealing with security issues. This applies to internal governmental processes as well as to international relations, with open systems being seen as the best protection against excesses of all types. In the Asia Pacific region, the increasingly widespread practice of publishing national defense white papers—even when they reveal conflicting views and interpretations—and the growth of open discussion of security matters in international forums such as ARF are considered particularly positive developments.

17 Vietnam

The Security Environment

EXTERNAL SECURITY CONCERNS Developments in Southeast Asia and the wider Asia Pacific region in the past year have had a tremendous impact on the security environment of the overall region and of each country in the region. Vietnamese policymakers and the Vietnamese public paid particular attention to the region's unfolding economic crisis; the subsequent adjustments of relations among the major powers, particularly the United States and China; and political instability in some Southeast Asian countries, especially Indonesia and Cambodia.

The financial crisis originating in Thailand in July 1997 spread rapidly to other economies in Southeast and Northeast Asia and eventually affected major stock markets around the world. The crisis had two main characteristics: widespread economic, political, and social impacts on all affected countries; and a virulent contagion effect that threatened to engulf more and more economies.

At the regional level, the economic crisis has shifted the relative balance of power in favor of the United States and China and against Japan, Russia, and member countries of the Association of Southeast Asian Nations (ASEAN). In addition, problems and disputes among some regional countries surfaced or reemerged, thus bringing new challenges to the process of promoting regional multilateralism. On the other hand, the economic aspects of the crisis have occupied much of the attention and resources of the region's countries and leaders, thereby helping to reduce the possibility of near-term military conflict or a "mini arms race" that might have otherwise tended to threaten regional stability and security. At the same time, the crisis also stimulated some efforts to promote improved regional cooperation, especially in the economic field.

At the national level, the prolonged economic crisis has to varying degrees devastated many individual economies in the region and thus challenged several East Asian governments' legitimacy, which had been based on rapid economic growth. In particular, social problems such as high inflation and unemployment resulting from the crisis are causing political destabilization. These domestic troubles in turn have influenced the broader regional security environment, even to the extent of disenabling ASEAN from playing its previously active role in international and regional organizations and forums. Be that as it may, many in Vietnam consider the crisis to be only a temporary phenomenon and believe that regional countries will emerge from it in improved competitive condition.

Well after the start of the crisis, some Vietnamese observers still believed that Vietnam would not be greatly affected, citing the facts that the country is not yet fully integrated into the region and its currency is not yet convertible. Yet as the crisis developed, Vietnam increasingly felt its economic impact—namely, sharp declines in exports and investment, a slower growth rate, higher unemployment, and a scarcity of hard currency. In 1997, Vietnam's export earnings dropped about US$500 million from the previous year, and its export growth rate is estimated to be flat in 1998 (compared with 13 percent in 1997 and 25 percent in 1996). Foreign direct investment in 1998 declined 30–40 percent from 1997 levels, and unemployment increased from 6 percent in 1996 to more than 8 percent in 1998.

Also, the crisis has narrowed the breathing space that is so important to an economy in transition such as Vietnam, especially as its reforms are now entering their most challenging stages including the transformation of state-owned enterprises, the establishment of a stock market, and the creation of a more effective and transparent administrative system. The current situation may in fact be Vietnam's greatest challenge since its initial implementation of the "Doi Moi" (renewal) policy in 1986.

MAJOR POWER RELATIONS The relationships among the major powers, especially the United States, China, and Japan, have a major influence on the peace, stability, and development of the Asia Pacific region. The interactions among these powers in the region are undergoing important changes within an overall framework of mixed competition and cooperation. However, the prevailing trend continues to be one of peaceful relations.

U.S. President Bill Clinton's visit to China in June–July 1998 contributed to strengthening this peaceful trend inasmuch as it was an important step toward improved Sino-American relations, which until recently had been seen as mostly antagonistic and a potential source of instability in the region. In general, Vietnamese analysts viewed the visit as favorable because it created a solid base for a more predictable pattern of interactions between the United States and China and thus greatly reduces the possibility of confrontation between them.

Like observers in a number of other countries in the region, including Japan and North Korea, some in Vietnam believe that the improvement in Sino-American relations may come at the expense of a deterioration in relations with other countries in the region and that it might have negative impacts on the process of finding peaceful solutions to outstanding territorial disputes, especially in the South China Sea.

Vietnam's own bilateral relations with all the major powers were strengthened in 1998. In October 1998, Prime Minister Phan Van Khai visited China. The two sides exchanged views on their experience with economic reform, agreed to boost bilateral relations in all fields, and reaffirmed their determination to complete a border agreement covering their land boundary and the Gulf of Tonkin before the year 2000.

Vietnam-U.S. relations also continued their steady improvement, with the two countries now engaged in negotiations for a trade agreement as well as exchanges of high-ranking military delegations and a dialogue on security issues. A major boost to Vietnam's relations with Russia was marked by the visit of President Tran Duc Luong to Moscow in August 1998, when the two sides agreed to step up bilateral cooperation in all fields, including military and security. In October, Russia's defense minister visited Vietnam for discussions of measures to enhance cooperation between the two countries' armies.

SOUTHEAST ASIA Social instability and political transformation in Southeast Asian countries, especially Indonesia and Cambodia, were major focuses of attention for Vietnamese policymakers and public opinion in 1998. Although such developments were basically domestic in nature, protracted destabilization in one country could have serious repercussions for regional stability as countries in the region become increasingly integrated, and this is of concern to other countries.

The most serious social and political consequences of economic turbulence were seen in Indonesia, where economic meltdown deteriorated into political crisis, President Suharto had to step down, and social unrest persists. Indonesia's destabilized situation raised at least two concerns on the part of other regional countries, including Vietnam. First, possible Indonesian disintegration or ethnic and racial conflict might produce refugee flows, threaten strategic trade routes for energy supplies through Malacca, Lombok, or the Sunda Strait, and create tensions between Indonesia and its neighbors, particularly Singapore and Malaysia. Second, Indonesia's domestic difficulties inhibit it from playing an active role in ASEAN, thereby potentially causing strains in the ASEAN grouping and processes as well.

In Cambodia, political reconciliation has proved to be slow and difficult. Although the July 1998 general election was praised by the international community, including Vietnam, as a success, the domestic power struggle in Cambodia remained complicated. Vietnam welcomed the formation of the new coalition government finally announced on November 13. One continuing concern of the Vietnamese government is that at times opposition parties within Cambodia have not only provoked anti-Vietnamese sentiment but also incited discrimination and even violence against the ethnic Vietnamese minority living in Cambodia, which inevitably has affected relations between the two neighbors. In late 1998, the Vietnamese government worked with the Cambodian government to resolve this issue peacefully, resulting in an improved situation.

DOMESTIC SECURITY   After more than 10 years of reform, Vietnam has made significant progress in promoting economic growth, enhancing living standards, and bringing itself out of a state of embargo and isolation. However, new problems have arisen that could cause social instability, including an increased gap in living standards between the urban and rural areas (in 1998, urban income levels were reportedly five times higher than rural levels), high unemployment, increased social problems, and corruption, among others. In fact, in 1997 social unrest erupted in several provinces owing to citizens' anger at corrupt local officials and low rice prices.

In 1998, Vietnam's greatest domestic security concerns were coping with the contagion effects of the regional economic crisis and accelerating the reform process launched in 1986. Debates on policy measures have intensified among the Vietnamese leadership, which is determined to push through the reform process as a means of bringing the country out of its current difficulties. Vietnam's reforms are centered on the following directives:

- Mobilize internal strength for economic development while promoting international cooperation and integration;
- Enhance the efficiency and competitiveness of the economy;
- Expedite agricultural and rural development to keep pace with industrialization and overall modernization;
- Make more effective use of domestic and foreign investment;
- Accelerate the process of increasing the efficiency of state-owned enterprises;
- Reform the financial and banking system;
- Promote administrative reforms; and
- Combine economic growth with cultural development and social equity.

DEFENSE POLICIES AND ISSUES

In 1998, the Ministry of Defense published Vietnam's first defense white paper, entitled "Vietnam—Consolidating National Defense, Safeguarding the Homeland." The white paper is not yet in the standard format for such documents, but nevertheless represents a major step toward promoting transparency and enhancing confidence building through the ASEAN Regional Forum (ARF) process. The paper consists of three parts.

Part 1 presents the Vietnamese government's overall assessment of and viewpoints on the regional and world situation, with an emphasis on the opportunities and challenges facing Vietnam. It also outlines Vietnam's defense policy, including the following key principles:

- Peace and self-defense are the bases for Vietnam's national defense policy;
- The defense policy is designed to defend national interests,

independence, autonomy, sovereignty, and territorial integrity; to prevent and punish crimes of all types; and to safeguard social order and safety; and

• Defense supports the overall national policy of openness, diversification, and multilateralization of external relations. Vietnam opposes alliances, confrontation and aggression, and the production or proliferation of weapons of mass destruction. It supports noninterference in internal affairs and the peaceful resolution of disputes.

Part 2 of the paper deals with "building a strong all-people's national defense," emphasizing that, given limited annual defense budgets, the national defense strategy must be based on mobilizing all the country's people as well as its other resources—spiritual, political, economic, and scientific-technological. Within this framework, Vietnam plans to build a modern military appropriate to the country's economic and technological capacity.

Part 3 of the white paper covers the tradition of Vietnam's people's army and provides guidelines for "building strong people's armed forces." These forces include regular forces, local forces, militia and self-defense forces, and the reserve force. In peacetime, Vietnam has radically reduced the number of its regular forces so as to allocate a larger portion of the defense budget to maintaining and modernizing existing arms and equipment. At the same time, local and regional forces are to be strengthened, and a large reserve force is being built to supplement the regular forces in case of war.

CONTRIBUTIONS TO REGIONAL AND GLOBAL SECURITY

In the context of the current economic crisis, Vietnam's major direct contributions to regional security are its efforts to reform its own economy and to cope with the severe impacts of the crisis, as well as its continued commitment to the processes of regional and global integration.

The crisis has reinforced the Vietnamese leadership's awareness and understanding of the concept of mutual security—that security can only be achieved by the joint efforts of all countries. Although its 1998 economic performance was not as good as that of preceding years, Vietnam was still able to achieve a growth rate of about 6 percent while maintaining social and political stability. In this way, Vietnam has made a modest contribution to preventing the crisis from further shaking the region economically, politically, and socially.

In addition to enhancing its internal strengths to cope with the regional crisis, Vietnam has also made determined efforts to further integrate itself into the region and the world. A new member of ASEAN, Vietnam considers the association to be an important factor promoting the security and development of Southeast Asia. Despite the difficulties that the ASEAN countries currently are facing, Vietnam still views ASEAN as an active player in the Asia Pacific region and the world through its intensive interactions with its dialogue partners and various international and regional organizations, as well as its activities in ARF, the Asia-Europe Meeting, the Asia-Pacific Economic Cooperation forum, and the United Nations.

Demonstrating its enthusiastic support for ASEAN, Hanoi hosted the Sixth ASEAN Summit in December 1998. The main theme of the summit was "to strengthen solidarity and expand cooperation for an ASEAN of peace, stability and equitable development." ASEAN leaders adopted the Hanoi Declaration and Hanoi Plan of Action, as well as a "Statement on Bold Measures" addressing the economic crisis and accelerating the implementation of the ASEAN "Vision 2020" of reducing economic barriers among member nations. Vietnam supported the admission of Cambodia into ASEAN at this meeting to finally achieve the founding members' vision of an ASEAN-10. This objective was reaffirmed, even though Cambodia was not actually admitted at the Hanoi meeting.

Regarding the sovereignty disputes over Hoang Sa (Paracel Island) and Truong Sa (Spratly Islands), Vietnam has requested that all parties to the disputes refrain from any activities that may further complicate the situation, to ensure free international maritime navigation, and to find peaceful solutions to the disputes through negotiations and on the basis of international law, especially the 1982 United Nations Convention on the Law of the Sea. For the immediate future, Vietnam supports any efforts at cooperation that are acceptable to all parties concerned.

At the global level, Vietnam supports efforts toward comprehensive and significant arms reductions, especially the elimination of weapons of mass destruction. Vietnam also supports efforts to restructure the United Nations in the direction of greater democratization, enhanced transparency, and increased responsibility of the Security Council to the General Assembly. In this final regard, Vietnam believes it is necessary that there be a developing country as a permanent member on the UN Security Council.

Although only recently elected a member of the UN Economic and Social Council, Vietnam has already made great efforts to fulfill its responsibility in this role and thereby contribute to UN activities for peace and development.

Abbreviations

ABRI   Angkatan Bersenjata Republik Indonesia (Indonesian Armed Forces)
ADB   Asian Development Bank
ADF   Australian Defense Force
AFP   Armed Forces of the Philippines
ANZAC   Australia–New Zealand Army Corps
ANZUS   Australia-New Zealand-United States defense alliance
APEC   Asia-Pacific Economic Cooperation forum
ARATS   Association for Relations Across the Taiwan Strait (China)
ARF   ASEAN Regional Forum
ASDF   Air Self-Defense Force (Japan)
ASEAN   Association of Southeast Asian Nations
ASEAN-ISIS   ASEAN Institutes for Strategic and International Studies
ASEM   Asia-Europe Meeting
ASG   Abu Sayaf Group (Philippines)
AUSMIN   Australia–United States Ministerial Consultations
BIG   Bougainville Interim Government
BJP   Bharatiya Janata Party (Indian People's Party)
BTG   Bougainville Transitional Government
BIMST-EC   Bangladesh-India-Myanmar-Sri Lanka-Thailand Economic Co-operation grouping
BRA   Bougainville Revolutionary Army
CBMs   confidence-building measures
CDR   Closer Defense Relations (Australia–New Zealand)
CINPAC   Commander-in-Chief, United States Pacific Command
CIS   Commonwealth of Independent States
CLOB   Central Limit Order Book (Singapore)
CSCAP   Council for Security Cooperation in Asia Pacific
CTBT   Comprehensive Test Ban Treaty
CWC   Chemical Weapons Convention

DAP   Democratic Action Party (Malaysia)
DFAIT   Department of Foreign Affairs and International Trade (Canada)
DND   Department of National Defense (Canada)
DPR   Dewan Perwakilan Rakyat (national parliament of Indonesia)
DSO   Defense Science Organization (Singapore)
EASR   East Asian Strategy Report (United States)
ECSCAP   European Council for Security Cooperation in Asia Pacific
EEZ   Exclusive Economic Zone
EU   European Union
EURATOM   European Atomic Energy Commission
EVSL   Early Voluntary Sectoral Liberalization
FBS   Federal Border Service (Russia)
FPDA   Five Power Defense Arrangements (Australia, Malaysia, New Zealand, Singapore, and the United Kingdom)
GAGASAN   Gagasan Demokratik Rakyat (Coalition for People's Democracy, of Malaysia)
GERAK   Gerakan Keadilan Rakyat Malaysia (Malaysian People's Movement for Justice)
GSDF   Ground Self-Defense Force (Japan)
GUAM   Georgia, Ukraine, Azerbaijan, and Moldova
IOR-ARC   Indian Ocean Rim Association for Regional Cooperation
IMF   International Monetary Fund
ISA   Internal Security Act (Malaysia)
JDA   Joint Development Area (Malaysia-Thailand)
JWG   Joint Working Group (India-China)
KEDO   Korean Peninsula Energy Development Organization
LAC   Line of Actual Control (India-China)
LC   Line of Control (India-Pakistan)
MCDVs   Maritime Coastal Defense Vessels (Canada)
MD   military district (Russia)
MILF   Moro Islamic Liberation Front (Philippines)
MNLF   Moro National Liberation Front (Philippines)
MOD   Ministry of Defense (Russia)
MOI   Ministry of the Interior (Russia)
MPR   Majelis Permusyawaratan Rakyat (People's Consultative Assembly, of Indonesia)
MSDF   Maritime Self-Defense Force (Japan)
MTDP   Mid-term Defense Program (Japan)
NATO   North Atlantic Treaty Organization
NDPO   National Defense Program Outline (Japan)
NGO   nongovernmental organization
NORAD   North American Air Defense system (U.S.-Canada)
NPT   Nonproliferation Treaty

NSC   national security council (India)
OAS   Organization of American States
ODA   Official Development Assistance
OIS   Organization of Islamic Countries
OPM   Organisasi Papua Merdeka (Free Papua Movement)
OSCE   Organization for Security and Cooperation in Europe
PAS   Islamic Party of Malaysia
PLA   People's Liberation Army (China)
PMG   Peace Monitoring Group (for Bougainville)
PNGDF   Papua New Guinea Defense Force
QDR   Quadrennial Defense Review (United States)
RIMPAC   U.S.-sponsored military exercise
RP-U.S. VFA   Republic of the Philippines–United States Visiting Forces
   Agreement
RSAF   Republic of Singapore Air Force
RSN   Republic of Singapore Navy
SAARC   South Asian Association for Regional Cooperation
SACO   Special Action Committee on Okinawa (Japan–United States)
SAF   Singapore Armed Forces
SAFTA   South Asian Free Trade Area
SDF   Self-Defense Forces (Japan)
SDR   Strategic Defense Review (India)
SEF   Strait Exchange Foundation (Taiwan)
SFOR   Stabilization Force (of NATO in Bosnia)
SIMLAB   Simulation System for Land Battles (Singapore)
SOFA   Status of Forces Agreement (Philippines–United States)
SRF   Strategic Rocket Force (Russia)
START-1   Strategic Arms Reduction Treaty 1 (Russia–United States)
START-2   Strategic Arms Reduction Treaty 2 (Russia–United States)
TMD   theater missile defense
TMG   Truce Monitoring Group (for Bougainville)
UMNO   United Malays National Organization
UNDOF   United Nations Disengagement Observer Force (Golan Heights)
UNIFIL   UN Interim Force in Lebanon
UNIKOM   UN Iraq-Kuwait Observer Mission
UNSCOM   United Nations Special Commission (in Iraq)
WEU   Western European Union
WTO   World Trade Organization

The APSO Project Team

A distinctive feature of the *Asia Pacific Security Outlook* is that it is based on background papers developed by analysts from the region. These analysts, many of them younger specialists, meet at an annual workshop to examine each country paper and discuss the overall regional outlook. They also fill out a questionnaire, which is used to develop the regional overview and provide an assessment of changing perceptions over time.

Those involved in the process of developing the 1999 *Asia Pacific Security Outlook* include the following people. (Note: Paper writers participated in their individual capacities; their views do not necessarily represent those of the institutions with which they are affiliated.)

COUNTRY ANALYSTS
(BACKGROUND PAPER WRITER IDENTIFIED BY AN ASTERISK)

AUSTRALIA   Ross Cottrill, Australian Institute of International Affairs*

CANADA   Brian L. Job, Institute of International Relations, University of British Columbia*

CHINA   Chu Shulong, China Institute of Contemporary International Relations*

EUROPEAN UNION   Hanns Maull, University of Trier, Germany*

INDIA   Dipankar Banerjee, Institute of Peace and Conflict Studies*

INDONESIA   Kusnanto Anggoro, Centre for Strategic and International Studies*

JAPAN   Katahara Eiichi, Kobe Gakuin University*

REPUBLIC OF KOREA   Song Young Sun, Korean Institute of Defense Analyses*

MALAYSIA   Mely Caballero-Anthony, Institute of Strategic and International Studies (ISIS) Malaysia*

NEW ZEALAND   David Dickens, Centre for Strategic Studies, Victoria University of Wellington*

PAPUA NEW GUINEA   Ronald J. May, Australian National University*; Ray Anere, University of Papua New Guinea

PHILIPPINES   Gina Pattugalan, Institute for Strategic and Development Studies*

RUSSIA   Dmitri V. Trenin, Carnegie Moscow Center, Carnegie Endowment for International Peace*

SINGAPORE   Lam Peng Er, National University of Singapore*

THAILAND   Julaporn Euarukskul, Thammasat University*

UNITED STATES   Richard W. Baker, East-West Center*

VIETNAM   Bui Thanh Son, Institute of International Relations*

OVERVIEW

Charles E. Morrison, President, East-West Center

EDITORS

Charles E. Morrison, President, East-West Center
Richard W. Baker, International Relations Specialist, East-West Center

PROJECT DIRECTORS

Charles E. Morrison, President, East-West Center (United States)
Nishihara Masashi, Professor of International Relations, National Defense Academy (Japan)
Jusuf Wanandi, Chairman of the Supervisory Board, Centre for Strategic and International Studies (Indonesia)

STAFF SUPPORT

Marilu Khudari, East-West Center
Kumai Mariko, Program Assistant, Japan Center for International Exchange
Suzuki Tomoko, Program Assistant, Japan Center for International Exchange

Index

Afghanistan, 68, 71, 73, 191
AFTA (ASEAN Free Trade Area), 119, 146
Alliance Party, of New Zealand, 124
Anwar Ibrahim, 10, 84, 112–117, 144, 163, 165–166
APEC, 11, 13, 28, 84, 101, 120, 128, 153, 186
ARF, 23, 29, 49, 63, 71, 88, 96, 111, 119–120, 128, 147, 170, 192–193
arms control: Asia Pacific, 17, 182; Australia, 22, 29–30; Canada, 36, 39–40; China, 48, 52–53; the European Union, 63; India, 65, 74, 77; Indonesia, 89; Japan, 93, 101–102; New Zealand, 126, 128; the Philippines, 146; Russia, 159–160; Vietnam, 199
arms sales
  Australia, to New Zealand, 125
  China, 67
  European Union, to East Asia, 61
  Germany, 62
  India, 76
  Israel, to India 69
  Russia: 160; to China, 153–154; to India, 69, 153–154, 156; to South Korea, 155; to Vietnam, 156
  United Kingdom, 62
  United States, 175
ASEAN, 10–11, 63–64, 84, 88–89, 111, 119, 144–148, 165–166, 173, 180–181, 194–195, 197, 200. See also under economic crisis, in Asia
ASEAN-ISIS, 40, 170
ASEM, 58, 63–64, 147
Asian Development Bank (ADB), 58

Australia
  armed forces (see also under military-to-military contacts): personnel, number of, 26
  and ASEAN, 23
  and China, 24
  defense: budget, 25–26; policy of, 21, 24
  and Indonesia, 22, 29–30, 87
  major power relations, view of, 23
  and New Zealand, 27–29, 125, 127
  See also under arms control; economic crisis, in Asia; nuclear tests, in South Asia; peacekeeping missions; security; weapons procurement

Bangladesh. See India, and Bangladesh
Bhutan. See India, and Bhutan
BJP (Bharatiya Janata Party, or Indian People's Party), 66–67, 76
Blair, Tony, 56, 59
Bougainville. See peacekeeping missions, Australia; peacekeeping missions, New Zealand; separatist movements, in Papua New Guinea

Cambodia, 51–52, 102, 119, 172, 179–180, 196–197, 200
Canada
  and Africa, 42
  armed forces (see also under military-to-military contacts): deployment of, 36; misconduct in, 38; personnel, number of, 37–38
  defense: budget, 37; policy, 37

Canada (*continued*)
and Europe, 42
human rights policy of, 41, 59
human security agenda and, 35, 39–40, 42
and Japan, 41
and North Korea, 34, 41
and Russia, 42
See also under arms control; economic crisis, in Asia; land mines, antipersonnel; NATO; peacekeeping missions; security; UN; weapons procurement
Chernomyrdin, Viktor, 150
China, 23–24, 59, 172, 195
armed forces (*see also under* military-to-military contacts): personnel, reductions in, 48; reorganization of, 49
and Cambodia, 51
defense: budget, 50–51; policy, 47–48
domestic affairs of: political stability, 44; social stability, 44; state of the economy, 43–44
and India (*see also under* territorial disputes), 45, 47, 52, 66–67
and Indonesia, 47, 84
and Japan (*see also under* territorial disputes), 14–16, 45–46, 50, 54, 91, 94–95, 97, 99
and the Korean peninsula: Four-Party Talks, 51
and the Middle East, 52
and Myanmar, 67
and North Korea, 51
and the Philippines (*see also under* territorial disputes), 143–144
and Russia, 14–15, 45, 52–53, 161
and Taiwan, 14–15, 43–46, 50, 97, 122–123
and the United States: 14–15, 34, 45, 52–54, 192–194, 196; Guidelines for U.S.-Japan Defense Cooperation, 50, 94, 97, 187; theater missile defense, 50, 99, 186–187
and Vietnam (*see also under* territorial disputes), 46, 196
See also under arms control; arms sales; economic crisis, in Asia; nuclear tests, in South Asia; security
Chirac, Jacques, 56
Chuan Leekpai, 10, 171, 178–179
Clinton, Bill, 14, 34, 45, 52–53, 93–94, 122, 126, 154, 166, 183–188, 196

CSCAP (Council for Security Cooperation in Asia Pacific), 35, 40, 71, 89, 111, 128, 147, 170
CTBT (Comprehensive Test Ban Treaty), 29–30, 39, 76–77, 160, 188

Democratic Party of Japan, 92
Democratic People's Republic of Korea. *See* North Korea
Diaoyu Islands. *See* territorial disputes, between China and Japan

East Timor. *See* separatist movements, in Indonesia
economic crisis, in Asia
ASEAN and, 11, 23–24
Australia's view of, 22–23
Canada and, 33, 40
China and, 43–46, 83, 117, 121–123
the European Union and, 55, 57–58
Indonesia and, 9, 12–13, 162, 188, 197
international relations and, 9–10, 183, 194
Japan and, 9, 11, 57, 83, 93, 117, 121, 166, 176
Malaysia and, 12, 163–164
New Zealand and, 122–123, 164
the Philippines and, 138–139
Singapore and, 162–163
South Korea and, 9, 11
Thailand and, 9, 11, 171–172, 175
United States and, 83, 175, 183–184, 187–188
Vietnam and, 195, 199
weapons procurement and, 16–17, 109, 176–178
ECSCAP (European Council for Security Cooperation in Asia Pacific), 63
Estrada, Joseph, 117, 138–145, 165
European Union
defense: expenditures, 60; policy, 59–60
and East Asia (*see also under* arms sales; economic crisis, in Asia): 55–63; ARF, 63; ASEAN, 63; ASEM, 58, 64; KEDO, 62; North Korea, aid to, 63; Official Development Assistance, 62; security interests in (*see also under* security), 57, 60; trade with, 57
internal change in, 55–56
military personnel in, deployment of, 60
See also under arms control; nuclear tests, in South Asia

Fissile Material Cut-off Treaty, 30, 76, 128
France, 45, 53, 56, 60–61, 111, 169

Gandhi, Rajiv, 66
Germany, 56, 60–62, 111
Goh Chok Tong, 116, 166, 168
Gujral, Inder Kumar, 65, 69
Gulf of Tonkin. *See* territorial disputes, be-
    tween China and Vietnam

Habibie, B. J., 12, 79–82, 84, 86, 117, 131,
    163, 165
Hashimoto Ryūtarō, 92–93, 95
Hoang Sa, 200

IMF, 10–12, 58, 113, 171, 176, 183, 187–
    188
India
    armed forces (*see also under* military-to-
        military contacts): 72; equipment of,
        69–71, 73–75, 156; personnel, number
        of, 74–75; structure of, 74
    and ASEAN, 66, 71
    and Bangladesh, 70–71, 73, 77
    and Bhutan, 71
    defense: budget, 75; policy, 65, 68, 73–74
    and Central Asia, 71
    and China (*see also under* territorial dis-
        putes), 47, 54, 65–67
    and the Indian Ocean region, 66, 72
    and Myanmar, 63–64, 67, 73
    national security, view of, 66, 68
    and Nepal, 70–71, 73
    nuclear policy of (*see also under* nuclear
        tests, in South Asia), 76
    and Pakistan (*see also under* territorial
        disputes), 69–70, 76
    regional policy of, 65, 69
    and Russia (*see also under* arms sales), 75
    security, internal: 72, 74; nonmilitary di-
        mensions of, 73
    and Sri Lanka, 70–71, 72, 77
    state of the economy, 73
    and the United States, 67–69, 182, 188
    and West Asia, 72
    See also under arms control; arms sales;
        BJP; land mines, antipersonnel; peace-
        keeping missions; security; weapons pro-
        curement
Indonesia, 9–13, 21–24, 180, 196–197
    and ARF, 88
    armed forces (*see also under* military-to-

military contacts): dual function concept
    of, 85; misconduct of, 82; personnel,
    number of, 86; "total people's defense"
    concept, 86
and ASEAN, 13, 84, 87–89
and China, 47, 84
defense budget of, 87
domestic affairs of: ethnic strife, 33, 47,
    81, 144; political upheaval, 22, 81, 130
foreign policy of, 87–88
and India, 84, 89
and Japan, 83–84
and Malaysia, 84, 87, 117, 197
and Russia, 84, 155
secessionist movements in (*see under* sep-
    aratist movements)
and Singapore, 77, 84, 162–163, 169
state of the economy, 79–80, 113
and the United States, 83, 188
See also under arms control; economic cri-
    sis, in Asia; nuclear tests, in South Asia;
    peacekeeping missions; security; weap-
    ons procurement
International Criminal Court, 36, 39, 128
Iran, 71, 153
Iraq, 29, 125–126, 128–129, 146, 152,
    161, 190–191
Irian Jaya. *See* separatist movements, in In-
    donesia
Italy, 56, 60

Jammu and Kashmir. *See* territorial disputes,
    between India and Pakistan
Japan, 9–11
    and APEC, 101, 120, 186
    and ARF, 96, 101, 120
    armed forces: personnel, number of, 98;
        role of, 97
    and ASEM, 101
    and China (*see also under* territorial dis-
        putes): 14–15, 43, 45, 50, 53–54, 91,
        94, 97, 99; apology, concerning wartime
        aggression, 95
    defense: budget, 98; policy, 96; reconnais-
        sance satellites, 100
    elections in, 92, 100
    and North Korea: 14, 187; KEDO, 93;
        missile launch, 14, 91, 93, 99–100; Six-
        Party Talks, 34, 101, 110
    Official Development Assistance, 103
    and Russia (*see also under* military-to-
        military contacts; territorial disputes):

Japan, and Russia (*continued*)
91, 154–155, 161; peace treaty with,
95–96, 154–155
and South Korea (*see also under* territorial disputes): apology, concerning colonial rule, 94, 107
state of the economy, 11, 83, 91–92, 186
and the United States: 93–94, 182, 186;
Guidelines for U.S.-Japan Defense Cooperation, 50, 94, 97, 187; Okinawa,
U.S. bases in, 98, 100, 187; theater missile defense, 15, 50, 99, 187; U.S.-China
relations, view of, 94, 187
See also under arms control; economic crisis, in Asia; land mines, antipersonnel;
nuclear tests, in South Asia; peacekeeping missions; security; weapons procurement
Japan Communist Party, 92
Jiang Zemin, 15, 34, 44–46, 52–53, 67, 94–95, 122, 153, 185

KEDO (Korean Peninsula Energy Development Organization), 29, 41, 51, 62, 93, 106
Kim Dae Jung, 14, 34, 94, 105–106
Kiriyenko, Sergei, 150
Kohl, Helmut, 56
Korean peninsula. *See* North Korea; South Korea
Kosovo, 36, 38, 42, 45, 53, 56, 60, 152, 160, 182, 190–191
Kuril Islands. *See* territorial disputes, between Japan and Russia

Labor Party, of Australia, 27
Labour Party, of New Zealand, 124
land mines, antipersonnel: 53, 63; Canada and, 39; India and, 77–78; Japan and, 102; the Philippines and, 146; United States and, 192
Laos, 40, 129, 146, 148, 172, 174
Lee Kuan Yew, 84, 116, 163–164
Liberal Democratic Party, of Japan, 92
Li Peng, 44, 153

Mahathir bin Mohamad, 10, 113–114, 116–117, 144, 163, 165, 184
Malaysia, 10–12
and APEC, 84, 117–118, 120, 144
and ARF, 119–120
and ASEAN, 11, 24, 117, 119, 144

and China, 122, 148
defense: budget, 118; FPDA, 61, 118, 127, 164–165, 170; policy, 118–119
and Indonesia, 84, 87, 117, 197
and Japan (*see* economic crisis, in Asia)
and New Zealand, 127
political upheaval in (*see also* Anwar Ibrahim; Mahathir bin Mohamad), 10–12, 112, 115–118, 163
and Singapore, 84, 116–118, 162–165
state of the economy (*see also* economic crisis, in Asia), 112, 114, 116, 118
and Thailand, 172–174
and the United States, 11, 118, 184–185
See also Estrada, Joseph; Habibie, B. J.;
peacekeeping missions; military-to-military contacts; UN; weapons procurement
military-to-military contacts: Australia, 27–29, 125, 127; Canada, 36, 42; China, 53–54; European Union, 61; India, 69, 71, 77; Indonesia, 87; Japan, 96; Malaysia, 118, 127, 165; New Zealand, 125, 127–128; Papua New Guinea, 134–135;
the Philippines, 143–145; Russia, 152–153, 161; Singapore, 169; South Korea, 107, 111; Thailand, 175; United States, 185
Mischief Reef. *See* territorial disputes, between China and the Philippines
Myanmar, 41, 63–64, 67, 73, 147–148, 172–174, 180

National Party, of New Zealand, 123
NATO: 56, 60, 151–152, 191; Canada and, 36. *See also* peacekeeping missions
Nepal, 70–71, 73
New Zealand
armed forces (*see also under* military-to-military contacts): operational doctrine, 124; personnel, number of, 124
and Australia: 28; Bougainville (*see also under* peacekeeping missions; separatist movements), 125; CDR, 125
and China, 53, 122
defense budget of, 123–124
and Iraq, 125–126, 128
and Malaysia: FPDA, 61, 118, 127, 164–165, 170
and Singapore: 61, 164; FPDA, 127
and the United States, 121–123, 125–127
See also arms control; economic crisis, in

Asia; nuclear tests, in Asia Pacific; peacekeeping missions; security; UN; weapons procurement
Nonproliferation Treaty (NPT), 30, 76–77
Northern Territories. *See* territorial disputes, between Japan and Russia
North Korea, 9, 17, 53, 191, 196. *See also under* arms control: Asia Pacific; Canada; European Union; Japan; Russia; South Korea; United States
nuclear tests, in South Asia: 17; American view of, 52, 69, 182, 188; Australian view of, 21, 30, 52; Canadian view of, 34; Chinese view of, 52; European Union view of, 63; by India, 9, 21, 34, 52, 63, 66–67, 76, 89, 122, 188; Indonesian view of, 89; Japanese view of, 93; New Zealand view of, 122; by Pakistan, 9, 21, 34, 52, 63, 66, 89, 122, 188; Papua New Guinean view of, 137; Russian view of, 153

OAS (Organization of American States), 181
Obuchi Keizō, 92–94, 96, 155, 166
OIC (Organization of Islamic Countries), 181
One Nation Party, of Australia, 28
OSCE (Organization for Security and Cooperation in Europe), 60, 160–161

Pakistan, 30, 45, 52, 66–71, 73, 76, 126. *See also under* nuclear tests, in South Asia; territorial disputes
Panganiban Reef. *See* territorial disputes, between China and the Philippines
Papua New Guinea
armed forces (*see also under* military-to-military contacts): personnel, number of, 136; security role of, 134–136
and ASEAN, 137
Bougainville (*see* separatist movements, in Papua New Guinea)
defense budget of, 136
and Indonesia (*see also under* separatist movements), 30, 130–131
internal security, 132–133, 135
and the Solomon Islands, 127, 131–132
See also nuclear tests, in South Asia; security
Paracel Island, 200
peacekeeping missions: Australia, 30–31,

133; Canada, 38–42; India, 78; Indonesia, 89; Japan, 102; Malaysia, 120; New Zealand, 126–127, 129, 133; the Philippines, 146; Singapore, 170; South Korea, 110–111; Russia, 160–161
Phan Van Khai, 196
Philippines, the, 10, 12, 118
armed forces (*see also under* military-to-military contacts): personnel, number of, 145; restructuring of, 145
and ARF, 147
and ASEAN, 89, 144, 146–147
and ASEM, 147
and China: 53, 143, 147; Panganiban Reef (*see* territorial disputes, between China and the Philippines)
domestic affairs of: communist and rebel movements (*see under* separatist movements); elections, 138; state of the economy, 139; terrorism in, 140–141
foreign policy objectives of, 141, 146
and Indonesia, 117, 144
and Malaysia, 144
and the United States: Visiting Forces Agreement, 142–143, 192
See also under arms control; land mines, antipersonnel; peacekeeping missions; security; UN
Primakov, Yevgeny, 69, 150–151, 156
Prodi, Romano, 56

Ramos, Fidel, 138–142, 146
Republic of Korea. *See* South Korea
Russia, 12, 14–15, 42, 55, 75, 84, 87, 95–96, 108, 111, 169, 188
and APEC, 153
armed forces (*see also under* military-to-military contacts): combat readiness of, 157–158; conventional forces development, 160; moral degradation of, 159; personnel, number of, 157–158; reorganization of, 157; role of, 157, 179
and ASEAN, 155, 161
and China (*see also under* arms sales), 14–15, 45–46, 52–53, 161
and CIS: 152–153; Kazakhstan, 152–153; Uzbekistan, 152–153
defense: budget, 158; policy, 156
domestic affairs of: government, reshuffling of, 150; internal security, 150; military discontent, 151
foreign policy of, 151

Russia (*continued*)
and India (*see also under* arms sales), 69, 75
and Iran, 153
and Iraq, 152, 161
and Japan: 91, 161; Kuril Islands (*see under* territorial disputes); peace treaty with, 95–96, 154–155; trade with, 155
and the Middle East, 142, 161
and NATO, 152, 156, 160
and North Korea, 155
nuclear forces of (*see also under* arms control), 157
and South Korea (*see also under* arms sales): 101, 108, 110–111; Four-Party Talks, 155
state of the economy, 149
and the United States: 151, 153–155, 159–161; presence in Asia, view of, 156
and Vietnam, 196
See also under nuclear tests, in South Asia; peacekeeping missions; separatist movements; weapons procurement

SAARC (South Asian Association for Regional Cooperation), 65, 70–71
SAFTA (South Asian Free Trade Area), 71
security
in Asia Pacific, assessment of: 9, 13, 16; Australia, 21; Canada, 33–34, 40; China, 49; European Union, 60; India, 65; Indonesia, 13, 79–80, 82–83; Japan, 91–98; New Zealand, 121–122; Singapore, 162, 166; United States, 182; Vietnam, 194
bilateral cooperation concerning: Australia, 29; Canada, 41; European Union, 61; Philippines, 148; United States, 192–193
global, assessment of: 21–23, 30; Canada, 32
multilateral cooperation concerning: 34; Australia, 21; Canada, 35, 39–40, 42; China, 54; European Union, 63; India, 71; Indonesia, 89; Japan, 96, 101; New Zealand, 128; Papua New Guinea, 136–137; Philippines, 141–142, 147; Singapore, 170; South Korea, 110–111; United States, 182, 192–193
in Northeast Asia, 17, 34, 40, 93, 101, 108, 110–111
Senkaku Islands. *See* territorial disputes, between China and Japan

separatist movements
in Canada, 33
in India, 72
in Indonesia: 130; Aceh Province, 81–82; East Timor, 28, 63, 81–82, 88; Free Papua Movement (OPM), 130, 135; Irian Jaya, 81, 130–131
in Papua New Guinea: 130; Bougainville, 131-133
in the Philippines, 140–141, 145
in Russia, 151
in Thailand, 172–173
Shipley, Jenny, 126
Singapore
armed forces (*see also under* military-to-military contacts): arsenal of, 170; personnel, number of, 168; training, and high technology, 168–170
and ASEAN, 11, 165–166
and China, 44, 166–167
defense budget of, 168
and Indonesia, 162–163, 169
and Japan, 166–167, 195
and Malaysia: 11, 116–118, 162–165; FPDA, nonparticipation in, 61, 118, 127, 164–165
state of the economy, 167
and the United States, 166
See also under economic crisis, in Asia; peacekeeping missions; security; weapons procurement
Skate, Bill, 131, 133–134, 136-137
South Korea, 9–15, 62
armed forces (*see also under* military-to-military contacts): personnel, number of, 108
and China, 101, 107, 110
defense: budget, 108–109; policy, 108
and Japan: 101; apology, for colonial rule, 94, 107
and North Korea: 13–14, 34, 101, 105–107, 110–111; Four-Party Talks, 106; KEDO, 51, 62, 93; Sunshine Policy, 14, 106–108, 110
and Russia, 101, 108, 110–111, 155
state of the economy: 104; political situation and, 105
and the United States: 108, 110–111; military personnel, number of in South Korea, 108
See also under peacekeeping missions; security; UN; weapons procurement

Spratly Islands, 16. *See also* territorial disputes, between China and the Philippines

Sri Lanka. *See* India, and Sri Lanka

Suharto, 12–13, 29, 58, 79, 81–82, 114, 162–163, 188, 197

Taiwan. *See under* China; United States

Takeshima Island. *See* territorial disputes, between Japan and South Korea

territorial disputes: between China and Japan, 15–16, 46; between China and the Philippines, 15–16, 46, 138, 143, 200; between China and Vietnam, 46, 196; between India and China, 66–67, 69; between India and Pakistan, 34, 67–68, 70, 188; between Japan and Russia, 95, 154–155; between Japan and South Korea, 94; between Thailand and Laos, 174; between Thailand and Myanmar, 173

Thailand, 9–12, 183, 192
  armed forces (*see also under* military-to-military contacts): restructuring of, 178–179
  and ASEAN, 119, 144–145, 166, 173, 180
  and Cambodia: 172, 179–180; national reconciliation, efforts toward, 179
  and China, 172, 175
  defense: budget, 177; policy, 176, 178
  drug trafficking in, 172
  and Japan, 176, 192
  and Laos, 172, 174
  and Malaysia, 172–174
  and Myanmar (*see also under* territorial disputes), 172–173, 180
  OAS (Organization of American States), membership in, 181
  OIC (Organization of Islamic Countries), membership in, 181
  state of the economy, 113, 172
  and the United States, 175–176, 183, 192
  and Vietnam, 172, 174
  See also under economic crisis, in Asia; separatist movements; weapons procurement

Tokdo Island. *See* territorial disputes, between Japan and South Korea

Tran Duc Luong, 174, 196

Truong Sa. *See* territorial disputes, between China and the Philippines

UN: and Canada, 35, 38–39; and India, 78; and Malaysia, 120; and New Zealand, 127; and the Philippines, 146; and South Korea, 110–111; and Vietnam, 201. *See also* peacekeeping missions

United Front government, of India, 65

United Kingdom: 29, 56, 60–62, 111; and China, 45, 53, 59

United States, 23, 194–196
  armed forces (*see also under* military-to-military contacts): personnel, in Asia Pacific, 183, 189, 191
  and China: 14–15, 34, 52–54, 94, 192–196; comprehensive engagement policy, 185; defense consultations, 185; human rights, 185–186; theater missile defense, 50, 99, 186–187
  defense: budget, 189–191; policy, 189, 190–192
  and India (*see under* nuclear tests, in South Asia)
  and Indonesia, 188
  and Iraq, 52, 190–191
  and Japan: 98–101, 182, 186; Guidelines for U.S.-Japan Defense Cooperation, 50, 94, 97, 187; Okinawa, U.S. bases in, 98, 100, 187; U.S.-Chinese relationship, view of, 94, 187
  and Malaysia, 11, 101, 118, 120, 184–185
  and North Korea, 14, 107–108, 187, 192
  and Pakistan (*see under* nuclear tests, in South Asia)
  and Russia, 151, 153–156, 159–161
  security issues (*see also under* security): nontraditional, 193; transparency of, 193
  and South Korea, 107–108
  state of the economy, 184
  Taiwan policy of, 45, 185–187
  and terrorism, 193
  and Vietnam, 192, 196
  and Yugoslavia, 190
  See also under economic crisis, in Asia; land mines, antipersonnel; weapons procurement

Vietnam, 40
  armed forces: personnel, reductions in, 199; structure of, 199
  and ASEAN, 200

Vietnam (*continued*)
  and Cambodia, 197
  and China (*see also under* territorial dis-
    putes), 46, 196
  defense policy of, 198–199
  domestic affairs of: reform, economic, 198;
    social instability, causes of, 197; state of
    the economy (*see also under* economic
    crisis, in Asia), 195, 197–199
  and Indonesia, 196–197
  major power relations, view on, 195–196
  and Russia, 155–156, 196
  and Thailand, 172, 174–175
  and the United States, 192, 196
  See also under arms control; security;
    UN

weapons procurement: 16–17; Australia, 26–
  27, 123; Canada, 37; India, 69–70, 74–
  75; Indonesia, 86–87; Japan, 98–100;
  Malaysia, 118; New Zealand, 123–124;
  Philippines, 145; Russia, 160; Singapore,
  169–170; South Korea, 109; Thailand,
  175, 177; United States, 189
WEU (Western European Union), 63
World Bank, 58, 187
WTO (World Trade Organization), 57, 186

Yeltsin, Boris, 42, 69, 95, 150
Yugoslavia, 36, 38, 53, 56, 60, 101, 129,
  182, 190–191

Zhu Rongi, 44

Asia Pacific Agenda Project

The Asia Pacific Agenda Project (APAP) was established in November 1995 to enhance policy-oriented intellectual exchange at the nongovernmental level, with special emphasis on independent research institutions in the region. It consists of four interconnected components: (1) the Asia Pacific Agenda Forum, a gathering of leaders of Asia Pacific policy research institutes to explore the future agenda for collaborative research and dialogue activities related to the development of an Asia Pacific community; (2) an Asia Pacific policy research information network utilizing the Internet; (3) annual multilateral joint research projects on pertinent issues of regional and global importance undertaken in collaboration with major research institutions in the region; and (4) collaborative research activities designed to nurture a new generation of Asia Pacific leaders who can participate in international intellectual dialogues. APAP is managed by an international steering committee composed of nine major research institutions in the region. The Japan Center for International Exchange has served as secretariat since APAP's inception.

ASEAN Institutes for Strategic and International Studies

ASEAN-ISIS (Institutes for Strategic and International Studies) is an association of nongovernmental organizations registered with the Association of Southeast Asian Nations. Formed in 1988, its membership comprises the Centre for Strategic and International Studies (CSIS) of Indonesia, the Institute of Strategic and International Studies (ISIS) of Malaysia, the Institute for Strategic and Development Studies (ISDS) of the Philippines, the Singapore Institute of International Affairs (SIIA), and the Institute of Security and International Studies (ISIS) of Thailand. Its purpose is to encourage cooperation and coordination of activities among policy-oriented ASEAN scholars and analysts, and to promote policy-oriented studies of, and exchange of information and viewpoints on, various strategic and international issues affecting Southeast Asia's and ASEAN's peace, security, and well-being.

East-West Center

Established by the United States Congress in 1960 to promote mutual understanding and cooperation among the governments and peoples of the Asia Pacific region, including the United States, the East-West Center seeks to foster the development of an Asia Pacific community through cooperative study, training, and research. Center activities focus on the promotion of shared regional values and the building of regional institutions and arrangements; the promotion of economic growth with equity, stability, and sustainability; and the management and resolution of critical regional as well as common problems.

Japan Center for International Exchange

Founded in 1970, the Japan Center for International Exchange (JCIE) is an independent, nonprofit, and nonpartisan organization dedicated to strengthening Japan's role in international affairs. JCIE believes that Japan faces a major challenge in augmenting its positive contributions to the international community, in keeping with its position as one of the world's largest industrial democracies. Operating in a country where policy making has traditionally been dominated by the government bureaucracy, JCIE has played an important role in broadening debate on Japan's international responsibilities by conducting international and cross-sectional programs of exchange, research, and discussion.

JCIE creates opportunities for informed policy discussions; it does not take policy positions. JCIE programs are carried out with the collaboration and cosponsorship of many organizations. The contacts developed through these working relationships are crucial to JCIE's efforts to increase the number of Japanese from the private sector engaged in meaningful policy research and dialogue with overseas counterparts. JCIE receives no government subsidies; rather, funding comes from private foundation grants, corporate contributions, and contracts.